P9-CDX-930

Dedication

For Kyla and all those we love who have left us too soon

The one absolutely unselfish friend
that man can have in this selfish world,
the one that never deserts him,
the one that never proves ungrateful or
treacherous, is the dog.

—*Samuel Taylor Coleridge* (Table Talk, *1830*)

Acknowledgments

With thanks to David Bishop, Beth Bishop, Jan Green, Sue Goolsbee, Robert at Clifftop Inn, Megan, and Brandy for their support, thoughtfulness, and help throughout the time I devoted to hiking and writing this book—and always.

CONTENTS

Part 1: Hiking Tips for Dogs and People

Part 2: The Trails

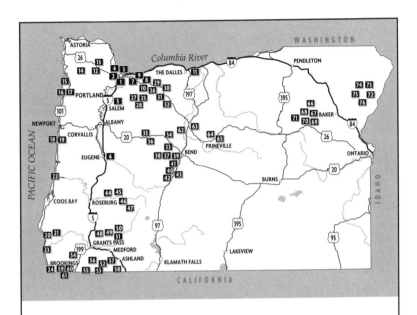

LEGEND

═══════════ Interstate Highway	🛡84 Interstate
━━━━━━━━ Paved Road	⬭20 U.S. Highway
═══════════ Gravel Road	⬭410 Oregon Route
= = = = = = = = = Dirt Road	▱9712 Forest Road
▪—▪—▪—▪—▪—▪ Featured Trail	⟋643⟍ Trail Number
·················· Connecting Trail	] [Bridge
·—·—·—·—·—·—· Wilderness Boundary	) (Pass/Saddle
▬—▬—▬—▬—▬ State Boundary	🛑 Trailhead
～～～～～ River/Creek	▲ Campground
🝆 Lake	▲ Peak
·—·—·—·—·—·— Power Transmission Line	☥ Ranger Station
	▪ Building
	⛷ Ski Area

HIKE SUMMARY TABLE

Trail	Easy on paws	Easy hike	Possible overnight trip	Alongside stream most of hike	Lake(s) to swim in	Unleashed okay	Solitude	Alpine scenery	Forested trail for the entire hike	Good for senior dogs	Best for well-conditioned dogs
Willamette Valley and Portland Area											
1 Tryon Creek State Park	•	•	•						•	•	
2 Forest Park Wildwood Trail (whole trail)	•								•	•	•
3 Sandy River Delta	•	•				*				•	
4 Sauvie Island: Warrior Rock Trail	•					•				•	
5 Silver Falls State Park: Perimeter Trail	•						•		•		
6 Howard Buford County Recreation Area: Mount Pisgah		•									
Columbia River Gorge											
7 Larch Mountain (almost) to Multnomah Falls	•					*			•		•
8 Gorge Trail 400–406: Wyeth Campground to Herman Creek Campground							•		•		
9 Oneonta Gorge: Triple Falls				•					•		
10 Wahclella Falls		•	•						•	•	
11 Atiyeh Deschutes River Trail						*	•			•	
Coast and Coast Range											
12 Banks–Vernonia State Trail: Vernonia to Braun									•	•	
13 Banks–Vernonia State Trail: Tophill to Buxton	•								•	•	
14 Gravelle Brothers Trail: University Falls	•	•				•			•		
15 Bayocean Peninsula County Park: Bayocean Spit		•					•			•	
16 Cape Lookout: South Trail		•							•		
17 Cape Lookout: North Trail	•								•		

	Easy on paws	Easy hike	Possible overnight trip	Alongside stream most of hike	Lake(s) to swim in	Unleashed okay	Solitude	Alpine scenery	Forested trail for the entire hike	Good for senior dogs	Best for well-conditioned dogs
Coast and Coast Range (cont.)											
18 Cape Perpetua: Cummins Creek to Gwynn Creek			•			•	•		•		•
19 Cape Perpetua: Giant Spruce Trail	•	•							•	•	
20 Humbug Mountain State Park: Summit Trail									•		
21 Humbug Mountain State Park: Coast Trail, Old Coast Highway									•		
22 John Dellenback Dunes Trail							•				•
23 Samuel H. Boardman State Scenic Corridor							•		•		•
24 Francis Shrader Old-Growth Trail	•	•							•	•	
Cascade Mountains											
25 Ramona Falls			•			•			•		
26 Burnt Lake	•		•	•	•	•			•		•
27 Old Salmon River Trail	•	•		•					•	•	
28 Salmon-Huckleberry Wilderness: Upper Salmon River Trail				•		•	•		•		
29 Mount Hood Wilderness: Elk Meadows Trail			•	•		•	•		•		
30 Tamanawas Falls Trail		•		•	•	•			•	•	
31 Dog River Trail						•			•		•
32 Pacific Crest Trail: Twin Lakes	•	•	•		•	•			•		
33 Three Sisters Wilderness: Matthieu Lakes and Collier Cone			•		•	•			•		•
34 Metolius River Trail	•			•					•	•	
35 South Breitenbush River Gorge National Recreation Trail	•					•			•	•	
36 South Breitenbush Trail: Jefferson Park			•		•	•		•	•		•
37 Devils Lake to Moraine Lake Loop			•		•	*		•			•

HIKE SUMMARY TABLE 13

	Easy on paws	Easy hike	Possible overnight trip	Alongside stream most of hike	Lake(s) to swim in	Unleashed okay	Solitude	Alpine scenery	Forested trail for the entire hike	Good for senior dogs	Best for well-conditioned dogs
Cascade Mountains (cont.)											
38 Three Sisters Wilderness: Sisters Mirror Lake	•		•		•	•			•	•	
39 Todd Lake			•		•	•		•	•		•
40 Bend: Deschutes River Trail				•					•	•	
41 Shevlin Park: Tumalo Creek Trail	•	•		•					•	•	
42 LaPine State Park: Fall River Loop				•						•	
43 Newberry National Volcanic Monument: Peter Skene Ogden Trail	•			•				•	•		
44 North Umpqua Trail: Tioga Segment, Miles 1–16						•	•		•		•
45 North Umpqua Trail: Hot Springs Segment, Miles 47–54	•		•			•			•		
46 North Umpqua Trail: Dread and Terror Segment, Miles 54–63	•		•			•	•		•		
47 North Umpqua Trail: Maidu Lake Segment, Miles 69–79	•		•	•	•	•	•	•	•		•
48 Upper Rogue River Trail: Takelma Gorge Segment, Miles 6–10	•		•			•			•	•	
49 Upper Rogue River Trail: Knob Falls Segment, Miles 10–14			•	•	•	*	•				•
50 Upper Rogue River Trail: Natural Bridge to Big Bend Segment, Miles 14–21				•		*			•	•	
51 Union Creek Trail	•			•					•	•	
Klamath Mountains											
52 Summit Lake						*	•		•		
53 French Gulch–Payette Trail: Applegate Lake	•		•		•	•				•	
54 Little Falls Trail	•	•		•		•				•	
55 Cook and Green Trail			•			•	•		•		•

	Easy on paws	Easy hike	Possible overnight trip	Alongside stream most of hike	Lake(s) to swim in	Unleashed okay	Solitude	Alpine scenery	Forested trail for the entire hike	Good for senior dogs	Best for well-conditioned dogs
Klamath Mountains (cont.)											
56 Middle Fork Applegate River			•			•				•	•
57 Wagner Butte Trail							•				•
58 Pacific Crest Trail: Mount Ashland to Siskiyou Gap			•			•	•				•
59 Rogue River Trail: Illahee to Paradise Bar				•	•	•			•		
60 Vulcan Lake	•					•		•			
61 Sourdough Trail #1114							•	•			
Blue Mountains, Wallowa Mountains, and Eastern Oregon											
62 Deschutes River: Scout Camp Trail							•	•			•
63 Crooked River National Grasslands: Cole Loop Trail						•	•				
64 Lookout Mountain Trail						•	•	•	•		
65 Round Mountain Trail						•	•	•			
66 Elkhorn Crest Trail to Anthony Lake						•	•	•			
67 Hoffer Lakes	•	•		•	•				•	•	•
68 Crawfish Lake			•				•				
69 Baldy Creek Trail	•		•	•	•		•	•	•	•	•
70 North Fork John Day Wilderness: Elkhorn Crest Loop			•	•		•	•	•			•
71 North Fork John Day Wilderness: North Fork Campground to Granite Creek			•	•		•	•			•	•
72 Bonny Lakes and Aneroid Lake			•	•		•	•	•			•
73 Eagle Cap Wilderness: McCully Creek Trail				•			•			•	
74 Eagle Cap Wilderness: Hurricane Creek	•		•	•						•	•
75 Eagle Cap Wilderness: Maxwell Lake			•		•		•		•		•
76 Eagle Cap Wilderness: East Fork Lostine River			•	•							•

NOTE: Under "Unleashed okay", the asterisks (*) indicate where there are seasonal or spatial leash requirements.

PART 1

Hiking Tips for Dogs and People

*No matter how little money
and how few possessions you own,
having a dog makes you rich.
—Louis Sabin
(All About Dogs as Pets, 1983)*

According to their DNA, dogs have been intertwined with human culture and history since at least the close of the last Ice Age about fifteen thousand years ago. Some evidence, from Goyet Cave in Belgium, suggests there was human-canid cohabitation more than thirty-one thousand years ago. More controversial finds suggest that as long as one hundred and forty thousand years ago, dogs had become domesticated and were helpful participants in human society.

However ancient our bonds, modern dogs provide vital companionship, service, and even levity. Who has not laughed at canine antics or unintended jest?

Today we find ourselves in an increasingly restrictive and litigious society, bounded by rules for everything from boarding aircraft to walking Fido in the park. The world has become a more stressful place, and our dogs, be they jokesters, partners, or therapists, are evermore essential parts of our lives. We may not need them to hunt mammoths anymore, but we still need dogs to navigate life.

Megan enjoys a game of Fetch the Stick on almost any hike!

This second edition of *Best Hikes with Dogs, Oregon*, provides 25 new hikes and revises many hikes from the first edition. We've deleted some hikes that impinged upon habitat for snowy plovers, ventured through areas that have burned in recent forest fires, or simply had become more popular and, hence, more crowded. In their place are hikes on trails in different areas, new or rarely used trails, or trails that simply were not included in the first edition.

There are some new regulations for dogs since the first edition, and there is a tendency for more strict enforcement of existing rules—6-foot leashes and removal of dog wastes in Oregon state parks, for example—as more and more hikers—and more and more of them with dogs—explore the out-of-doors. Many parks have more stringent rules for staying on designated trails. In some parks, such as Silver Falls State Park, some major trails are newly off-limits to canines. In other parks, newly posted areas prohibit dogs. And national parks (in Oregon, that's Crater Lake) remain the *worst* of places to take a dog, because dogs are simply not allowed on trails and seem barely allowed to get out of the car, even in campgrounds. Taking a dog into a national park sentences your friend to long stints alone in a hot car. Don't go there.

Where you and your dog(s) *do* go depends on your interests, fitness level, and how much you want to travel. A well-trained, well-behaved dog can enhance your backcountry experience, opening up a new world of smells and textures and offering protection simply by being along for the trip—a dog in the hiking party makes you less likely to be threatened by predators of all species.

And dogs can be great icebreakers on the trail. Other hikers are more likely to pause to greet the two of you, though they usually address the dog first. Dogs just seem to make us better people—who hasn't heeded the bumper-sticker mantra of trying to be the person your dog thinks you are?

Like humans, dogs need training, conditioning, and the right gear if they are to enjoy their hikes. Regular daily exercise is essential for you both. Up-to-date vaccinations, a current identification tag, along with good obedience skills and socialization training, are important prerequisites for any pet on the trails.

Taking a dog on a hike, or anywhere, especially in a litigious culture where dogs may be viewed as a walking liability lawsuit, means assuming extra responsibilities, including cleanup, acceptable canine social behavior, and proper care of the dog's health on the trail. Whenever you are in the backcountry with your dog, you are an ambassador for all dogs who accompany hikers.

Hikers are generally tolerant of dogs, but a small, vocal minority would like to ban them from the trails. Their objections rest on three concerns: (1) potential harassment of or harm to wildlife and ecologically sensitive environments, (2) dogs and dog waste creating unsanitary conditions, and (3) dogs biting or presenting other hazards to people, especially children. Some who object to dogs on the trail also incorrectly believe that dogs communicate disease to wildlife, spread giardiasis and other waterborne diseases, and, by their presence, discourage wildlife from using an area or cause harm and even death to wild creatures of all sizes.

So when you and your best friend go for a hike, don that halo or cape at the trailhead and be a canine superhero team. Protect and respect wildlife. Admire and sniff, but don't dig up the plants. Keep the waters unmuddied, and carry and use a trowel or poop bag. Be friendly, and yield to other hikers on the trail. The following tips are designed to help you develop a well-trained, tail-wagging trail dog; achieve this, and the two of you—and everyone else—will better enjoy any trail you choose.

Gear for Fido and You

When hiking with your dog, you should always take along a few supplies. And with a proper dog pack, Rover can help carry them.

The Ten Essentials for People

For decades hikers have been coached to pack the Ten Essentials, key items to help them survive a wilderness emergency. The list has recently been modified into ten functional systems that hikers need to consider when heading into the outdoors.

1. Navigation (map and compass). Carry a topographic map of the area you will hike, and learn how to read it. Also carry a compass and learn how to use it, including the local magnetic declination. An altimeter can be even more useful but is more expensive. Better yet, learn how to use a global positioning system (GPS) receiver, but don't blindly rely on it for direction to—or on—the trail.

2. Sun protection (sunglasses and sunscreen). Ultraviolet light damages your eyes as well as your skin. Always wear UV-blocking glasses when hiking at altitudes above 5000 feet.

Your dog should remain close to you and on the trail without harassing wildlife during your hike.

3. Insulation (extra clothing). Rain and cold weather can develop quickly in the backcountry. Carry raingear and enough extra clothing to keep you warm should you become lost or injured.

4. Illumination (headlamp or flashlight). Even the best-laid plans can go awry. Should darkness overtake you on a hike, you'll need artificial light to follow the trail. Take a light with good batteries and a strong beam.

5. First-aid supplies. Make your own or purchase a prepackaged kit designed for hikers and campers. Bandages, antiseptic, adhesive wrap, and aspirin are essential kit items. Include an emergency space blanket and an instant cold pack as well. Your dog also needs a first-aid kit, described later in this chapter, so you might want to combine the two kits into one all-purpose kit.

6. Fire (firestarter and matches or lighter). An emergency campfire provides warmth and a signal if you become lost. Many good commercial firestarters are available, such as tubes of fire-starting ribbon. A candle works too. Pack waterproof matches (they light even when wet) and also carry regular, strike-anywhere matches or a lighter in a waterproof case.

7. Repair kit and tools (including a knife). A knife has a multitude of uses in normal hikes as well as in emergency situations.

Offer some water periodically during your hike and when you return to your car or camp. You don't need a fancy dog bowl—any open, accessible bowl will do.

Always carry a knife or, better yet, a stout multitool with a knife blade and highly functional accessories including pliers, wire cutters, and so on.

8. Nutrition (extra food). Carry the food you intend to eat on the trail or while camping, plus extra in case of an emergency. A few extra energy bars weigh little but will help if your hike is longer than you anticipate or if you stray from your intended hike.

9. Hydration (extra water). Clean drinking water is essential for health. Carry at least a quart, and on longer hikes take a purification system so you can safely drink water from streams.

10. Emergency shelter. In the backcountry, weather can change and accidents happen. Carry a lightweight emergency shelter—an emergency space blanket or space tent. It weighs only ounces, but it may save your life.

The Ten Canine Essentials

Ten tangible and intangible systems keep your dog safe and healthy when away from home. Be sure you consider these before you head out with your dog.

1. Obedience training. Before you set foot on a trail, make sure your dog is trained and will obey your commands when faced with other hikers, other dogs, wildlife, and an assortment of strange scents and sights in the backcountry. A dog that can't behave should be left at home.

2. Water and water bowl. Don't count on water being available for your dog along the trail. Streams are great for keeping Fido cool, but dogs, like humans, are susceptible to giardiasis and other waterborne disease. Give dogs ample water before you begin your hike, and offer water during the trek as well. Having enough drinking water will lower your dog's risk of heatstroke. Pack as much water for your dog as you do for yourself. Carry a small bowl for Fido, too. Collapsible nylon bowls work well, as do lightweight metal or plastic bowls.

3. Leash and harness or collar. Have a 6-foot leash with you at all times, even if not required by local regulations. Flexible leads are relatively fragile and can tire your arms. For hands-free hiking, run your belt through the leash handle. An inexpensive and versatile alternative to a commercial leash is to buy a length of small-diameter climbing rope and use small carabiners to latch one end to your dog's collar and the other end to your belt. Consider a harness instead of a collar if your dog will be leashed for the entire hike.

4. Basic first-aid kit and sturdy multitool. Dogs are prone to injury, bee stings, and other traumas. In the backcountry, they may encounter snares set for wildlife—you will need wire cutters to release your pet—or porcupines (you'll need reliable pliers to remove porcupine quills). Take a canine first-aid course and read up on canine first aid. Kit contents are listed later in this chapter.

5. ID tags, microchips, and picture identification. It's a fact that dogs do get lost, left behind, or wander. Make sure that whoever finds yours can reunite the two of you. Your dog should always wear ID tags that are easy to read. Be sure your cell phone number and/or email is legible.

One night, when driving Highway 197 literally in the middle of nowhere, I came upon two Great Pyrenees looking a bit bedraggled by the side of the road—many, many miles from any sheep I might have thought they were guarding. Fortunately, one dog had a collar—with a cell phone number on it. I called. The owners answered—in Salt Lake City. They were on a trip without their dogs. If they hadn't put their cell phone number on the collar, I would never have found them. From

Salt Lake City, they called a neighbor who met me on the highway, and together we got the dogs home.

A microchip—a small plastic object about the size of a grain of rice implanted just under the skin by a veterinarian—is also recommended. Microchips, which contain the animal's ownership and contact information, never fall off, are inexpensive, and can be read at most animal shelters and clinics. Be sure your contact information is registered with the chip maker!

Pictures of your dog are helpful to have in your pack and/or on your phone. If your dog gets lost far from home, you can show the image to local residents and make flyers and handbills to post in the surrounding communities.

6. Compact roll of plastic bags and trowel. Even on a short hike, be prepared to remove or bury dog waste. Carry it out or bury it, according to what is most appropriate for the area.

7. Preventive shots and insect repellent. Before venturing out on the trail, be sure immunizations are up to date. In addition, ask your vet about shots for heartworm, giardia, and snake bites. Take insect repellent to ward off ticks. Be aware that some animals and some people have strong negative reactions to DEET-based repellents. Before leaving home, dab a little repellent on a patch of your dog's fur to see if there is a reaction. Look for signs of drowsiness, lethargy, or nausea. Remember to restrict repellent applications to those places the dog can't lick—shoulders, back of the neck, and around the ears (staying well clear of the ears and inner ears)—which are also near the most logical places mosquitoes will be looking for exposed skin (at the eyes, nose, and inner ears) to bite.

8. Dog food and trail treats. Pack more food than your dog normally consumes, because hiking burns more calories than normal. If you have to spend an unplanned night in the backcountry, you need to keep your best friend fed too. Trail treats serve the same purpose for a dog as they do for you: providing quick energy during a strenuous day of hiking. Treats made for dogs usually provide better nutrition for your dog than human snacks will.

9. Doggie backpack. This is one of the first—and usually least essential—things we rush out and buy. It's clever that dogs can pack their own food, water, and other gear in a doggie backpack, and they look, oh, so cool. Trouble is, they don't *stay* cool. The pack may actually contribute to overheating Fido on hot days. If it's hot, ditch the backpack idea. But in cooler weather (less than about 70°F), dogs wear backpacks quite comfortably.

The pack should fit snugly. Don't buy a pack that's too big or overload your dog. A general rule is 1 pound in the pack per 20 pounds of dog.

If your dog likes to immerse herself in streams, you might want to package everything in her backpack in waterproof plastic bags.

10. Dog booties. Booties also look really cool on your dog. But be very judicious in their use. Dogs sweat through their feet and can overheat if booties are left on too long in which case they will *not* be cool!

That said, appropriate use of booties can protect footpads on short stretches where the trail is rocky or noxious weeds stab into paws. Booties can also keep bandages secure in case your dog damages his footpads. Practice putting them on and having your dog wear them at home at first.

Tips for Safe and Comfortable Canine Hiking

Keeping your dog in good health, including providing preventive vaccines, using pest controls for fleas, ticks, and heartworm, and

Daytona wears a properly sized and adjusted pack for the hike to Twin Lakes with Zach, Chris, and Kurt.

maintaining proper weight, is important for safe canine traveling and hiking. Ensure that your dog has up-to-date and appropriate vaccinations, including a vaccination for giardiasis and rattlesnake bites. A canine vaccine that protects against bites from western diamondbacks and related snakes is now available. When traveling, carry up-to-date vaccination and health records in case your dog should need veterinary care or an overnight stay in a kennel while you are away from home.

Groom your dog for the trail as well. Toenails and dewclaws should be short and rounded to avoid being caught and torn. Trim hair from between the toes to minimize damage by sharp-pointed seeds that can hide in fur and then burrow into the paw. On long-coated breeds, consider a trim of tummy hair and hindquarter feathers. In addition to the Ten Canine Essentials (listed above), bring a dog comb or brush on the hike. Periodic brushing during and after a hike can minimize problems from ticks, embedded seeds, and tangled plant materials.

If you are planning an overnight trip, make sure that your tent is large enough to accommodate both Rover and you. Keeping Rover safe in the tent at night protects him from wild midnight rovers such as raccoons, skunks, and porcupines. A dog appreciates creature comforts as much as humans do, so a sleeping pad just for the dog is another nice touch. And, trust me, that extra pad will keep you from waking up on the ground while Rover slumbers in comfort on your soft bed.

Choosing Trails for Dogs

Hikes in this book are selected for their suitability and safety for dogs. Most hikes in this book meet *most* of the selection criteria outlined below. This checklist can be used to determine the suitability of any trail as an appropriate and safe place for adventures with your dog. A trail is a good choice if it has all, or most, of these:

- Springs, streams, and/or lakes for your dog to take a dip in; dog use must not contaminate a human water source or disturb important fish or wildlife habitat
- Shade for much of the hike
- No major roads or vehicular traffic
- Minimal or no contact with livestock or pack stock
- No leash requirement (though a leash should be available at all times)

- No rare, threatened, or endangered species
- Minimal or no poison oak or ivy
- Minimal or no cliffs or other hazards for ambitious and highly energetic or inexperienced dogs (or owners . . .)
- Few other hikers or small children
- No off-road vehicles, including mountain bikes
- No long rocky stretches—especially over sharp rocks; trails should be easy on paws
- A trailhead that is easily accessible by car

Etiquette and Rules of the Trail

As trails become more crowded, the need for hikers with dogs to be courteous and helpful to others on the trail grows. Here are a few basic guidelines to follow. Ignore them, and the anti-dog forces gain more fodder for complaints. Follow them, and you might win a few for the dogs.

Protect wildlife and sensitive habitats by leashing or controlling your dogs. To keep wildlife (especially young animals) safe, your dog should be leashed at all times in the spring and early summer, from April through July, when deer fawns, elk calves, and nesting and fledgling birds are especially vulnerable. If your dog is off leash, ironclad obedience training is helpful. "Come" should be a nonnegotiable command, even if there is a rabbit trail (or rabbit) to follow. Keep your dog in the tent at night or leashed securely just outside the door. The backcountry at night can be an exciting place for your dog, and it will be exciting for you, too, if Rover encounters a skunk or porcupine during a late-night exploration. Defending the camp against nocturnal marauders, whether deer, bear, or raccoon, can result in injury to your dog.

Yield the right-of-way to other hikers, horse and llama packers, and mountain bikers. Not everyone loves dogs. Some people fear them. No matter how friendly Rover might be, step off the trail with your dog when you meet oncoming hikers and allow them plenty of room. Likewise, yield to horses and llamas. They'll thank you for it. Where possible and safe, step off the trail on the downhill side to be less threatening, and always speak to livestock and make your presence known to them as soon as you see them on the path. This keeps your dog safe, alleviates any sense that she is a threat or is being threatened, and creates a fine impression of dog-owner courtesy.

Can't we walk FASTER? Wasn't that a SQUIRREL? Leashes are a good idea on trails where temptations abound.

Ask if it's okay for your dog to approach when you encounter other hikers. The answer is usually an enthusiastic yes, but check first. Other hikers might be allergic to dogs. They might fear dogs. Or they might not want to share their lunch. Make sure your dog does not rush up to other hikers, especially children. No matter how affable your dog's intent, the rapid approach of an unfamiliar dog, especially a big one, can frighten a child or an adult. So ask first and keep your dog on a leash and by your side in any group you meet, especially one with children.

Clean up and properly dispose of dog waste. It's a surprisingly major contributor to watershed pollution, with clear DNA evidence that at least 20 percent of organic wastes in Seattle's watershed comes from dogs. You wouldn't leave your dog's poop in your yard or on the city sidewalk, so please don't leave dog waste along the trail. There are no waste cans in the woods, but there is a giant compost heap just under your feet. You can dispose of your dog's waste by digging a 6-inch-deep hole with your trowel or a stick, placing the poop in it, and covering it with soil. In smaller parks or rest areas, remove dog waste with a plastic bag and pack it out to the nearest garbage can.

Consider where you let Fido take a doggie dip. Keeping your dog cool is critical, but please don't let her muddy or contaminate water sources that are used by people or that are important to wildlife. (Dogs don't know the difference—you'll have to help.)

Pay attention to your dog at all times, especially when Fido is off leash. Your dog's exquisite senses alert her to wildlife and people long before you will notice them. She can alert you to danger early on.

And if she seems ready to chase an unseen bunny, you can regain her attention and call her back before the pursuit begins.

Go Lightly on the Land

Both you and your dog love a walk in wilderness, but this landscape is shared with an increasing number of other hikers—human and canine. To keep the backcountry as pristine as possible, practice Leave No Trace hiking. The goal of the national nonprofit Leave No Trace organization (www.lnt.org) is to "avoid or minimize impacts to natural area resources and help ensure a positive recreational experience for all visitors." Following are the basic principles of Leave No Trace.

Plan ahead and prepare. Know the trails you plan to hike and what to expect when you get to your destination. Take what you need so that you don't have to modify or destroy vegetation and other wilderness assets along the way. Take a backpacking stove and fuel if you need to cook, rather than building a campfire. Carry a sleeping pad so you don't have to collect pine needles to have a soft bed. Repackage food and other consumables to minimize waste that must be packed out. Know your route and stick to the trail.

Travel and camp on durable surfaces. Use existing campsites rather than disturbing a pristine forest floor or grassland. If there are no prehardened sites—or if overused sites are being restored—choose

a rocky or sandy area to camp to minimize disturbing plants. If you must camp in a meadow or on top of plant cover, remember that those plants need light and air to survive. Minimize the time your tent covers them. Set up your tent in the evening; take it down in the morning. The grass will thank you for it.

Dogs and humans have been companions on the trail for around 15,000 years, and some research suggests our partnership began at least 100,000 years ago.

Dispose of waste properly. If you pack it in, pack it out. Even seemingly biodegradable items such as orange peels should be packed out with you.

Leave what you find. That nifty stick that you think you might make into a hiking staff when you get back home is better left in the forest where it will someday contribute to forest duff and soils.

Minimize campfire impacts. Take and use a small gas stove if you must cook. Fires are entrancing but leave unsightly charcoal scars, contribute to global warming, and can start a wildfire if not completely extinguished. Put on a good down jacket, cuddle up with Rover, and watch the stars instead. If you crave firelight, consider candles.

Respect wildlife. Take care that your dog does not damage habitat or harass wild animals.

Be considerate of other visitors. Yield to other hikers on trails. Clean up after your pooch.

When to Leave Your Dog at Home

Well-trained and properly socialized dogs are a joy to hike with. But in some situations, dogs simply don't belong or cannot go. It is far more humane to leave Rover comfortably and safely at home than to bring him into places or conditions where his health could be endangered or where he is not allowed.

Hot weather. In very hot weather, leave your dog at home—or in a kennel, if you are away from home. Hint: Check the weather report for your destination before you leave. The National Oceanic and Atmospheric Administration (NOAA) has an excellent weather site. Dogs cannot cool themselves as readily as we can. As a result, dogs are prone to heatstroke and possible death when temperatures rise above 90°F and there is limited shade or water. Dogs that are not acclimated to heat may suffer when temperatures are only in the 70s or 80s. In these conditions, leave your dog at home with shade and water. If you are away from home and the weather turns hot, board your dog at a good local kennel or cancel the day's hike and relax together at a cool, shady streamside instead.

Crowded trails. If you plan to hike crowded trails, especially trails with a lot of children, horse packers, or mountain bikers, consider leaving Fido at home. You won't have to worry about your dog's safety and interaction with other hikers. If Fido does accompany you, she should

Not all trails are open to dogs, especially in national parks.

remain on a leash or under close control. Another option is to explore popular, congested trails in off-peak seasons and days.

Prohibited trails. Keep in mind, too, that some places, such as national parks and Nature Conservancy preserves, do not allow dogs on trails. Not even on a leash. Not even if you carry the dog or zip her into a backpack. These places are probably wary of cars with bumper stickers like "Wag More, Bark Less." Just don't go there with the dog. You'll have to leave your best friend in the car for long stretches, and even in cool weather it's not a good idea.

For example, there's the couple who visited Crater Lake in September 2010. Like any good national park visitor, they left their Akita-dingo mix, Haley, in their Volkswagen Passat. The car's brakes failed, and it rolled over the crater's edge and plunged 1100 feet down the cliff and into the lake. Fortunately, Haley, who was not wearing her seatbelt, was ejected from the car before it hit the lake and was able to scramble upslope to safety and her stunned owners.

Not all sagas of dogs in cars at national parks are this extreme. But still—consider leaving Fido at home on the Crater Lake National Park trip.

Sensitive habitats. Don't take the dog if you will be hiking where there are sensitive habitats or endangered or threatened species. Or if you must take him, keep him leashed. Dogs on the trail are less destructive than reputed, but the fact remains that dogs can't tell the difference between a Shasta daisy (common) and a Columbia Gorge daisy (endangered).

Livestock areas. Leave your dog at home or keep him under close control (leashed) when hiking where livestock might be present. Cattle, sheep, and horses often share federal and state lands with hikers. Dogs that harass livestock can legally be shot in Oregon. If there is a herding club in your community, or if you can find a cattle owner who is willing to work with you, train your dog in the presence of livestock to leave the animals alone and respond instantly to your command "Come!"

Unfamiliar dogs in your group. Likewise, consider leaving your dog at home if there will be unfamiliar dogs (and their unfamiliar owners) in your group. Leaving your dog at home becomes an even better idea if your dog is very submissive or very dominant. If you do take Rover, pay attention to her and the other dogs and be prepared to leave the group if the situation (human or canine) gets tense. Allow dogs to socialize before you set off on a hike. Keep in mind that a dog might believe that he needs to defend you if he is leashed and other dogs are not. The greater the number of unfamiliar dogs on a hike, the more likely it is that trouble will occur.

Preparing Dogs for Hiking

Most hikers maintain a fitness program of sorts, wear hiking boots, pack clothing and other gear to be ready for bad weather, and try to eat the

Dogs of any size make cheerful hiking companions.

right foods. Even though dogs have a different physiology than humans, they also need to be prepared.

Conditioning. A half hour of exercise each day will help to keep your dog fit. Ideally, that exercise should include running as well as walking. A half-hour aerobic stroll will build your dog's muscle tone, circulation, and lung capacity and also begin to toughen her footpads for the trail. A walk that includes some jogging or a chance to chase a ball provides additional canine fitness benefit.

Begin your dog's fitness program slowly. Start with a visit to your veterinarian to ensure there are no hidden health problems, such as hip dysplasia, that might cause trouble on the trail. A walk each day is a good beginning. Quicken your pace as time goes by, and soon you'll both be walking briskly. Teach Fido to swim, too, so he can keep cool on the trail.

Older dogs, like older humans, need patience and special consideration. Dogs reach their prime at about age four, and larger breeds are considered senior citizens by age seven or eight. Be prepared to go slowly and hike shorter, less-challenging trails if your dog is older, and consult your veterinarian for appropriate pain-relieving medications or food additives that can help keep joints limber. Older dogs benefit both mentally and physically from time spent on the trail, so if you can adjust your pace and distance, by all means take an older dog.

Importantly, when you are on the trail, monitor your dog's condition. Not long ago, on a climb up the 800-foot-high staircase and trail at Beacon Rock, I met a very nice couple with a Chihuahua in tow. The tiny dog was panting, overheated, and literally being dragged up the stairs. The owners were busy looking at the view rather than their pet. When I politely pointed out the dog's condition to her owners, they were suddenly concerned—and immediately the 300-pound man picked up the 3-pound dog. They didn't have any water, so I provided some from my water bottle. "Lady" got a ride the rest of the way.

Leash training. During your conditioning walks, reacquaint Fido with the etiquette of walking on a loose leash, at your pace, and in response to basic commands, including "heel." A dog who pulls on the leash can be a real nuisance on the trail.

Other fitness activities. Dogs are sentient and intelligent creatures. Their wild, wolfy ancestors planned hunts, raised families, and maintained a complex, disciplined social hierarchy. Modern dogs need food for thought as well as exercise and a nutritious dinner. Each dog, like each human, has individual aptitudes and interests. Activities that develop discipline, mental agility, and physical fitness—especially activities that appeal to your dog's innate abilities—will also foster a strong bond between you and your dog. Recommended activities include obedience and agility training and participation in search and rescue or animal-assisted therapy, as well as activities that are breed-specific, such as herding, water rescue, field trials, and retrieving.

For a better companion on the trail, interact with your dog at every opportunity. For example, if you watch television, you can make commercials a time to practice obedience or learn new tricks. Taking the dog along on a car trip to the store? Spend an extra five minutes on a short walk down the street to meet and greet people. The more situations you face together, and the more opportunities you provide for learning, the more responsive your dog will be when you are on the trail together.

Essential Commands

Even if your dog never darkens the door of a formal obedience class, Rover should obey basic commands without hesitation on the trail. I have found several commands to be especially useful over the past three decades of hiking with dogs. Some are obedience-class standards. Others are specialized. Three commands—"Come!" "Leave it!" and "Wait!" (or "Stay!")—are helpful for safety. A book on dog training can help you teach your dog these commands if a trainer or class is not an option.

"Come!" This is the most critical command. Make your dog understand that this must be obeyed at all times. Practice "Come!" and other commands at places where there are people, noise, and other distractions. Reward liberally for instant obedience.

"Leave it!" Has Fido discovered a most wonderful cow pie to sample for a snack or roll in? Or, more critically, is he about to raid the unknown contents of a bag or plastic wrapper? This command, taught by rewarding the dog for turning away from the questionable object, can save your dog's life. At the very least, it will help you avoid a ruined hike and possible veterinarian bills.

"Wait!" This command can stop your dog from advancing into danger—unexpected traffic, a rushing stream, or a turn in the trail that carries her out of your line of sight. "Wait!" is the word I yell instinctively when I see danger ahead. "Wait!" is not the same as "Stay!" It does not

Meesha and Dundee wait "off trail" while other hikers head toward Twin Lakes.

freeze your dog in one spot for a prolonged time period or imply that you are going to go someplace else while Rover remains in place. It *does* mean that she needs to stop instantly and wait until you get your mitts on her or release her from the "Wait!" command.

I learned to give this command quite by accident. Wolf, a malamute then about a year old, was sauntering toward a road crossing about 20 yards ahead of me. I could hear a car coming, and the only thing I could think to shout was "Wait!" Wolf stopped in his tracks. The car missed him. He never forgot that "Wait!" is a command to be obeyed instantly. Since then, I've taught it to all my dogs. Begin by shouting urgently at them to wait when you are close by, and reward them for standing there until you reach them. Gradually increase the distance. Chances are they'll catch on quickly.

"Off trail!" This unorthodox command tells your dog to move off the trail and sit while other hikers, horses, or bikers pass by. While the majority of hikers seem to like dogs, some are afraid of them or simply prefer not to share the trail with them. Courtesy on the trail includes yielding the right-of-way to other hikers. Giving the command "Off trail!" while pointing at the place of direction where you expect your dog to go eliminates risk to your dog and to other hikers—and it usually earns a smile from other hikers.

This command is easy to teach by instructing "Off trail!" while pointing to the spot you want the dog to go. Then reward correct behavior. Research shows that dogs have an instinctive knack for going to a place pointed at by a human. Combining "Off trail!" with "Stay!" will soon have your dog responding to the command by moving to the place you point and then sitting or lying down until you release him. This command is especially useful if you encounter a horse pack string, a flock of mountain bikes, or a thundering herd of off-road vehicles (ORVs).

Hazardous Wildlife

Dogs tend to seek wild animals, so in the backcountry your dog might come face-to-face with a number of risks that a more hazard-savvy human would avoid. Keeping your dog leashed and/or under firm voice control minimizes the likelihood of unsavory encounters. Even benign encounters should be controlled. Never allow your dog to disturb, harass, or chase any wildlife. Oregon does have some large and/or hazardous fauna, such as cougars, bears, and rattlesnakes.

Cougars

Cougars are generally solitary and reclusive. Encounters are extremely rare. While their presence should not be taken lightly, cougars are not a great hazard. According to the U.S. Fish and Wildlife Service, in the 120 years between 1890 and 2010, there were only 70 confirmed cougar attacks and about one fatality every seven years from a cougar encounter in the entire United States. In Oregon there have been no fatalities and only seven documented attacks. To put this in perspective, more than fifty thousand people are killed annually in the United States in automobile accidents, about 90 are killed by lightning strikes, 40 by bee stings, and 80 by dog bites. Your likelihood of being attacked by a cougar while you are on the trail is far less than your chances of having a debilitating or fatal accident driving to the trailhead or being struck by lightning while on the hike.

Your chances of a cougar encounter are further reduced if you are hiking in a group of adults or if you have a dog. However, biologists note that cougars may be attracted to the high-pitched voices of young children, especially if they are yelling and screaming, which a cougar might interpret as a distress call.

For five years I lived along a major cougar corridor on the western flank of the Wallowa Mountains, yet my hikes with or without dogs never crossed the path of a cougar, to my knowledge. We occasionally found cougar tracks. Even more rarely, neighbors saw one crossing the road or padding through a field.

The only time I saw a cougar was when I was invited to accompany a team of wildlife biologists who used hounds to track and tree a female cougar near our house. They needed to capture and sedate her to change the batteries in her radio collar. The treed cougar looked down at us—biologists, dogs, and tourists—with pure malevolence in her eyes. Before the biologists could dart her, she leapt 30 feet to the ground and ran away, a tawny, angry, and frightened blur across the snow. She passed within about 10 feet of the astonished biologists but never bothered them. We let her go. Two weeks later, she was treed again, and this time her collar did get new batteries.

Following are some tips developed by the U.S. Fish and Wildlife Service and the Oregon Department of Fish and Wildlife to minimize your chances of provoking a cougar attack when hiking in cougar habitat:

- **Go in groups and make enough noise for your approach to be heard.** You don't have to shout and ring bells to do this.
- **Keep children quiet and physically close to adults, preferably within arm's reach.** Do not allow children to run far in front of or behind adults. Their high-pitched voices and rapid movements can attract cougars. About half of documented cougar attacks involved children.
- **Carry a sturdy walking stick.** (Those nice titanium hiking poles might not be "sturdy.") It can be used as a weapon against a cougar.
- **Never approach a dead deer, elk, or other animal.** It might be a recent cougar kill, with a cougar nearby guarding it. Partially covered animals are an indicator that a cougar might be in the vicinity, because cougars cover their prey between feedings. Immediately call your dog away from any such "find" and place the dog on leash.
- **Keep a clean camp.** Reduce odors that can attract small mammals such as raccoons, which in turn attract cougars. Store meat, other foods, pet food, and garbage in double plastic bags.

- **Keep your dog leashed.** Some experts recommend leaving your dog at home when hiking in cougar territory. My preference is to bring a dog, especially if it is a large dog (bigger than 50 pounds), but keep her leashed at all times. This prevents the dog from approaching a cougar or a cougar's kill. A cougar might take you on alone, or it might attack your dog alone—a reason for keeping your dog leashed and close to you when in cougar territory—but a cougar is very unlikely to attack you and a large dog together. Talk to your dog and play with her as you hike. The louder, more boisterous, and more aggressive you appear, the less likely you are to be viewed as vulnerable prey.
- **Do not allow your dog to roam at night.** Keep your dog inside your tent or shelter. Dogs, especially small dogs, can attract cougars and stand little chance of fighting one off.
- **Never approach a cougar.** They are unpredictable but will usually avoid a confrontation.
- **If you do encounter a cougar, give it an escape route, and do not run.** Work to convince the cougar that you are dominant and will put up a fight that the cat might lose. Throw rocks. Yell. Wave sticks. Tell it in no uncertain terms that you will not be easy prey. If you establish eye contact, maintain it; eye contact is a test of dominance. Keep your dog with you.
- **Lastly, if attacked, fight back.**

Bears

The only wild bears documented in Oregon today are American black bears. These animals tend to be shy and reclusive—with three major exceptions: (1) when they are hungry and you have food, (2) when a mother bear needs to defend her cubs, and (3) when defending themselves against attack.

Dogs usually will know there is a bear in the area long before you do. They might refuse to move forward along the trail, or they might run toward the bear with the intent of chasing it. If your dog balks at continuing, you should consider it a fair warning. Make sure your dog is leashed before you proceed farther, and use caution along the trail.

When hiking the North Fork of the John Day, my dog Meesha, then about two years old, simply sat down and refused to continue along the trail. We made camp right there (it was late in the afternoon). The next morning, fresh bear scat and ripped-open logs adorned the trail about a quarter mile farther along our trip.

Unleashed dogs might choose to pursue a bear. This confrontation is likely to provoke the intended quarry. Bears usually turn the tables on any dog that tries to chase them. Aggressive dogs that stand and fight will inevitably lose. Dogs that retreat to you for protection can lead an angry, combative bear to you. Preventing either scenario is a good reason to keep dogs leashed in the backcountry.

To lessen chances of an unsavory encounter with a bear, watch for bear "sign" along the trail. Look for rocks that have been overturned in a search for grubs and ants; scratch marks on tree trunks; dead trees and snags that have been ripped open recently; berry bushes stripped of leaves and fruit; and bear scat—droppings that look like a very, very large dog has been up the trail.

If you see any sign of bears, leash dogs and stay close together. Loud conversation—even if it is just you talking to your dog—alerts bears to your presence and allows them to move away.

The rules for encounters with bears are slightly different from those for cougars:

- **Remain calm.** Talk calmly in a low-pitched voice.
- **Do not look the bear directly in the eyes.** Eye contact can be construed as a challenge and might provoke the bear to attack.
- **Move slowly and allow the bear room to escape.** Work your way upwind from the bear so it can smell you and identify you as a human—an animal from which it prefers to retreat.
- **Do not run.** During a standoff, a bear might "bluff charge" to see if it can stampede you. If a bear charges, stand your ground and do not run. A bluff charge could turn into the real thing if you run, and your chances of outrunning a bear are small. Black bears can charge at speeds of 35 miles per hour.
- **If you surprise a bear, behave passively.** Keep your dog as calm as possible. Back away or lie down. Allow the bear to leave.
- **As a last resort, fight back.** If the bear sees you and charges from a distance, it likely considers you prey or a threat too serious to ignore. This behavior is rare in black bears, but possible. Fight back by kicking, gouging, and punching. Once it realizes that you are not easy prey, the bear might leave.

Wolves and Other Wild Canids

In Oregon, there are two documented wolf packs: the Imnaha Pack, with territory in and near Hells Canyon, and the Wenaha Wolf Pack, in very wild country north of Troy—both in northeastern Oregon. No hikes in this book are within these areas. Wolves are also known to have been in the Elkhorn Mountains and North Fork of the John Day River. More recently, roving individual wolves have been reported in the southern Cascades, but no permanent, residential presence has been confirmed as of this printing.

Wolves (*Canis lupus*) are reclusive animals and, like cougars and bears, are highly overrated as devastating predators of humans. Coyotes (*Canis latrans*), like wolves, have an undeserved reputation for ferocity. However, as with all wild animals, it is best to be aware and to exercise caution.

Both these species may view dogs, especially small dogs, as prey. Small, active, and vocal children may possibly be placed into the same category if they are alone. (Wolves have been implicated in, but not proven to be responsible for, two fatal animal attacks on lone humans in Alaska and Canada in the past fifty years.)

Your best defense is simply to be aware of your surroundings and talk quietly as you hike. In the unlikely event that you are approached by any wild canid, it can be easily scared away by yelling and arm-waving.

While I was hiking in Montana long ago, Wolf, my two-year-old 50-pound Alaskan malamute, trotted purposefully around a tall outcrop—and then returned with a lovely silver coyote at his side. The two of them played. Then they sat down together. Wolf looked at me quizzically, a bit like a teenager asking Mom if she approved of his date. It seemed that they had in mind developing a family and that I could just come back to visit periodically, maybe, as grandmothers do, bringing treats for the soon-to-be furry grandchildren. I called Wolf. He came, but the young coyote didn't budge. Then Wolf, sitting next to me, did his best to howl. The coyote responded. I chimed in. We all sat on the ridgetop howling back and forth for perhaps five minutes before the coyote decided that this was just not going to work out and softly padded away. It was an unforgettable experience—for me and probably for the other two as well.

Rattlesnakes

The warning buzz of a rattlesnake inspires fear in humans but often incites curiosity in dogs. Encounters between dogs and snakes are usually one of two kinds: The dog finds a snake in the open and tries to sniff it, or the dog finds a well-fed snake in a vacant gopher or mouse hole. Once again, the best way to avoid these encounters is to keep your dog on a leash. Keep dogs close and under control when hiking in snake territory: central, eastern, southern, and southeastern Oregon. Snakes are more common near streams and places where they find rodents and shade.

There is now a vaccine that is effective in developing substantial immunity to bites from western diamondback and related rattlesnakes. If you will be hiking in places where snakes might lurk anyplace in Oregon, consider having your dog vaccinated. The vaccine is administered in a series of two or three shots, so work with your vet and plan ahead.

The effects of a rattlesnake bite include swelling and respiratory distress. There is little you can do for a snake-bitten dog except head for a veterinarian and a dose of antivenom as quickly as possible. Immobilize the dog and place ice or cold packs on the bite areas. Administering a two-tablet (for a 50-pound dog) dose of antihistamine will help keep swelling down. When my malamute was bitten in central Oregon, the veterinarian was a 30-minute drive away. The dog, given a dose of antivenom less than an hour after being bitten, survived with minimal swelling and respiratory problems. But quick treatment is essential.

Most snakes that you encounter on hikes are harmless. Some—especially bull snakes—resemble rattlesnakes but lack fangs and venom. In any encounter with a snake, it's best to just leave the snake alone and provide an escape route for it.

Porcupines, Raccoons, and Skunks

While porcupines, raccoons, and skunks may not seem as fearsome as cougars, bears, and wolves, your chance of an encounter with one of these smaller animals is infinitely greater. Veterinary costs, nationwide and in the Pacific Northwest, for treatment of dogs injured by bears, cougars, and wolves are virtually undocumented (probably because they are not significant enough to be tracked), but costs for treatment of dogs injured by these smaller animals are counted in millions of dollars. All three of these animal species are more active after dark than during the day—hence the wisdom of keeping Fido in the car or tent at night.

Porcupine encounters leave a painful assembly of sharp, hooked quills in your dog's face, nose, eyes, and mouth. There is no easy method of removal, despite folk tales of cutting the end off the quills to "deflate" them or soaking them in vinegar to "dissolve" them. Quills simply have to be pulled out, and if there are more than one or two, it is extremely painful—and doubtful that your dog will allow you to do the job. Sedation and veterinary help are essential.

A study published in the *Canadian Journal of Veterinary Medicine* showed that longer times between quill injury and obtaining medical help by a veterinarian were associated with an increased risk of complications. Owners were strongly encouraged to bring the dog in as soon as the quill injury is discovered. Dogs treated after 24 hours of the porcupine encounter should be monitored closely during the first three weeks after injury, as most complications occur during this time. Spring and fall are the most likely times for porcupine encounters, according to this study.

Raccoons, which can be aggressive, are attracted to campgrounds and food of all sorts. A raccoon encounter with a dog may result in serious bites and injury. Raccoons may also carry rabies. Should your dog be bitten by a raccoon, or if you suspect that an injury was inflicted by a raccoon, seek veterinary treatment as soon as possible.

Skunks usually present a different problem, but they, like raccoons, carry rabies, so if your dog tangles with a skunk, check him for any bites and seek veterinary care if it appears he was bitten by the skunk. The most obvious result from an encounter with a skunk, however, is their spray, which is very oily and contains sulfur (hence the stench). Common remedies for skunk odor include these:

- In a plastic container, combine 1 quart hydrogen peroxide, ¼ cup baking soda, and 1 to 2 teaspoons liquid dishwashing detergent. Add lukewarm water if needed (for larger dogs). Mix ingredients well. The solution will fizz as a chemical reaction occurs. Use immediately—do not store. Without prewetting the dog, rub this solution over the affected areas (don't get it into the dog's eyes and ears!) and allow it to remain on the dog for about 5 to 10 minutes. Rinse with lukewarm water. Repeat two or three times, as needed. (From www.Aboutdogs.com.)
- A commercial enzymatic cleaner of the type commonly used to clean odors from urine "accidents" is more expensive and probably not as quick or effective as the remedy described above.
- Tomato juice bath—marginal and messy!

Canine First Aid and Trauma Prevention

This book and this section are meant to supplement, not take the place of, a comprehensive canine first-aid manual (recommendations are listed in Appendix B). The Oregon Humane Society and other organizations offer canine first-aid courses. It's a good idea to take one.

Poisons

Some common substances and foods that humans relish are directly or indirectly poisonous to dogs. When hiking, pack a separate lunch or separate treats for your dog, even for a day hike. Take only foods that are safe for dogs. If you tend to share your snacks, choose dog-friendly foods, such as soy or oatmeal bars, and avoid anything with chocolate or raisins. Below are some foods and substances that are harmful to dogs, along with treatments if they are ingested.

Antifreeze. Antifreeze is a deadly poison that rapidly destroys a dog's kidneys and neurological function. Even minuscule amounts of antifreeze—the amount that leaks into a puddle beneath a car radiator—can kill your dog or cause irreversible kidney damage, especially on a hot day after a long hike when the dog might be dehydrated. Immediate veterinary attention is essential if your thirsty dog ingests even a tiny amount of antifreeze from a radiator puddle. If you cannot get to a vet within minutes to have your dog's stomach pumped or an antidote administered, you can help stave off death or disability until you do get to a vet by inducing vomiting. To do this, place a few tablespoons of hydrogen peroxide or ethyl alcohol deep in the dog's mouth and ensure that the dog swallows it. These measures alone might not save your dog, but they might diminish kidney damage sufficiently that veterinary care can save him.

Acetaminophen (Tylenol) and ibuprofen (Motrin, Advil, Nuprin). Even small doses (two tablets) of these familiar pain remedies can kill a small dog (less than 15 pounds) and cause significant pathological responses in larger dogs. These drugs provide no pain relief for a dog. Instead, ibuprofen produces bleeding stomach ulcers, kidney damage, and possible death; acetaminophen produces liver failure and damage to red blood cells. Symptoms include vomiting, dehydration, bloody stools, lethargy, and abdominal pain. Veterinary treatment is essential. When hiking with your dog, bring only coated aspirin as your anti-inflammatory pain-control medication. Aspirin can be administered to dogs without harm in small doses of one tablet. Acetaminophen and ibuprofen cannot.

Chocolate. A mere 5 ounces of baking chocolate can kill a 50-pound dog. While for humans "death by chocolate" is a sort of joke, for dogs it is no laughing matter. Some dogs have ingested a fatal dose of chocolate by eating a pan of brownies or another chocolate dessert, particularly one containing baking chocolate. A 60-pound Labrador died after eating a 1-pound bag of semisweet chocolate pieces. Although dogs might vomit up such excesses and avoid death, they can remain ill for some time. When you hike with your dog, it is best to leave chocolate in any form, including "healthy" snack bars, at home.

Salmon, steelhead, and trout. Although many boutique dog foods now offer "salmon" flavors, the fish in these foods is fully processed and cooked. But ingesting small amounts of undercooked, raw, or dead salmon, steelhead, or trout (salmonid fish) can kill your dog. Prompt veterinary treatment is essential. It is not the fish itself that causes canine salmon poisoning but the presence of a bacteria—*Neorickettsia helminthoeca*—that lives in one of the salmon's internal parasites. This parasite, a fluke, travels throughout the fish's circulatory system, invading its muscles as well. When a dog eats uncooked fish, he ingests these flukes—and the pathogenic bacteria they contain. The flukes pass through the dog's intestinal tract, but the lethal bacteria remain behind, causing disease and often death.

The first symptoms are slight fever followed by loss of appetite. The dog's temperature will rise, often to levels high enough to kill it (above 107°F is considered a lethal temperature for a dog). Even if the dog survives this high fever, there are worse effects still to come, which also are often lethal, including severe diarrhea and dehydration. Few dogs survive untreated.

Loki, my healthy, boisterous, 100-pound two-year-old Newfoundland, nearly died from salmon poisoning after he ate a few ounces of freshly caught, barbecued coho salmon. The tiny piece of fish that Loki ate was from the interior of the fish. It was cooked—but not enough. For two days following the barbecue, Loki hiked happily with me through the Strawberry Range in eastern Oregon. But on the third day, he lagged behind. On the fourth day, he would not leave his bed in camp. By the time I got him to a veterinarian, he could not move and had to be carried from the car into the veterinary clinic. His temperature was 106°F—nearly lethal and verging on brain damage. Loki recovered fully but only after massive doses of antibiotics, intravenous fluids, a week of hospitalization, and a month of diminished activity. If we had arrived at the vet a few hours later, he would have died.

Troublesome Plants

Several plants commonly encountered on hikes in Oregon can cause problems for dogs. Some produce seeds that can invade skin or paws,

Meesha works at removing "beggars ticks" seeds from her lovely tail. A comb would make the job easier.

causing pain and, eventually, a large vet bill. Be aware of vegetation along your hike, and take precautions. Groom Fido before and after your hike to inspect for seeds and other hazards. Plants of concern include these:

Poison oak and/or poison ivy. Dogs, like humans, can develop severe reactions to these plants, either on exposed underbelly skin that brushes against the plants or in tissues of the mouth and esophagus if the dog chews the leaves or licks the plant's sap off his fur. Poison oak and poison ivy are common in the dry areas of the Columbia River Basin, where they grow in profusion in moist valley bottoms; in eastern Oregon's Hells Canyon area; on the eastern slopes of the Wallowa Mountains; and in the Rogue River and Kalmiopsis Wilderness of southwest Oregon.

Rhododendrons and azaleas. These seemingly benign plants contain a toxin that affects canine heart rhythm and function. This compound is most concentrated in leaves and flowers, but it is present throughout the plant, including the branches. Avoid using these branches as throwing sticks. Symptoms of ingesting this poison include weakness, decreased heart rate and blood pressure, and arrhythmia. Other plants that are similarly toxic to dogs include yew and the berries and leaves of most ivies. While poisoning from these plants is rare, if your dog begins to act lethargically during or after a forest hike, get Fido to your vet promptly.

Grasses and grass seeds. Some grasses, especially those found in overgrazed or disturbed areas (cheatgrass, rip-gut brome, bottlebrush squirrel-tail grass, foxtail, etc.), have seeds with sharp points that can puncture a dog's skin and paws—especially between the toes. If you are hiking where these grasses occur, trim the hair between your dog's toes before you begin the hike. This makes seeds that invade this vulnerable area easier to spot and remove. Seeds can also lodge in a dog's ears, eyes, nose, and throat, as well as penetrate the fur. As a precaution, brush your dog well after a hike through grass, removing seeds caught in her coat and between her toes before they begin to dig into the skin. If grass seeds become lodged in your dog's nose, she will sneeze repeatedly. If seeds are lodged in the throat, your dog will cough. If you can see the seed, you might be able to pull it out. Otherwise, veterinary attention is essential.

Insects, Pests, and Other Small Animals

Critters to look out for include ticks, bees, and *Giardia lamblia*.

Giardia. Most hikers are quite religious about taking purified water and/or water filters on any outdoor adventure to avoid acquiring internal

Brown dog ticks and deer ticks are common in areas where livestock and/or deer forage. Combing around the legs, ears, and belly can remove them before they attach to your dog.

parasites. The most notorious of these is *Giardia lamblia*, a tiny flagellated protozoan, often referred to simply as "giardia." Dogs are as susceptible as humans to giardia. But dogs are more likely than humans to drink from streams, ponds, and puddles where giardia awaits. Giardiasis can be especially serious in dogs, causing rampant diarrhea, flatulence, weight loss, listlessness, discomfort, and malaise, and it can slow the growth of puppies.

To help your dog avoid giardiasis, make sure she has plenty of safe water before you begin your hike and that she drinks frequently from the water you brought with you. A preventive vaccine is available for dogs. If you hike throughout the year, it should be renewed annually along with your dog's other regular shots. If you are an occasional or summer-only hiker, then be sure that your dog has a giardiasis shot before you begin your summer of traveling and hiking.

Ticks and Lyme disease. When hiking in areas grazed by livestock, you and your dog are likely to pick up ticks. The most common are the brown dog tick (dark red-brown), the American dog tick (slate-gray when engorged), and the deer tick (light brown with dark legs and a dark "shield" on its back). The deer tick is the principal carrier of Lyme disease; the American dog tick is the principal carrier of Rocky Mountain

Hikes with small springs and streams allow your dog to cool off effectively on warm summer days.

spotted fever. Dogs can get—and die from—both. While you can't prevent ticks from hitching a ride on Fido, frequent checks of fur on the legs, belly, head, and ears may detect them before they bite. Insect repellent applied to head, legs, and belly may also deter them.

If you don't remove ticks while they are crawling around on your dog, they will attach themselves and engorge on blood. Ticks' mouthparts have reverse harpoonlike barbs, designed to penetrate and attach to skin. Ticks secrete a cementlike substance that helps them adhere firmly to the dog (or to you). If this happens, a tick can best be removed by using either tweezers or a tool manufactured for tick removal. Grasp the tick with the tweezers as close to your dog's (or your) skin as possible. Do not use fingers, which can squeeze the tick's body, forcing it to regurgitate your dog's (or your) blood and any microbes the tick is carrying. Once you have a firm grasp near the tick's head, lift gently until the surface of your dog's (or your) skin puckers. This is enough force to make it difficult for the tick to remain attached. Hold this position until the tick lets go. This can take several seconds, so you and your dog might need a bit of patience. Once you have removed the tick, be sure you kill it, but don't touch it with your fingers. My personal preference is to pulverize it with a rock.

Bees. Few dogs can resist snapping at a bee. Fortunately, most dogs are not badly affected by bee stings. The best remedy is to remove the stinger, if it is present, using tweezers, then give your dog an antihistamine tablet and apply a cold pack to the sting. However, as with humans, some dogs react badly to bee stings. If your dog has trouble breathing after a sting or is stung multiple times, seek veterinary care immediately.

Heat and Heatstroke

Heatstroke is one of the gravest dangers to dogs who go hiking in the summer and early fall. It is a life-threatening condition in which your dog's internal temperature exceeds the level compatible with his normal life functions. Put more simply, your dog literally cooks in his own skin. Early symptoms include rapid panting, bright red gums, increased heart rate, elevated temperature (above 103°F), and excess salivation. Heatstroke becomes progressively more severe as your dog's temperature rises. Above 103°F, your dog is at risk of damage to internal organs, including the brain and brain function. If your dog's temperature exceeds 105°F, it is an emergency situation. Symptoms of advanced heatstroke include vomiting, diarrhea, and gums that have gone from bright red to pale pink or white as the body goes into shock. Death can quickly follow if the dog's body temperature is not reduced.

Dogs are perhaps the least heat-tolerant animals that go hiking. They are engineered to sweat only through their footpads and tongue, a very inefficient cooling mechanism. Dogs can suffer heatstroke on warm, sunny days, especially if traveling through places where there is limited shade and water. As an aid to canine comfort and safety, most hikes in this book follow shaded streams or provide access to water every half mile or so.

To minimize the chance of heatstroke, keep your dog lean and fit. You also should acclimate both yourself and your dog to hot weather before attempting backcountry hikes. Remember how warm a 70°F day feels in April—and then how cold that same temperature feels in August after your system has made a seasonal adjustment?

To help prevent heatstroke, give your dog a drink before you begin your hike, and keep her hydrated throughout the trek. Carry plenty of water for your dog. When temperatures rise, stay in the shade and near cold water. Slow down when the weather warms, and if Rover decides it is time to dig a hole in cool forest dirt and lie down, stop and rest a bit yourself while he cools off. If a stream or even a puddle is nearby, immerse your dog.

Heatstroke can overtake and kill your dog in weather that you find comfortable: temperatures of 70°F and above. A black Labrador retriever died of heatstroke in Portland on a sunny spring day with temperatures in the 70s. The dog had trotted for several miles in the sun with its owner—without a drink, shade, or a swim.

Overweight, muzzled, and dehydrated dogs are more susceptible to heatstroke, as are dogs on some medications. And, importantly, dogs that suffer previous heatstroke are then more susceptible to recurrent heatstroke.

To diagnose heatstroke, use a digital rectal thermometer to take the dog's temperature. Normal dog temperature is between 100°F and 102.5°F; above 103°F, your dog is at risk of heatstroke. Do what it takes to cool your dog before heatstroke becomes more serious. If your dog appears hot, provide water, seek shade, and, if possible, immerse the dog in cold water or wet its coat for temporary cooling. If water is not available, apply a cold pack to the dog's head while getting the dog to water. If your dog's temperature exceeds 105°F, carry the dog to avoid further overheating. Immerse the dog in cold water or spray him with cold water to reduce his temperature as quickly as possible. Get Rover into a stream or a puddle.

If your dog suffers heatstroke on the trail but seems to have recovered, it is still wise to visit a veterinarian for a checkup, especially if the dog's temperature was in the danger zone.

Emergency Care

The general approach to canine emergency first aid is a four-step process: restraint, bleeding control, wound care, and transportation. It is also a good idea to scope out the location of the closest veterinarians as you travel to a trailhead—just in case you need to find one quickly.

1. Restraint. An injured dog may misconstrue your actions as causing more pain. He may bite defensively or try to escape. Be prepared to restrain your dog before you administer first aid. For body restraint, roll the dog in your jacket or shirt. A muzzle can prevent bites from an injured dog while you clean or bandage its wounds. A lightweight, humane, and effective temporary muzzle can be made from pantyhose. Wrap the wide portion of the pantyhose once around your dog's muzzle, then cross it in a figure eight and tie the remaining fabric "legs" around your dog's neck.

2. Bleeding control. If bleeding is severe, first stop major bleeding by applying pressure on an artery. If the wound is on a dog's leg, you can slow bleeding by applying pressure to arterial pressure points. On the front legs, grasp the leg just above the elbow and apply pressure between your thumb on the outside and your fingers on the inside. On a rear leg, you can find the large artery on the inside of the dog's leg just below the groin.

3. Wound care. Wounds should be cleaned with water if possible. Lessen minor bleeding by applying petroleum jelly (such as Vaseline) or a triple antibiotic ointment (such as Neosporin) to the wound before bandaging.

Bandaging bleeding wounds. If your dog gets a cut or other bleeding wound, it is likely you will have to wrap the wound. Wounds should be cleaned, covered with a gauze pad, wrapped with gauze wrap, and then secured with self-adhering veterinary wrap (available in human first-aid kits as the slightly more frail "self-adhering tape"). Be careful not to apply this final elastic layer too tightly. You might wish to rewrap the wound after bleeding has stopped.

Torn dewclaws. Active dogs can catch long toenails and dewclaws—the toenails on the upper part of front legs—on rocks or brush; a torn dewclaw can bleed profusely. Clean and bandage the wound as described above until you reach veterinary care.

Puncture wounds. Deep wounds such as puncture wounds are potentially life-threatening. Do not remove any object that has penetrated your dog's body; you might need to apply a light bandage to hold the item in place. Try to find immediate veterinary aid. Assume that shock will occur and keep your dog warm, with hindquarters slightly elevated (see "Treating for shock," below).

Bites. Ragged wounds and shallow puncture wounds such as those that result from bites by other dogs or wild animals can bleed profusely. Some bleeding helps cleanse a deep wound, but, if possible, clean the wound with water, then control bleeding by applying pressure with a gauze pad and bandage the wound as described above. Be careful not to wrap the wound so tightly that you create a tourniquet. Seek veterinary care.

Embedded fishhooks. Dogs are attracted to fishy smells. As they explore these attractive scents along a stream, they can pick up fishhooks in paws, gums, or noses. First restrain and muzzle your dog before attempting to remove a fishhook. If the barbed end of the hook is visible, cut it off with wire cutters and gingerly pull the rest of the hook out. If the barb is not visible, use pliers to push the barbed end through the skin, then cut it off and pull the rest of the hook out. Clean and bandage the wound as described above.

Treating for shock. A dog that sustains cuts or other serious injury might need treatment for shock as well as its injuries. Shock shows up immediately and should be considered in initial treatment. Signs of shock are pale white gums, shallow breathing, a cool body temperature (below 98°F), and a rapid heartbeat. If these symptoms are present, treatment is essential. Place your dog on his side and extend his head and neck to help breathing. Keep the dog warm by wrapping him in a blanket—an emergency space blanket works well. Do not give him anything to eat or drink. Transport him to veterinary care immediately.

Inducing vomiting. If your dog has eaten raw salmon or steelhead, or other potentially lethal material, you can induce vomiting by administering hydrogen peroxide. The dosage is approximately 3 tablespoons for a 70-pound dog. Hold the dog's mouth closed to ensure he swallows the peroxide. If vomiting does not occur in about five minutes, repeat the dosage.

Performing CPR. If your dog has no heartbeat or is not breathing, as might be the case in the event of a near-drowning or a traumatic injury, you can administer cardiopulmonary resuscitation. Canine CPR is similar to human CPR. Clear your dog's airways and pull his tongue forward. Hold his mouth closed, place your mouth over his nose, and breathe into his nose at the rate of 10 to 20 exhalations per minute. Perform heart massage by placing the dog on his right side, positioning your hands on his chest just behind the dog's elbow, and pressing down strongly and abruptly, repeating at the rate of one and a half compressions per second (100 per minute). Perform heart massage for 15 seconds and then breathing for 10 seconds, alternating them until the dog revives.

4. Transportation. To transport an injured dog, you can make an impromptu dog stretcher from a variety of materials, including your tent fly, jacket, or sleeping pad. An emergency space blanket can serve as a stretcher for dogs that weigh no more than 30 pounds. For larger dogs, consider carrying a 36-by-48-inch piece of lightweight nylon or Kevlar fabric in your backpack as part of a basic canine first-aid kit.

Basic Canine First-Aid Kit

Humans need a first-aid kit; dogs need one too. Below is a list of items you need to carry when you hike with your dog. Most of this kit fits nicely into a small nylon sack.

- Tweezers
- Stout, serious, functional multifunction pocket tool (should include scissors, serious wire cutters, pliers, and knife)
- Plastic digital rectal thermometer
- Pantyhose or nylons for muzzle or other restraint

Dundee and Kyla put themselves on a pedestal at Balanced Rocks above the Metolius River in the Deschutes National Forest.

- Gloves (heavy enough to avoid being bitten when handling an injured dog)
- Benadryl or other antihistamine
- Betadine or other antiseptic to disinfect and clean wounds
- Enteric-coated aspirin (aspirin only; no ibuprofen or acetaminophen)
- Hydrogen peroxide
- Petroleum jelly and/or antibiotic ointment
- Gauze bandage
- Veterinary wrap or other semi-elastic, self-sticking outer bandage
- Emergency space blanket
- Chemical cold pack

Be sure that the multitool you carry will cut stout wire and cable, especially if you venture off major park trails—or off trail at all—with your dog. Recently, while I was hiking backcountry in eastern Oregon with my border collie, Kyla, she was caught in an illegal cable snare (set to catch coyotes) located next to the trail. The cable tightened every time she moved, threatening to choke her in a matter of minutes. Fortunately, my stout multitool wire cutters were able to cut the cable so I could free her before she choked to death.

Your canine first-aid kit might also include:

- An oversize dog booty or a soft vinyl camera-lens bag (available in the used bins of camera stores for a dollar or two) to cover an injured paw
- An 8-foot soft nylon rope to use as a spare leash
- Lightweight nylon fabric for use as a stretcher, shade, or shelter
- A handkerchief for washing wounds

How to Use This Book

An information block at the beginning of each hike gives an at-a-glance overview of the hike length, difficulty rating, and other important elements. Information in these blocks is defined as follows:

The hike's total mileage is given as a **round trip** or **one-way trip**. Most round-trip hikes are out and back from a single trailhead. For one-way trips, hikers can either turn around and retrace their steps or arrange for a shuttle or pickup from the far end of the hike. Several hikes offer options for shortening or lengthening a hike.

Elevation range is the hike's lowest and highest elevation, in feet. Commonly, the trailhead is the lowest elevation and the destination is the highest. Where the trailhead is highest and the trail heads downhill, the higher elevation is provided first. Elevations were determined from United States Geological Survey (USGS) topographic maps and a GPS receiver.

Difficulty ranking evaluates the hike's length, steepness, and trail conditions. It is a subjective judgment based on how quickly one works up a sweat or how slowly one must go to navigate challenging terrain. Steep, rough trails that might require crossing fallen trees, include pitches of greater than 6 percent grade, or skirt a cliff for a short distance are judged strenuous. Broad, flat trails are judged easy. Most hikes are classified as moderate, though virtually all vary in difficulty from start to finish.

Hiking time assumes that Fido will want to take a break from time to time, will want to explore a bit and sniff a lot, and that in between doggie dips and sniffing stations you both maintain an average hiking pace of about 2 miles per hour on an easy-to-moderate trail. These are relatively leisurely hikes with more time allotted than for human-only hikes. Fido is in no big hurry.

Best canine hiking season is determined by seasonal trail accessibility, the need for dogs to keep cool, and your need to return to the car with a dog that is relatively clean.

Regulations regard parking permits and leash requirements. All national forest parking areas require a daily or annual Northwest Forest Pass ($5 or $30, respectively, in 2011). Most Oregon state parks require a daily or annual State Parks parking permit ($5 or $30, respectively, in 2011). Many county facilities also charge a parking fee. Portland and Multnomah County Parks offer free parking.

Parking permits are widely available at Forest Service offices, visitor centers, and private retailers or by depositing a fee in a drop box. Travel into the wilderness requires that you fill out a free wilderness permit at a kiosk near the trailhead specifying how many dogs or livestock are going along.

Dogs must be on a 6-foot leash at all times in Oregon state parks. This rule also applies to many Forest Service interpretive and recreational trails and to about half the hikes in this book. Dogs are banned on all national park trails in Oregon, though leashed dogs are permitted in Crater Lake National Park on the park's segment of the Pacific Crest Trail.

The **maps** listed are from the United States Geological Survey (USGS) 7.5-minute quadrangle series. These maps are available in many bookstores, sporting goods stores, and other retailers, online, by phone, and at ranger stations and information centers.

Information includes the name and telephone number of the agency responsible for the hiking area.

Getting there provides driving directions to the trailhead from a nearby town.

Appendix A at the back of this book lists the agencies responsible for the hiking areas in this book, as well as contact information.

Appendix B provides a list of recommended reading.

A Note About Safety

Safety is an important concern in all outdoor activities. No guidebook can alert you to every hazard or anticipate the limitations of every reader. Therefore, the descriptions of roads, trails, routes, and natural features in this book are not representations that a particular place or excursion will be safe for your party. When you follow any of the routes described in this book, you assume responsibility for your own safety. Under normal conditions, such excursions require the usual attention to traffic, road and trail conditions, weather, terrain, the capabilities of your party, and other factors. Keeping informed on current conditions and exercising common sense are the keys to a safe, enjoyable outing.

The Mountaineers Books

PART 2

The Trails

Dog, n. A kind of additional or subsidiary
Deity designed to catch the overflow
and surplus of the world's worship.
—Ambrose Bierce
(The Devil's Dictionary, 1911)

WILLAMETTE VALLEY AND PORTLAND AREA

1. Tryon Creek State Park

Round trip: 3.8 miles
Elevation range: 115–260 feet
Difficulty: Easy
Hiking time: 1.5 hours
Best canine hiking season: Year-round
Regulations: No park fee; dogs must be on leash
Map: USGS Lake Oswego 7.5' quadrangle
Information: Tryon Creek State Park, (503) 636-9886; Oregon
State Parks, (800) 551-6949

Getting there: From Interstate 5 in Portland, take exit 297 (Terwilliger Boulevard). Turn east onto Terwilliger Boulevard and go 2.3 miles to the entrance to Tryon Creek State Park on the right. Follow the entry road 0.1 mile to the parking area. Trailheads are west of the parking lot near the Nature Center.

This 645-acre state park is tucked away in the southern hills of Portland, just north of Lake Oswego. It offers a variety of rolling trails through forest. Don't expect solitude here. You'll share the trails with hikers, horses,

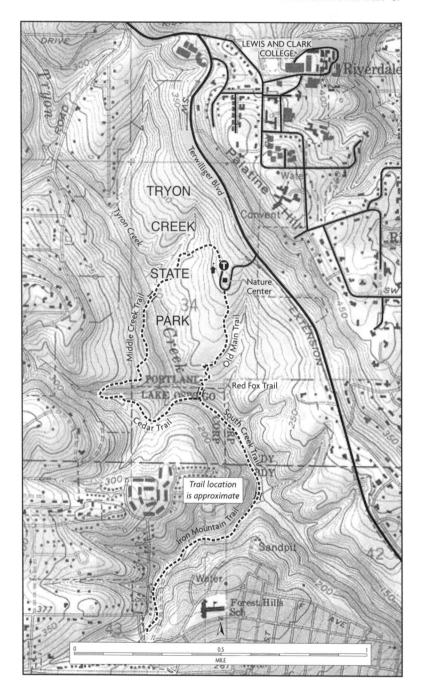

LEWIS AND CLARK
COLLEGE

Riverdale

TRYON

CREEK

STATE

34

PARK

Convent Hill

Nature
Center

Middle Creek Trail

Tryon Creek

Old Main Trail

PORTLAND
LAKE OSWEGO

Red Fox Trail

Cedar Trail

South Creek Trail

*Trail location
is approximate*

Iron Mountain Trail

Sandpit

Water

Forest Hills
Sch.

Terwilliger Blvd

Palatine

EXTENSION

DRIVE

Tyron
Road

300

350

450

250

350

300

200

377

350

0   0.5   1
                              MILE

Michelle and her golden retriever, Dasha, hike a shaded trail in Tryon Creek State Park.

and, on some paths, mountain bikers. It is green and quiet, however, and a quick getaway at the edge of the city. This is a state park, so dogs must be on a leash no more than 6 feet long.

The hike begins at the Nature Center. Turn left (south) on the Old Main Trail—a relatively broad, flat thoroughfare. The path strides through a largely alder and big-leaf maple forest that replaced the conifer forest logged in the late 1800s. The path forks in 0.2 mile. Turn left heading down the winding, switchbacking Red Fox Trail as it scoots into the canyon of Tryon Creek. Here's a good place for a quick doggie dip—on leash, of course.

Cross the sturdy bridge here and turn left onto the South Creek Trail. This leads to an out-and-back hike of 2 miles. Follow the South Creek Trail along the ivy-festooned alder and Douglas fir forest of Tryon Creek for 0.4 mile to its junction with the Iron Mountain Trail at a bridge. Both chinook salmon and steelhead spawn in Tryon Creek. Keep an eye out for fish here in the fall and winter, and don't let your dog sample any of the spawned-out adults.

At the bridge, turn right and continue uphill on the Iron Mountain Trail another 0.6 mile to the trail's end on Iron Mountain Boulevard. Turn around here to return the way you came to the junction with the Red Fox Trail. Jog left at the junction to join the Cedar Trail—a path that clings to the steep canyon slope, ducking beneath cedars and Douglas fir.

The Cedar Trail crosses a small creek in 0.4 mile and contours northward to find Tryon Creek again. Continue north along the creek to High Bridge. Cross this bridge and follow the meandering Middle Creek Trail 0.3 mile upslope back to the parking area and Nature Center.

2. Forest Park Wildwood Trail

One-way trip: 21 miles
Elevation range: 240–820 feet
Difficulty: Moderate
Hiking time: All day
Best canine hiking season: Year-round
Regulations: Dogs must be on leash
Map: USGS Portland 7.5' quadrangle
Information: Portland Department of Parks and Recreation, (503) 823-7529

Getting there: To reach the south trailhead (Pittock Mansion) where this hike starts, from downtown Portland follow West Burnside Avenue 2.7 miles west from the Burnside Bridge or 1.3 miles west from Northwest 23rd Avenue. Turn right (north) onto Northwest Barnes Road, go 0.7 mile, and then turn right at the relatively obscure entry sign for Pittock Mansion. Follow the entrance road about 0.2 mile to the visitor parking lot. The trailhead is on the north side of the parking lot.

To reach the north trailhead (Germantown Road) where you will park a second car, from Portland take Interstate 405 west to its merger with U.S. Highway 30. Follow US 30/NW Yeon Avenue west for 5 miles. Continue another 0.2 mile past the Saint Johns Bridge. Turn left onto Northwest Bridge Avenue and in 0.24 mile make a sharp right onto Northwest Germantown Road. Follow Northwest Germantown Road 1.2 miles to a small pullout on the left and the north trailhead for the Wildwood Trail.

The trail in Forest Park offers solitude, mile-markers, and shade.

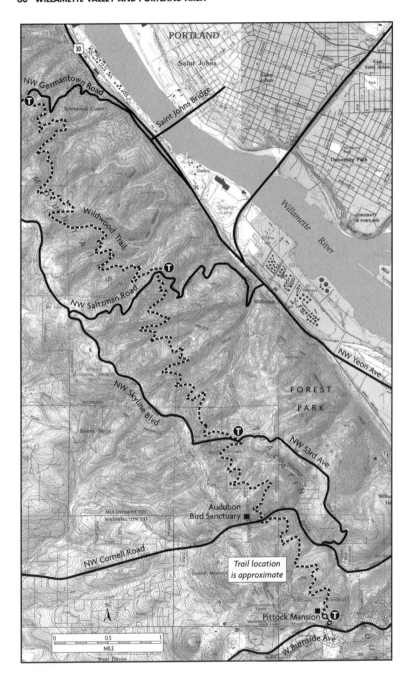

Trail location
is approximate

Even though it is within the city of Portland, the Wildwood Trail in Forest Park is a worthy wilderness hike. Many Portlanders drive for hours to access trails that are not much wilder than what they have in their own backyard. This 21-mile segment of the 24.6-mile Wildwood Trail crosses several streams and avoids the portions of the path with the most foot traffic. Road crossings along the way provide turnaround points for shorter hikes. Expect plenty of people along this trail, including runners and cyclists. Dogs must remain leashed in this enormous—more than 5000 acres—city park, which is the largest in the United States. Carry plenty of water for your dog in the summer.

Before you plunge into the forest at Pittock Mansion, take a moment to walk east, past the mansion, to take in the vista of Portland and Mount Hood. It's one of the few views on the entire hike. Although you'll be hiking along the top of the Tualatin Mountains—also known as Portland's West Hills—trees obscure the landscape. The forest here is mostly second-growth fir interspersed with alder and big-leaf maple, though you'll also find cedars and western hemlock along the way.

From the Pittock Mansion trailhead, the path plunges into a dense woodland as it heads north. The trail is broad and meanders downhill here, reaching Northwest Cornell Road and an Audubon Society reserve in about 2 miles. This first mile or two can be fairly congested, but the crowds thin once you get beyond Cornell Road. You can find water for a doggie dip at Balch Creek 3.5 miles from the Pittock trailhead.

All along the trail, the forest varies in its density of Douglas fir, incense cedar, hemlock, alder, and big-leaf maple. Look for the scraggly Pacific yew in moist, heavily shaded spots. Sword ferns dominate the forest floor, with salal running a close second. Watch for a few rhododendrons showing off in the spring. The trail contours along the intricate topography, sometimes dropping slightly to avoid steep slopes, sometimes rising gently to cross divides.

At 5.3 miles from the Pittock Mansion, the trail crosses Northwest 53rd Avenue—a point for easy automobile access if needed. The path then returns to its meandering through the trees. Watch for anachronisms along the hike. For example, you'll find fire hydrants tucked in the underbrush—what more could any dog ask for? Many are relics of efforts to develop the park in the early 20th century. The broad character of the Wildwood Trail belies its origin as a roadway for both development and logging. Look for white mileage posts marked ORRC—artifacts of the Oregon Road Runners Club.

At 12 miles from the Pittock Mansion, the path descends into the broad canyon of Saltzman Creek and intersects Northwest Saltzman Road. This road is a good destination for a day hike—consider it as a drop point if you wish to hike the 8 miles from this road to Germantown Road, the next easy access point. Parking is available in a small four-car area.

Your best bets for doggie dips along the Wildwood Trail include nameless creeks at about 7, 9, and 10 miles into the hike, as well as Saltzman Creek at mile 12. However, the trail tours the upper portion of these drainages, so the water is usually gone by midsummer.

Look for glimpses of Mount Hood about 16 miles into the hike. As the trail gradually descends to Germantown Road, it teases you with views of the Willamette River industrial parks. The sound of traffic presages your return to civilization about 0.2 mile before you reach the Germantown trailhead.

3. Sandy River Delta

Round trip: 2 miles on gravel trail; much farther if you wish
Elevation range: 0 feet
Difficulty: Easy
Hiking time: 1 hour or more
Best canine hiking season: Year-round
Regulations: Northwest Forest Pass required; dogs must be on
    leash on gravel path and within 100 feet of gravel path
Map: USGS Camas, WA, and Washougal, WA, 7.5' quadrangle
Information: Columbia River Gorge National Scenic Area, (541)
    308-1700

Getting there: From Portland, drive east on Interstate 84. Take exit 18 just beyond Troutdale. Turn right at the stop sign, and drive under the freeway. Bear left into the parking area just before you reenter the freeway on-ramp.

A decade ago, the Sandy River Delta park was a little-known refuge for Portland-area dogs and their human staffers to go on hikes. The parking

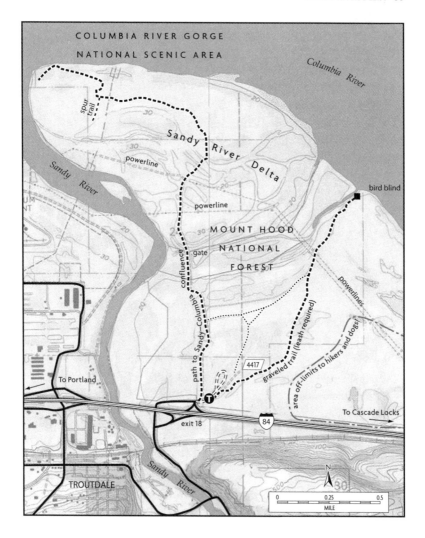

area was a mud hole perilously close to the freeway. The trails were a bewildering network that twisted through woods and berry patches with no signage and every opportunity to get lost. Occasionally a terrified deer would break from cover. It was a place to get away from it all with no regulation and a lot of area to roam.

Today, the Forest Service has tamed its 1400-acre jewel, with a nicely developed paved parking area (with restrooms!), a marked, signed gravel trail that leads to the Columbia River, rules for dogs and dog-staffers,

Pleeeeze throw the ball???!! On a cool, windy day, Jen gets ready to toss a ball for Murphy along a trail on the Sandy River Delta.

and areas preserved for wildlife and habitat restoration where neither humans nor canids may tread. All these changes are for the better, and the Sandy River Delta (a patch of land created by a huge mudflow from Mount Hood's 1705 eruption and noted by Lewis and Clark a century later as an area of low-growing alders and quicksand) remains an excellent place for people and pooches.

Start your exploration with a stroll down the mile-long, all-weather, handicapped-accessible graveled path (FS trail 4417) to the Columbia and a bird blind where you can watch migrating waterfowl aplenty in the spring and fall. This is the only trail that requires a leash, so keep Fido tethered to you on the pathway and within 100 feet of the trail.

Beyond the graveled FS trail 4417, there are no leash requirements, and you can hike the paths, play fetch, or make your way to the Sandy or Columbia river for a swim. It's a longish trek from parking area to shoreline, so carry plenty of water for yourself and Fido.

A favorite and (relatively) easy-to-follow off-leash 4-mile out-and-back trek is along an old road-dike from just west of the parking lot to the confluence of the Sandy and Columbia rivers. The trail starts at a green metal gate just fifty yards from the park entrance. The first portion is a very straight, built-up "dike" with a fine graveled road atop it that served to confine the Sandy River when the rest of its delta was grazed and farmed—and planned for some sort of development. Today a cottonwood forest occupies low areas adjacent to the dike, and a heavy, productive hedge of blackberries offers late summer snacking. In 0.5 mile, the trees fade and the path morphs into a softer trail. Bear right, and continue on the broad path—once a road.

In 0.5 mile from the start, the path crosses a broad wetland swale (once a small Columbia River channel) and then encounters a gate. Continue through the gate (please close it after you go through), and in 1 mile from the hike's start, scoot beneath the first of two huge powerlines. Beyond the powerlines, you'll find a fence and another dike—this one built to keep the Columbia River at bay. The path leads through an opening in the fence and to the top of the dike. Follow this path, which curves generally to the left, through grassy open spaces and tree groves. After another 0.5 mile, turn right at a trail intersection and follow this path to the Columbia.

The Sandy River Delta parkland offers an almost infinite variety of walks. Your main challenges will be keeping track of where you've been, so you can return to the car, and deciding which trails to follow next time.

4. Sauvie Island: Warrior Rock Trail

Round trip: 5.8 miles
Elevation range: 0 feet
Difficulty: Easy
Hiking time: 3 hours
Best canine hiking season: September–March
Regulations: Parking permit required at or near trailhead (applies to all Oregon Department of Fish and Wildlife trailheads on the island); daily or annual permits available at Cracker Barrel Store on Sauvie Island Road, 7-Eleven store in Linnton, and G.I. Joe's stores in Portland; dogs must be on leash
Map: USGS Sauvie Island 7.5' quadrangle
Information: Oregon Department of Fish and Wildlife, (503) 621-3488

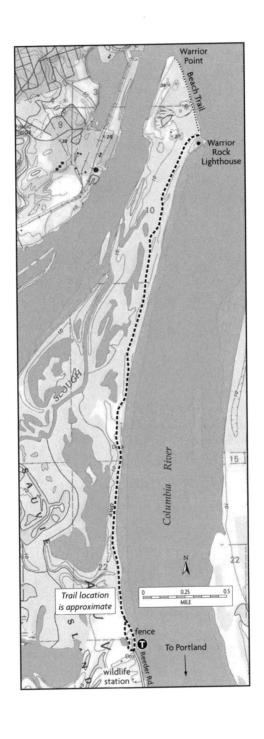

Warrior
Point

Beach Trail

Warrior
Rock
Lighthouse

10

10

10

SLOUGH

S A U V I E

Columbia River

10

15

10

22

N

22

Trail location
is approximate

0   0.25   0.5
MILE

fence

To Portland

T

Reeder Rd.

S L A N V

wildlife
station

The lighthouse at the north end of Sauvie Island overlooks the Columbia River near Warrior Rock.

Getting there: From Portland, take U.S. Highway 30 west 6 miles through the town of Linnton. Four miles west of Linnton, turn right to cross the Sauvie Island Bridge. Continue west (left) on Sauvie Island Road and at 3.2 miles, turn right onto Reeder Road. In another 8 miles, Reeder Road changes to a wide gravel road and continues as gravel for 3.4 miles to the trailhead at the road's end 14.6 miles from the Sauvie Island Bridge.

This 2.9-mile hike to Warrior Rock weaves along the Columbia River through cottonwood groves and grassy glades to a lighthouse and rocky point where Multnomah tribal members greeted Captain William Broughton and his ship in 1792. Broughton commanded one of the ships in the expedition with Captain George Vancouver, the first European to explore the Columbia River tidewater.

Sauvie Island is Portland's breadbasket—a farming community with lush pastures and rich soils. Its northern and western ends are also a wildlife refuge, and dogs must remain leashed on this hike. Migratory waterfowl and songbirds, as well as residents such as great blue herons, abound here. You might encounter cattle grazing in the pasture adjacent to the trailhead and along the first portion of the trail from the parking lot, so be doubly sure that your dog is under control as you begin your hike. Despite the proximity of the Columbia River, there's no potable dog water along the way, so carry extra for four-legged hiking companions.

From the parking area, the unmarked Warrior Rock Trail follows a narrow path through a wooden gate and then minces between a cow pasture and Columbia beaches that often host anglers or families on a summer outing. Just beyond the cow pasture, a blue stock gate offers an easy entrance to a grassy field. The narrow path leads through this gate to a service road. Alternatively, you can follow a path along the shoreline that joins the service road in 0.2 mile. This route thrashes its way through blackberries and crosses a partly downed barbed wire fence.

The main path leads through cottonwoods on a level grade. This path to the lighthouse is a double-track road that consistently bears to the right (toward the river) wherever it junctions with other trails. Two open areas are noteworthy. The first, encountered about 0.75 mile into the hike, flirts with the open sky for about 100 yards, then ducks back under trees. At 2 miles into the hike, another grassy open area about 200 yards long opens up.

The main trail reaches the northern tip of Sauvie Island at 2.9 miles. The lighthouse is to the right of the trail. Use caution in letting dogs swim at the lighthouse. The Columbia River currents can be treacherous here, and it is an abrupt plunge from rocks into deep water. Better swimming can be found to the left, where the beaches are sandy and the water is less turbulent.

During times where the Columbia's flow and the tides permit, you can return by walking along the beach on the Columbia side. If you choose this route, be ready to wade in a few places and be wary of oily flotsam and dead fish. Even a single taste of a dead salmon can kill a dog. This route offers the advantages of an open view of the river and its oversize cargo vessel traffic, as well as the Ridgefield and Bachelor Island wildlife refuges and the mouth of the Lewis River across the Columbia.

5. Silver Falls State Park: Perimeter Trail

Round trip: 10 miles
Elevation range: 1500–2200 feet
Difficulty: Moderate
Hiking time: 5 hours
Best canine hiking season: Spring, summer, fall
Regulations: Oregon State Parks parking permit required; dogs must be on 6-foot leash and able to respond to your commands, and you must be physically capable of restraining your dog
Maps: USGS Drake Crossing and Stout Mountain 7.5' quadrangles
Information: Silver Falls State Park, (503) 873-8681

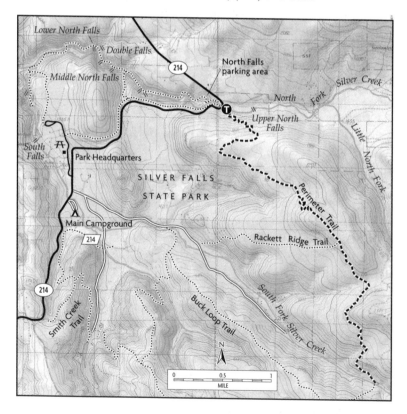

Many trails in Silver Falls State Park, including the Smith Creek Trail, provide for multiple uses.

Getting there: From Salem, take Interstate 5 to eastbound Oregon Route 22 (Santiam Highway). Drive 11.8 miles on OR 22 and turn north onto OR 214, marked for Silver Falls State Park. Follow OR 214 for 15 miles to the park boundary. Continue into the park on OR 214, and park in the North Falls parking area.

Unfortunately, although Silver Falls State Park showcases many waterfalls, including four more than 80 feet high, your pooches will never get to see them, as dogs are not allowed on the most popular of the park's trails—those that tour the waterfalls. This rule is imposed for the safety of both pooches and people, as trails to waterfalls are slippery and usually tour the edges of steep cliffs. However, the park offers 25 miles of interesting backcountry hikes for dogs, including the 214 Trail, the Smith Creek Trail, and the 15-mile Perimeter Trail.

Of all the dog-friendly paths in the park, the first 5 miles of the Perimeter Trail offer the best access to water. The trail crosses four creeks before descending to the south fork of Silver Creek, the destination of this hike. The Perimeter Trail leads to not a single waterfall, as the sign at its start forewarns. However, it is a delightful and usually private hike—most of the crowds flock to the waterfalls, leaving the hiking here to the more adventurous. The path explores a typical and diverse Cascade second-growth forest, with Douglas fir and hemlock stands and riparian areas replete with cedar, alder, and big-leaf maple. Please keep dogs leashed at all times in this Oregon state park.

The trail leads uphill—a total of 500 switchbacking feet in the first mile. The forest is shady and welcoming, and there's plenty for Fido to sniff. (Remember the leash rule, though . . .) Then the path curves right and tops out in a fir and big-leaf maple forest. The path remains flat and in about 0.3 mile encounters an old gravel roadway. Continue to the left here.

For the next mile, the trail is effectively flat, with small rises and falls through the forest. It encounters a series of marshy seeps and streams—welcome for Fido—with strategically located bridges, before climbing another 300 feet through irregular switchbacks to reach a higher forested plateau. Just beyond the summit, the Perimeter Trail intersects the Rackett Ridge Trail. Continue straight on the Perimeter Trail. (The Rackett Ridge's path leads down to the Howard Creek horse area—but nowhere near your North Falls Trailhead.)

Beyond the Rackett Ridge Trail intersection, the Perimeter Trail drops slowly into the gentle canyon of Silver Creek's South Fork. You'll reach the clear, shallow waters of the creek at 4.8 miles from the North Falls Trailhead. Return as you came.

Another hiking option in Silver Falls State Park is the 214 Trail–Smith Creek Trail system. This trail is accessed at the other end of the park, descending into Smith Creek canyon in a long, elegant switchback. It joins the Smith Creek Trail and continues about 1.5 miles to Smith Creek itself, then climbs again to a flat ridgetop. Ultimately in about 5 miles the Smith Creek Trail connects with the Buck Loop Trail, which in another 6 miles connects to the Perimeter Trail—a 15-mile hike. Consult Silver Falls State Park maps as guidance for navigating the complex trail system.

6. Howard Buford County Recreation Area: Mount Pisgah

Round trip: 7.8 miles
Elevation range: 510–1561 feet
Difficulty: Moderate
Hiking time: 4 hours
Best canine hiking season: Fall, winter, spring
Regulations: Park hours are dawn to dusk; leashes required on trails 1 and 2—dogs must be under voice command on all other trails; stay on designated trails and do not disturb vegetation; pick up and dispose of all waste
Map: USGS Springfield 7.5' quadrangle
Information: Lane County Parks, Mount Pisgah Arboretum, (541) 747-3817 or (541) 682-2000

Getting there: From Interstate 5 at Eugene, take exit 188, Oregon Route 58/Willamette Highway. Almost immediately after exiting I-5 (virtually at the end of the exit ramp), turn left (north) onto Seavy Loop Road marked for Buford Park. Follow Seavy Loop Road 1.8 miles to a T intersection, and then turn right (north) onto Seavy Way to cross a bridge over the Coast Fork of the Willamette River. Once across the bridge, turn left into a large parking area. The trailhead is at the west end of the parking area.

Whether you are looking for a short, scenic hike or an all-day outing, Mount Pisgah in the Howard Buford County Recreation Area is an excellent place for hikers and their dogs. This Lane County park features 2300 acres of an almost-native Willamette Valley hilltop oak savanna balanced between the Middle and South forks of the Willamette River. Park rules require that you keep dogs leashed on the main trail to the summit and under immediate control on other trails, that dogs do not harass wildlife (there are plenty of squirrels here, and chasing squirrels is a definite no-no), and that you clean up dog waste.

The most popular hike in the huge Buford Recreation Area starts on Trail 7, the Bridge Bowl Trail, from the North Trailhead about 0.6 mile west of the arboretum and winds its way to the summit in 3.8 miles. At a trail junction just past an entry gate to the trail, bear to the right. The trail meanders upward. Its mild switchbacks and curves make the walk interesting.

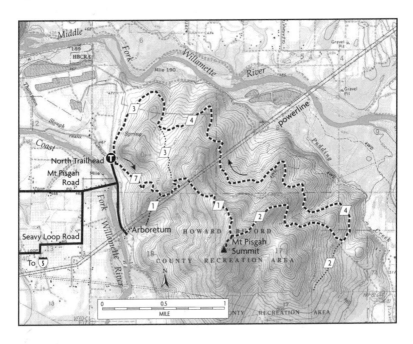

Trails on Mount Pisgah provide a hike through forest and native oak savanna, as well as a view of the surrounding Willamette Valley.

At 0.7 mile, the trail merges with Trail 1, Beistel's West Summit Trail. This hike explores a tiny remnant of the Willamette Valley's native oak woodland, though there are also plenty of tall Douglas firs here, mostly on more moist and sheltered slopes. The firs provide a welcome, deeper shade on summer hikes, but the gnarly countenance of the white oaks makes Mount Pisgah a special place. The landscape is being slowly restored from grazing. Watch for poison oak along the trail on sunny, open slopes and in oak glades.

The path navigates mostly oak savanna, providing exquisite views of the valley to the south as it climbs. The first 2 miles cross several small drainages that can provide a doggie dip in winter, but they are dry most of the year, so be sure to carry plenty of water for your dog, especially on sunny days, as much of the hike crosses open savanna. The main summit trail tours stands of Douglas fir about halfway to the summit, then remains on open ground for the rest of the trudge to the 1561-foot summit. From the top, Mount Pisgah provides a superior view of the Willamette Valley, the Cascades, and even hints of the Klamath Mountains to the southwest.

Take Trail 2, Beistel's East Summit Trail, to descend. This path is narrower, rockier, steeper, and rougher than the veritable freeway that leads to the summit. It tours grassland and oak savanna. It also boasts considerable poison oak along the path, so it's best to take this trail during the winter when poison oak is not in leaf.

Leading steeply down from the Mount Pisgah summit, Trail 2 meanders less than the main summit trail and reaches the East Trailhead on the Middle Fork of the Willamette in 2 miles. Before that, turn left onto Trail 4, the West Boundary Trail. The path wobbles toward the west, connecting with Trail 3, the West Slope Trail (a short loop hike around a small butte just west of Pisgah) in about 0.5 mile. It ducks under cover of fir trees as it swings west around the base of the mountain and turns toward the first trailhead. The path returns to the trailhead parking area 4 miles from the summit.

Five More Great Dog Hikes in the Willamette Valley and Portland Area

1. Marine Drive bike and hiking path, 12 miles one way along the Columbia River beginning at 33rd Avenue and Marine Drive. Portland Bureau of Parks and Recreation, (503) 823-2223 or (503) 823-7529.

2. Milo McIver State Park, Clackamas River, 4.3-mile loop. Milo McIver State Park, (800) 551-6949.

3. Powell Butte Perimeter and other trails; you can hike for more than 5 miles here easily. Powell Butte is crisscrossed by multiple trails, and most trails remain informal. Parking is off 162nd and Powell. Portland Bureau of Parks and Recreation, (503) 823-2223 or (503) 823-7529.

4. Portland Springwater Corridor, a 21-mile-long bike and hiking path from SE Ivon Street to the town of Boring, has a few stretches that need completion, but most of this trail along waterways and riparian areas is hikeable. The corridor connects several parks and open spaces, including Tideman Johnson Nature Park, Beggars-tick Wildlife Refuge, the Interstate 205 Bike Path, Leach Botanical Garden, Powell Butte Nature Park, and Gresham's Main City Park. Portland Bureau of Parks and Recreation, (503) 823-2223 or (503) 823-7529.

5. Little North Fork Santiam Trail, #3338, 9 miles round trip, follows the Little North Fork Santiam River, but there's nothing little about this hike; the trail is located about 25 miles east of Salem off Oregon Route 22 and not too far from Silver Falls State Park. Northwest Forest Pass is required at the trailhead. Opal Creek Wilderness, with 36 miles of trails, is also found farther along the North Santiam River Road, off OR 22. Detroit Ranger District, Detroit Ranger Station, (503) 854-3366.

COLUMBIA RIVER GORGE

7. Larch Mountain (almost) to Multnomah Falls

Round trip: 12 miles
Elevation range: 4056–150 feet
Difficulty: Moderate
Hiking time: 6 hours
Best canine hiking season: Spring, summer, fall
Regulations: Keep dogs leashed in Larch Mountain picnic areas and near Multnomah Falls
Maps: USGS Bridal Veil and Multnomah Falls 7.5' quadrangles
Information: Mount Hood National Forest Headquarters, (503) 668-1700; Columbia River Gorge National Scenic Area, (541) 308-1700; Multnomah Falls Lodge Visitor Center, (503) 695-2372

Getting there: To reach the Larch Mountain trailhead, from Portland follow Interstate 84 east to exit 22, Corbett. Turn right and follow the curving road 2 miles to a junction with Columbia River Gorge Highway (U.S. Highway 30). Turn left (east) onto the Columbia River Gorge Highway and drive 2 miles to Larch Mountain Road at a Y intersection. Follow Larch Mountain Road (Forest Road 15) 10 miles to the trailhead at the road's end.

While gazillions of people mob Multnomah Falls and millions hike the first mile of switchbacking Forest Service Trail 441 to the top of the falls, practically no one hikes the other end of this well-maintained and easy trail at Larch

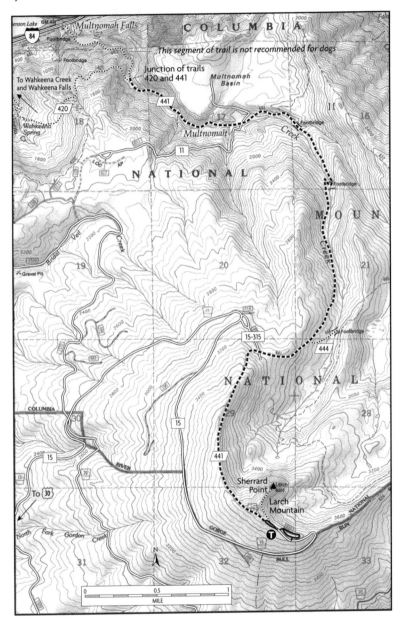

Mountain. Though the full length of the trail is 7 miles, it is recommended that you turn around at mile 6 during the high-volume summer months. If you must make this a through-hike from Larch Mountain all the way to Multnomah Falls, your dog will be a lot happier if you hike it in the spring or on a weekday when the trail is less crowded—otherwise, the last mile of trail can be a lot like waiting in line for concert tickets while taking a shower in the falls overspray.

Trail 441 departs from the Larch Mountain picnic area just west of the parking area. Before you head out, be sure to take the short walk to Sherrard Point, which has a spectacular view of the Portland Basin and Columbia River. Trail 441 leads along a ridge crest at an even and level pace through a dark forest of small Douglas firs, western hemlocks, and grand firs that provides shade and a sense of privacy. Listen for the flutelike song of the hermit thrush here early in the summer.

At 1.3 miles, the path and forest change. The trail turns more steeply downhill, crossing a road and entering an old-growth forest dominated by Douglas fir. At 1.8 miles, Trail 444 turns east and drops even more steeply downhill. If you are looking for a doggie dip, a short stroll downhill on this trail will bring you to Multnomah Creek. Return to Trail 441 and continue toward Multnomah Falls. At 2.5 miles, the trail touches the creek, then follows it for the remainder of the hike, crossing the water on sturdy footbridges at 3 miles and 3.5 miles and returning again to water at 4 miles just after crossing a gravel road.

From this point, Multnomah Creek gets very serious as it gears up for the falls. Its channel steepens and the creek enters a real canyon. It becomes a hazard for dogs, rather than a friend. Between 4 and 5.5 miles, the trail edges along the creek, sometimes on the brink of sheer and quite slippery cliffs. The final 1.5 miles largely spiral downhill, crossing the bridge across the falls and landing among the multinational crowds, outdoor vendors, and smells of espresso at Multnomah Lodge. Return as you came, or if you ventured all the way to the lodge, catch a ride back to your car with a friend.

8. Gorge Trail 400–406: Wyeth Campground to Herman Creek Campground

Round trip: 6.7 miles
Elevation range: 320–750 feet
Difficulty: Easy to moderate
Hiking time: 4 hours
Best canine hiking season: Year-round
Regulations: Northwest Forest Pass required to park at Wyeth Campground; dogs must be on leash
Map: Columbia River Gorge National Scenic Area trails map (this trail is not on most maps!)
Information: Columbia River Gorge National Scenic Area, (541) 308-1700

Getting there: From Interstate 84 in the Columbia River Gorge, take exit 51, Wyeth. Turn right and drive 0.25 mile to the entry to USFS Wyeth Campground. Drive south on this entry road to a parking area at the trailhead.

This segment of the Gorge Trail is relatively new and stays at low elevations for most of its length. It explores the heart of the Columbia River gorge and its steep topography, with very little need for climbing as it skirts the cliffs. In the spring, a profusion of wildflowers tickles your sense. Look for rare chocolate lilies near the trailhead and trilliums along the main trail in the spring.

Wyeth Campground and the entry road close in late September (usually September 30th) and open in late May. However, early- or late-season

hikers are welcome to park at the locked gate and walk 0.25 mile to the trailhead.

An excellent side excursion to a pretty waterfall invites, before or after your hike, to Herman Creek on the main Gorge trail. To find the falls, continue straight past the Gorge Trail bridge for about 0.5 mile. This trail is informal and not maintained, but is generally well-worn and easy to follow. The path stops at the falls. Return to the main trail as you came.

The trail begins at the Wyeth USFS Campground's trailhead, sequestered at the south end of the campground. About 10 yards into the woods here, turn right on Gorge Trail 400–406 and cross Gorton Creek on a nice, new (but appropriately rustic) wooden bridge. The trail rises ominously but within 0.5 mile flattens, and for the rest of its length, it retains relatively docile gradients.

A rustic bridge across Gorton Creek marks the start of the Gorge Trail portion of the Wyeth to Herman Creek hike.

At 1.1 miles into the hike the trail encounters Grays Creek, which tumbles down the impressive cliffs exposed above the trail. The trail dances with adjacent powerlines before slinking back into the forest. It rises to an elevation of about 750 feet before returning to near river level at Herman Creek Campground in 3.35 miles. Return as you came.

If you and your pooch are fitness fanatics, you might try a somewhat more demanding route to get from Wyeth to Herman Creek. From Wyeth Campground, turn left onto Trail 411 instead of right on 400–406. This route rises about 3900 feet in 4.5 zigzagging miles to reach North Lake. From North Lake, take Trail 423 for a flat mile to its junction with Trail 408. Trail 408 abruptly climbs a ridge and then drops back to Herman Creek Campground in about 8 miles. Both of these trails manage to avoid cliffs for most of their distance. However, water is scarce, and trail conditions are not as reliably good as on Trail 400–406.

9. Oneonta Gorge: Triple Falls

Round trip: 7.4 miles
Elevation range: 120–1430 feet
Difficulty: Moderate
Hiking time: 3.5 hours
Best canine hiking season: Year-round
Regulations: Dogs must be on leash
Map: USGS Multnomah Falls 7.5' quadrangle
Information: Columbia River Gorge National Scenic Area, (541) 308-1700; Multnomah Falls Lodge Visitor Center, (503) 695-2372

Getting there: From Portland, drive east on Interstate 84 to exit 28, Bridal Veil. Take this exit and turn left (east) onto the Columbia River Gorge Highway (U.S. Highway 30). Drive 3.5 miles to a parking area on the right with a poorly marked trailhead. If you cross Oneonta Creek, you've gone about 0.4 mile too far.

Most hikers to Triple Falls begin at Horsetail Falls, about 1.5 miles east of this trailhead. By starting at the less popular trailhead, you avoid crowds, a few slippery jaunts behind two waterfalls, and the botanically sensitive

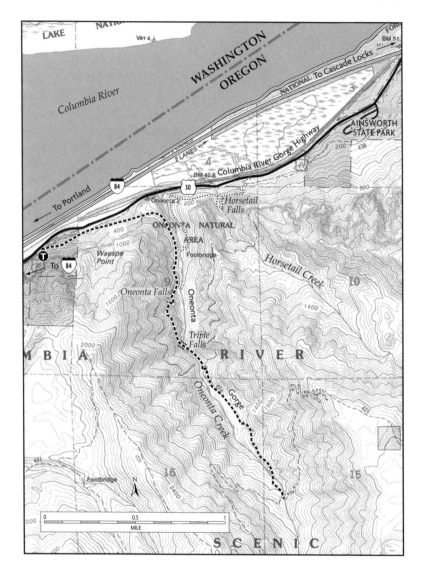

areas of Oneonta Gorge. There are some steep drop-offs and cliffs along the way, so keep dogs leashed.

The trail begins with a long, gentle ascent through a forest of Douglas fir and vine maple. At 1.1 miles the path enters Oneonta Gorge and turns to the south. There are several good views into the steep canyon, but for the most part, trees screen and soften the steepest trailside drops.

At 1.8 miles, the official Oneonta Falls Trail merges from the left. Continue straight ahead.

This portion of the route also hugs the canyon rim. The path is relatively flat and allows ample room for passing others. At 2.5 miles into the hike, the trail reaches a broad rock rim, providing a view of Triple Falls—a place where the creek divides into three separate plumes as it dives over a rock bench and enters Oneonta Gorge. From the overview (not a good place to hang out with dogs), the path leads down to a bridge across the creek.

From this point, the nearly level trail follows the creek closely. The trail beyond the creek crossing is little used and, for dogs, is the best part of the hike. It continues through spectacular old-growth forest for another 1.2 miles before

Tara, a seven-year-old Labrador mix, keeps a watchful eye on lunch below the bridge across Oneonta Creek.

it begins to climb away from the creek. Turn around where the trail begins its ascent away from water and return as you came.

10. Wahclella Falls

Round trip: 1.8 miles
Elevation range: 500–800 feet
Difficulty: Easy
Hiking time: 1 hour
Best canine hiking season: Year-round
Regulations: Dogs must be on leash
Map: USGS Tanner Butte 7.5' quadrangle
Information: Columbia River Gorge National Scenic Area, (541) 308-1700; Multnomah Falls Lodge Visitor Center, (503) 695-2372

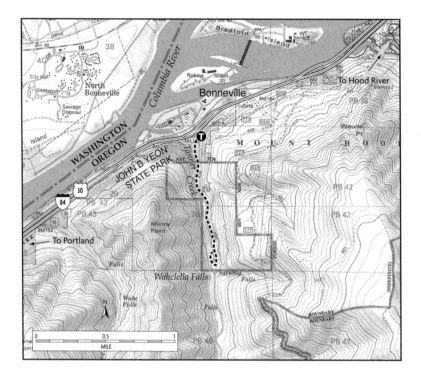

Getting there: From Portland, drive east on Interstate 84 to exit 40, Bonneville Dam. At the end of the exit ramp, turn right (south) and continue to a parking area at the end of the roadway.

This short hike dead-ends at a spectacular, 120-foot double falls. The trail is an easy grade, water is accessible, and use is fairly light for a Gorge trail.

From the parking area, the path skirts along Tanner Creek, keeping the creek within easy sight. The trail rises over several groups of creek-smoothed boulders and tours a forest of mostly Douglas fir. Side trails invite contemplative visits to Tanner Creek.

At 0.7 mile, the canyon opens up, providing a view of a huge, moss-covered cliff on the west. In winter and early summer, a misty waterfall plunges over this wall of rock. You can hear the roar of Wahclella Falls before you see it. At 0.9 mile, the trail rises a bit, providing a view of the double falls.

The path scampers downslope for a more intimate view and crosses an arching wooden bridge just downstream. The bridge leads to a rock-strewn

The double cataract at Wahclella Falls is breathtakingly scenic.

slope below the misty falls. This is a great place for dogs to explore and unwind before the trip back to the car. Return as you came.

11. Atiyeh Deschutes River Trail

Round trip: 2–34 miles
Elevation range: 180–500 feet
Difficulty: Easy
Hiking time: 2 hours–2 days
Best canine hiking season: Fall, winter, spring
Regulations: Oregon State Parks parking permit required; dogs must be on leash
Map: USGS Wishram, WA, and Emerson, OR, 7.5' quadrangle
Information: Oregon State Parks, (541) 739-2322 or (800) 551-6949, reservations (800) 452-5687

Getting there: From Interstate 84 eastbound, take exit 97 onto Oregon Route 206, 17 miles east of The Dalles; westbound, take exit 104 at Biggs Junction. Follow the signs on OR 206 to reach the park. Deschutes River Trail Park is on the east bank of the river and includes a campground with up-to-snuff facilities at 59 campsites.

The trail along the east bank of the Deschutes River was originally railroad, laid by Jim Hill as he raced up the Deschutes toward Bend and Central Oregon's presumed timber wealth. Hill lost the battle, and today his railroad right-of-way provides recreational areas for hikers, horseback riders, and mountain bikers. The campground closes in October and reopens in February, but the trails are accessible year-round. This trail makes a nice escape from Gorge gloominess in the winter.

Three trails start up the river and converge into a single trail that follows the old abandoned railroad grade after 1 mile. The preferred doggie hike starts out on the Blackberry Trail, which leaves from the far end of the campground and follows the river closely. As the weather warms, watch for snakes along the path.

After a mile of flat hiking, the trail turns upslope, offering three different opportunities for continuing the hike: (1) You may return on the Riverview Trail, which parallels the trail you've hiked but is a little

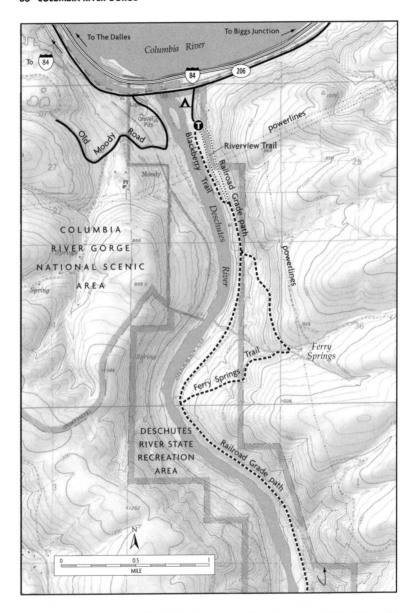

farther from the water. (2) A bit farther up the slope, you'll find the old railroad grade itself, which you may follow back to the campground. (3) Or you can continue upstream. This grade is publicly accessible as a trail for horses and bicycles, as well as hikers and dogs, for an additional 15 miles.

View upriver along the Deschutes from the Riverview Trail

If you are itching for a climb, follow an even higher calling on the Ferry Springs Trail. This adds an additional mile to your return trip, but you'll get a better overview of the canyon and its geology.

Five More Great Dog Hikes in the Columbia River Gorge

1. Trail 411, Wyeth Campground to North Lake and Rainy Lake, 4.5 miles one way to North Lake, 6 miles one way to Rainy Lake. Columbia River Gorge National Scenic Area, (541) 308-1700.

2. Herman Creek Trail and Trail 406 to Wahtum Lake, 11 miles one way. Columbia River Gorge National Scenic Area, (541) 308-1700.

3. Trail 414, Starvation Creek to Warren Lake, 5 miles one way with a hard initial climb. Columbia River Gorge National Scenic Area, (541) 308-1700.

4. Old Columbia River Gorge Highway Trail from near Mosier, 7 miles one way on the old highway, with a lot of bikes. Columbia River Gorge National Scenic Area, (541) 308-1700.

5. Gorge Trail 406 from Herman Creek trailhead to Cascade Locks via Dry Creek Falls, 8.6 miles round trip; this hike—relatively flat, with waterfalls along the way—is a continuation of Hike 8, Wyeth to Herman Creek. Columbia River Gorge National Scenic Area, (541) 308-1700.

COAST AND COAST RANGE

12. Banks–Vernonia State Trail: Vernonia to Braun

One-way trip: 5.5 miles
Elevation range: 660–750 feet
Difficulty: Easy
Hiking time: 2.5 hours
Best canine hiking season: Fall, winter
Regulations: Oregon State Parks parking permit required; dogs must be on leash
Map: USGS Vernonia 7.5' quadrangle
Information: Oregon State Parks, (503) 324-0606

Getting there: From Portland, take U.S. Highway 26 west about 30 miles to the junction with Oregon Route 47. Turn right (north) onto OR 47 and drive 14 miles to Vernonia. Turn right onto Weed Street and right again into the trailhead parking area. To leave a second vehicle at the Beaver Creek trailhead, return to OR 47, the Nehalem Highway, and follow it about 4.4 miles south to a bridge over Beaver Creek.

The ambitious, 20-mile Banks–Vernonia Trail was the first "rails-to-trails" park in Oregon. It follows a narrow-gauge rail line built in the 1920s that carried lumber and logs from a mill in Vernonia and passengers from nearby Keasey to Portland. When the mill closed in 1957, the line was converted to accommodate steam excursion train use. The last train ran in 1965, and the line was abandoned in 1973. The right-of-way has

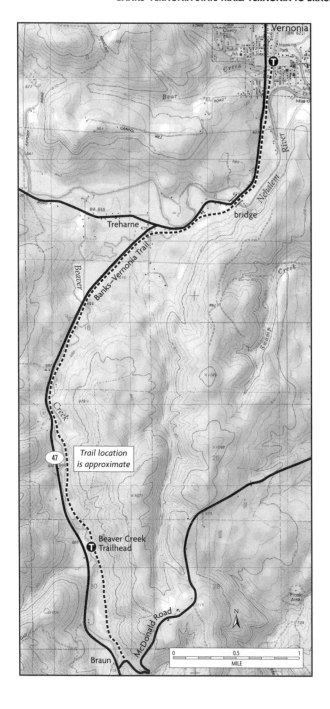

been an Oregon state park since 1990. Horses, bikes, in-line skaters, and families with small children are abundant on the trail near Vernonia. Dogs must remain on a 6-foot leash throughout this park. Pavement offers dry-footed winter hiking.

From Vernonia, the pathway heads generally south, paralleling Beaver Creek but staying well away from the water. In 1 mile it crosses the Nehalem River and in the next mile encounters a small tributary stream, a road, and Beaver Creek. The path never strays far from the Nehalem Highway (OR 47), and there is no fence to restrain dogs from traffic. Much of the first 2 miles crosses open meadows where summer shade is limited. After the first crossing of Beaver Creek, there is no water access for the next mile.

At 2.5 miles into the hike, the trail again crosses Beaver Creek. Now the path runs between highway and creek, with the road on your right and creek on the left. After another mile, the path crosses Beaver Creek yet again, then hugs the creek bank most of the way to a toilet and trailhead at mile 4.3. This is the Beaver Creek trailhead, a popular hiking objective and turnaround point—or a place to drop a second vehicle for use as a shuttle.

The paved segment of the trail continues another 2.5 miles. This segment is less popular. It is also more remote from water throughout its length. However, for winter hikes, it makes a fine, more private walk

A rustic picnic table awaits hikers at Beaver Creek's bridge.

than the first segment of the paved trail. At the end of the paved path, you can return as you came or continue on a rough railroad grade to the Tophill trailhead, 8 miles from Vernonia (see Hike 13).

13. Banks–Vernonia State Trail: Tophill to Buxton

One-way trip: 5 miles
Elevation range: 360–1040 feet
Difficulty: Moderate
Hiking time: 3 hours
Best canine hiking season: Spring, fall
Regulations: Oregon State Parks parking permit required; dogs must be on leash
Maps: USGS Vernonia and Buxton 7.5' quadrangles
Information: Oregon State Parks, (503) 324-0606

Getting there: From Portland, take U.S. Highway 26 west about 30 miles to the junction with Oregon Route 47. Turn right (north) onto OR 47 toward Vernonia. At mile 14, turn left into the trailhead parking area—you'll drive beneath a huge trestle just before the turn into the Tophill trailhead parking area. To leave a second vehicle or arrange for a pickup at the Buxton trailhead, from the town of Buxton take Bacona Road about 1 mile north to the large parking area.

This portion of the Banks–Vernonia Trail is more primitive and less developed than other parts. It is remote from roads, offering a good opportunity for solitude. There's no potable water at the trailheads, so be sure to bring plenty for you and your dog. And as this is an Oregon state park, dogs must remain on a leash throughout your hike.

From the Tophill trailhead, the old railroad grade turns west toward Beaver Creek, then swings south, climbing steadily to the summit 1 mile from the trailhead, then dropping to cross Nowakoski Road. It turns again, continuing its descent through woods cluttered with oak and maple, reaching OR 47 in 0.3 mile. The path plunges across the road and crosses the West Fork of Dairy Creek on a footbridge. From here it

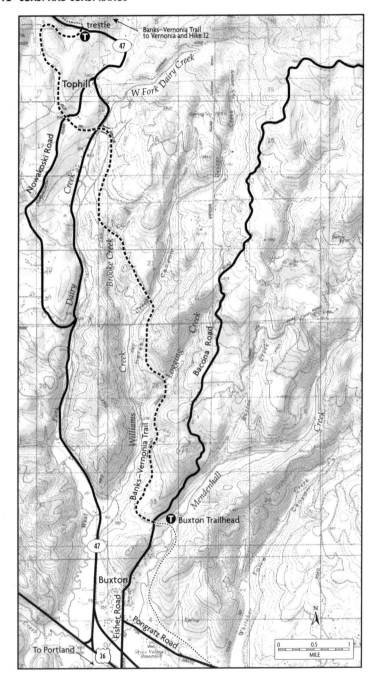

Most of the Banks–Vernonia Trail is graveled or paved.

passes through the wetland headwaters of a tributary and then climbs gradually once again.

The next 3 miles are the most remote and rugged on the trail. Cross Brooke Creek in another mile. The trail then rises slightly before dropping into the valley of Williams Creek. These woods offer a variety of big-leaf maple, white oak, and vine maple with an understory of ferns. Deer abound, so be doubly certain that dogs are leashed at all times on spring and summer hikes. (On fall hikes, unleashed dogs risk being mistaken for deer by hunters, so it's always best to heed park rules and keep a leash on your pet.)

Four miles from the Tophill trailhead, the trail finds the valley of Mendenhall Creek and winds downhill until it reaches and crosses Bacona

Road and then Mendenhall Creek. Here, the Buxton trestle towers above the Buxton trailhead 5 miles from the beginning.

You can arrange for a pickup here on Bacona Road or choose to continue as the trail crosses the road and continues along a slope for another 1.5 miles to the Banks–Vernonia State Park headquarters just off OR 47.

14. Gravelle Brothers Trail: University Falls

Round trip: 6 miles
Elevation range: 1740–1620 feet
Difficulty: Easy
Hiking time: 3 hours
Best canine hiking season: Year-round
Regulations: Northwest Forest Pass required
Map: Tillamook State Forest
Information: Oregon Department of Forestry, (503) 945-7200; Forest Grove District, (503) 357-2191; Tillamook District, (503) 842-2545

Getting there: From Portland, head west on U.S. Highway 26. Bear left on Oregon Route 6 toward Banks. Continue about 18 miles to a gravel road marked for the Rogers Camp trailhead. In about 100 yards, turn left on a spur road and continue another football-field-length to the parking area. Do *not* park in the tempting Oregon Highway Department gravel yard; you might get locked in!

This is an easy hike to a scenic waterfall in the Coast Range. It is one of the few trails in the area—west of Banks—where all-terrain vehicles have recently been banished, so it provides a scenic respite from civilization. But not from other hikers: it tends to be popular with the footloose crowd and kids and dogs on summer weekends. So it's recommended that you keep Fido close at hand.

The trailhead requires some persistence to find—head back toward OR 6 and look for a trail sign on the left, cross the Oregon Highway

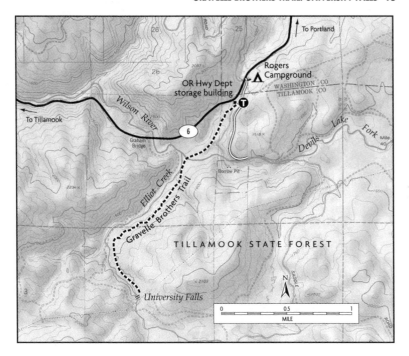

Department gravel yard, and look for the actual trailhead just behind a large, rusty yellow gate at the west end of the storage building. Rocks block vehicular access. (The location of this trail seems to be the hiker's little secret—one way to keep it safe from wheeled vehicles.)

From its secretive start, the wide trail follows an old roadway downhill about 0.25 mile to a contorted junction with the real trail—a footpath that veers right and then straightens into the Gravelle Brothers Trail (unsigned). Note that a broader and well-used ATV thoroughfare parallels much of the foot trail—but you and Fido will be much happier if you stay on the foot trail.

The Gravelle Brothers Trail continues downhill through a scrubby forest to the Wilson River (Devils Lake Fork), then changes its mind and climbs away from the riverbank. The path is irregular but, after the first mile, curves south, making a break with the ATV trail and following Elliot Creek. In another 0.3 mile, the trail begins a rapid descent to the imposing, 80-foot-high University Falls tumbling over a 15 million-year-old basalt flow. Here, Elliot Creek provides a welcome respite from summer heat. Return as you came.

The Gravelle Brothers Trail leads into the forest along an old road but soon transforms into a single-track trail.

15. Bayocean Peninsula County Park: Bayocean Spit

Round trip: 9 miles
Elevation range: 0–50 feet
Difficulty: Easy; moderate on windy days
Hiking time: 4–5 hours
Best canine hiking season: Year-round
Regulations: None
Map: USGS Garibaldi 7.5' quadrangle
Information: Tillamook County Parks Department, (503) 322-3477

Getting there: Take U.S. Highway 101 to downtown Tillamook. Turn west on Third Street (watch for signs for Three Capes Loop) and drive 1.7 miles, crossing the Tillamook River Bridge. Just past the bridge, turn right onto Bayocean Road NW and follow the bank of Tillamook Bay approximately

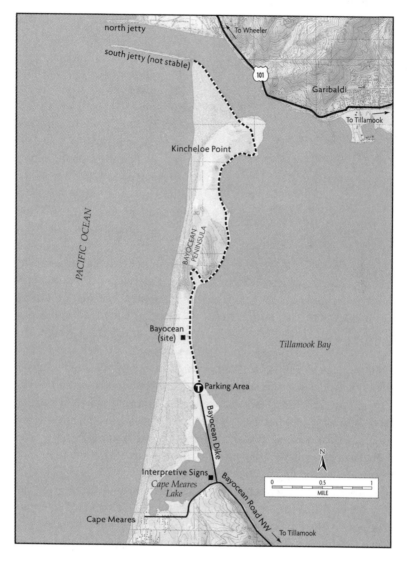

5 miles to the Bayocean sign and parking area on the right. You can drive several hundred yards onto the spit and park in a parking area on the Bayocean Dike.

This hike explores one of the coast's most quiet and historic locations, where the power of nature and geology trumped grandiose human dreams—the now-vanished city of Bayocean. Its history is chronicled

Sand dunes provide opportunities for romping with Fido on the Bayocean Spit.

in *Bayocean, The Oregon Town That Fell Into the Sea,* by Bert and Margie Webber.

In 1906, developer Thomas Potter envisioned a swank resort community ("The Atlantic City of the West") rising from the sands of a substantial, long spit then called the Tillamook Spit, west of Tillamook. With dunes up to 120 feet high, the features appeared stable. By 1910, Potter and others platted 4000 lots and built a narrow-gauge railway the length of the spit and erected a fine hotel (the Bay Ocean). By 1912, codevelopers installed water and telephone systems and a diesel power plant for the city. Three hotels opened: the Bayside, the Bay Ocean Inn Hotel, and Potter's Hotel Bay Ocean Annex. In 1914, a natatorium with a heated saltwater pool opened; it was the largest and most elaborate natatorium in the United States. Development also included a dancing pavilion, a bowling alley, tennis courts, a bakery, a cannery, a tin shop, a machine shop, a gas station, a boat dock, sidewalks, and streets (Potter's monthly newspaper touted nearly 4 miles of paved streets). All in all, by 1920 more than 2000 lots were sold and approximately 60 homes built.

However, spits are ephemeral geologic features, and their erosion can be induced if the currents and sediment sources that created them are changed. While Bayocean was growing, in 1917 the city of Tillamook began to build jetties, which cut off the sediment supply that maintained the (Tillamook) spit. Unable to rebuild itself with sands transported along the coastline, the Tillamook–Bayocean Spit fell victim to erosion and ocean currents. As early as 1920, some observers noticed that the beach was receding, if not downright disappearing. When Tillamook and the Army Corps of Engineers "improved" and extended the jetties in 1932–33, erosion of the spit increased. Major winter storms in the 1930s and '40s exacerbated the problem. By 1949, 20 houses had washed into the sea. In 1953 the townsite was essentially abandoned. In 1956 the ever-helpful Corps of Engineers bulldozed and cleared whatever was left. Ultimately, the huge Bayocean Spit disappeared almost completely, and its human trappings are long gone, save for a roadway that makes hiking the remaining spit's 4-mile length easy.

To explore the Bayocean Spit today, the easiest trail is the old roadway that effectively bisects the spit out to Kincheloe Point and jetty (the jetty is unstable). The 120-foot dunes are gone, leaving 30- to 50-foot-high mounds and sand dunes in their place. Recent efforts to stabilize the spit have included planting or encouraging grasses (nonnative) and shrubs (some nonnatives, including Scotch broom) as well as the lodgepole (coastal) pines that compose scattered groves along the spit.

Several other informal trails cross the spit and explore the dunes. It's a great place to romp with Rover and ranks among the most isolated, lonely, and reflective places on Oregon's coast. Return as you came.

16. Cape Lookout: South Trail

Round trip: 2.6 miles
Elevation range: 890–0 feet
Difficulty: Moderate
Hiking time: 3–4 hours
Best canine hiking season: Year-round
Regulations: Oregon State Parks parking permit required; dogs must be on leash
Map: USGS Sand Lake 7.5' quadrangle
Information: Cape Lookout State Park, (503) 842-4981 or (800) 551-6949

Getting there: From Tillamook, drive south 11 miles on U.S. Highway 101. Turn right (west) onto County Road 871. Continue 4.2 miles and turn right (north) onto Cape Lookout Road (Forest Road 11). The large parking area is 3 miles farther on your left (west) at the crest of a long hill.

The Cape Lookout Trail to the western tip of Cape Lookout is the most popular of the hikes that tour the cape. It is also the least suitable for dogs, with steep cliffs and places where there is no room to allow other

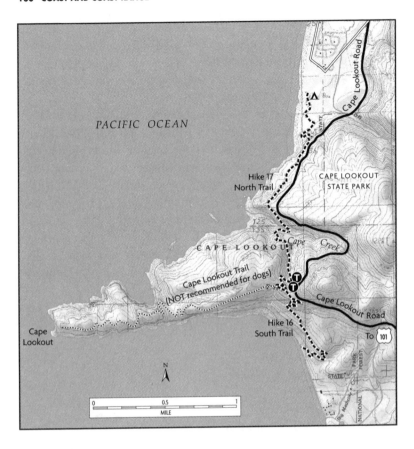

hikers to pass easily. The South Trail, described here, and the North Trail (Hike 17) are better alternatives, and both have the added advantage of beach access, as well as views every bit as good as the view from the west end of the cape.

From the east end of the parking area, start down the Cape Lookout Trail toward Cape Lookout. About 200 feet from the trailhead, turn sharply left and downhill on a spur trail that is poorly marked and appears to lead in the opposite direction. This path is the South Trail. It heads downhill in a straight line for the first 0.3 mile, then begins a series of elongated switchbacks.

The forest near the trailhead is mostly Douglas fir and western hemlock. Sword ferns and salal form a riotous understory. In late summer, the salal berries turn blue-black. They are plump and quite edible by

both humans and dogs. If your dog has learned to eat huckleberries, chances are that he'll also enjoy the slightly chewier salal.

The trail's switchbacks become shorter as it winds downhill. In 0.9 mile it crosses a small stream with enough water to cool canine feet. This water seeps from the base of a huge Sitka spruce, giving the spot a sort of fairy-tale feeling.

The South Trail at Cape Lookout leads to a cobbled beach and a good view of the cape's basalt cliffs.

Beyond the spring, the trail spirals downward more tightly, offering a view of Cape Lookout's cliff-lined south side and its outstanding columnar joints. The last 0.5 mile of the trail tours moist thickets of salal, then plunges to the log-laden beach. Depending on the previous season's storms, the last few yards to the beach can be perilous. From here, you can hike south toward Cape Kiwanda. At low tides, it can be fun to examine the base of Cape Lookout. Return as you came.

17. Cape Lookout: North Trail

Round trip: 5.2 miles
Elevation range: 890–0 feet
Difficulty: Moderate
Hiking time: 2–3 hours
Best canine hiking season: Year-round
Regulations: Oregon State Parks parking permit required; dogs must be on leash
Map: USGS Sand Lake 7.5' quadrangle
Information: Cape Lookout State Park, (503) 842-4981 or (800) 551-6949

Getting there: From Tillamook, drive south 11 miles on U.S. Highway 101. Turn right (west) onto County Road 871. Continue 4.2 miles and turn right (north) onto Cape Lookout Road (Forest Road 11). The large parking area is 3 miles farther on your left (west) at the crest of a long hill. See Hike 16 for the Hike 17 map.

The North Trail of Cape Lookout travels through a shady forest.

The North Trail down the north side of Cape Lookout leads to the beach and Cape Lookout State Park. Along the way, there are views of the Netarts Spit to the north, as well as a nice stream for cooling off. The trailhead on the northwest side of the parking area is separate from the trailhead to Cape Lookout's western point.

From the northwest trailhead, the path ambles through a forest sprinkled with mammoth Sitka spruce to reach Cape Creek in 0.9 mile. From the creek, the path climbs across a long and ingenious set of steps, then flattens and crosses a ridge where it offers a tantalizing view of the Pacific Ocean. From this spot 1.5 miles into the hike, the trail begins dropping. It edges briefly along the top of cliffs—the drop-offs are screened and cushioned by salal and shore pine. Occasional gaps in the salal fringe permit glimpses of the beach below.

At 2.2 miles, the trail begins an earnest, switchbacking descent to Cape Lookout State Park Campground. Before it enters the campground at 2.6 miles, the path crosses an inviting creek, offering another dog-cooling opportunity. Once on the beach, you can follow it northward past the camping area and along Netarts Spit. Return as you came.

18. Cape Perpetua: Cummins Creek to Gwynn Creek

Round trip: 7.8 miles
Elevation range: 430–1350 feet
Difficulty: Moderate
Hiking time: 5 hours
Best canine hiking season: Year-round
Regulations: Northwest Forest Pass required
Map: USGS Yachats 7.5' quadrangle
Information: Cape Perpetua Visitor Center, (541) 547-3289; Sius-
law National Forest, Waldport Ranger District, (541) 563-3211

Getting there: Starting from the Cape Perpetua Visitor Center located 11
miles south of Waldport on U.S. Highway 101, continue south on US 101
for 1.1 miles. Turn left (east) onto Forest Road 1050. Continue 0.3 mile to
the trailhead and a small parking area on the right (south) side of the road.

The Cummins Creek Trail tours the watershed of Cummins Creek, climbing through recovering logged areas that are now alder-laced forest and
arriving at a ridgetop to provide a nice view of the Pacific coast. Carry
water for Fido, as parts of the trail are in the open with limited water
after the first 0.3 mile.

From the trailhead, Trail 1382 enters the riparian environment along
Cummins Creek, following the stream closely for the first 0.3 mile. The
hike follows an abandoned logging road that rises above Cummins Creek
and then turns north, weaving through alder and young Douglas fir. The
path maintains an even grade through the alder. Salal and blackberries
line the trailside.

After 2 miles of easy walking, the path begins a steeper climb through
more recent clear-cuts. The trail up the south-facing slopes can be sunny
and hot in the summer, but it makes an ideal spring or winter hike. At
2.4 miles, the Cummins Creek Trail turns left, while a spur trail (also an
abandoned road) continues straight to dead-end after 0.6 mile. Bear left
here, climbing through a landscape of more recent clear-cuts. In time,
alder and fir will obscure the view here (and also provide more summer

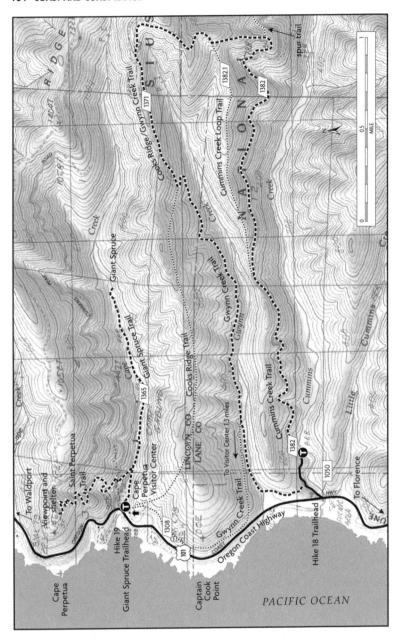

shade), but there are plenty of places along this rising trail segment where you can glimpse the coastline to the south.

The trail drops a bit and, about 0.5 mile from the spur-trail intersection, encounters Trail 1382.1 to the left. This path (Cummins Creek Loop) leads back to the main Cummins Creek trail, allowing a shorter 6-mile loop hike. You may return to the trailhead via this (more rugged, less developed) ridge-crest route, but the hike described here continues straight for a longer, more diverse loop.

At 3.4 miles, the Cooks Ridge/Gwynn Creek Trail bears to the left. Turn left onto this trail to return to the trailhead via old-growth forest and a moist creek bottom. The Cooks Ridge/Gwynn Creek Trail turns west to follow the ridge crest for about a mile, dropping gradually and finding deeper shade.

You reach a trail junction at 0.9 mile from the ridge crest. The trail straight ahead leads to the Cape Perpetua Visitor Center. To return to your vehicle, turn sharply left onto the Gwynn Creek Trail (Trail 1371). This path makes a long, single switchback, descending into the old-growth forest of Sitka spruce, hemlock, and diminishing

The coastal forest of mostly cedar and spruce provides ample shade along Cummins Creek.

numbers of Douglas fir. After a steady downhill track of about 2 miles, a path heads to the left (south), while the Gwynn Creek Trail continues straight toward the Cape Perpetua Visitor Center. To return to the trailhead, turn left (south) here, crossing Gwynn Creek in 0.1 mile—a welcome place for a refreshing doggie dip.

Beyond Gwynn Creek, continue 0.5 mile to FR 1050, then follow the road 0.2 mile back to the trailhead and your car.

19. Cape Perpetua: Giant Spruce Trail

Round trip: 4.6 miles including side trip
Elevation range: 160–800 feet
Difficulty: Moderate
Hiking time: 3.5 hours
Best canine hiking season: Winter, spring
Regulations: Northwest Forest Pass required
Map: USGS Yachats 7.5' quadrangle
Information: Cape Perpetua Visitor Center, (541) 547-3289; Siuslaw National Forest, Waldport Ranger District, (541) 563-3211

Getting there: From Waldport, drive 11 miles south on U.S. Highway 101 to the Cape Perpetua Visitor Center. Turn left (east) at the visitor center entrance, and drive 0.2 mile to the Giant Spruce trailhead on the right. See Hike 18 for the Hike 19 map.

Aptly named, the Giant Spruce Trail leads through spectacular old-growth forest. This is a popular path, especially in summer. You should keep Rover leashed. Hike during off-peak tourist seasons—in the winter or spring—for

The Saint Perpetua Trail to a viewpoint atop Cape Perpetua branches off the main trail to the Giant Spruce.

the easiest excursion with your dog. The trail follows Cape Creek and intersects several tributary streams, so cooling water is readily available. However, as always, carry drinking water for your dog.

From the trailhead, the path to the Giant Spruce plunges into coastal forest. Salal and a variety of berries, including salmonberry, thimbleberry, and huckleberry, line the trail. Massive Sitka spruce and a few hemlock and alder provide a rich canopy. The relatively flat trail follows Cape Creek through this forest of huge spruce. The grandmother of them all is the Giant Spruce at 1 mile. The Giant Spruce is more than 6 feet in diameter and ringed by the path, benches, and an interpretive sign.

As you return along the same path that brought you, look for a side trail to the north marked for the cape viewpoint. In its 1.3-mile length, the Saint Perpetua Trail (Trail 1365.1) crosses Cape Creek and rises out of the forest to visit Cape Perpetua's windswept brow, then bears left to a rock shelter and an overlook. The overlook offers a compelling view of the coastline, as well as a good binocular-based whale-watching post during the spring and fall migrations of gray whales. Return to the visitor center trailhead as you came.

20. Humbug Mountain State Park: Summit Trail

Round trip: 5.8 miles
Elevation range: 40–1756 feet
Difficulty: Moderate
Hiking time: 3–4 hours
Best canine hiking season: Year-round
Regulations: Oregon State Parks parking permit required; dogs
   must be on leash
Map: USGS Port Orford 7.5' quadrangle
Information: Humbug Mountain State Park, (541) 332-6774 or
   (800) 551-6949

Getting there: Take U.S. Highway 101 south of Port Orford 5.5 miles to Humbug Mountain State Park. The parking lot is on the west side of the highway just past where the road swings away from the beach. The

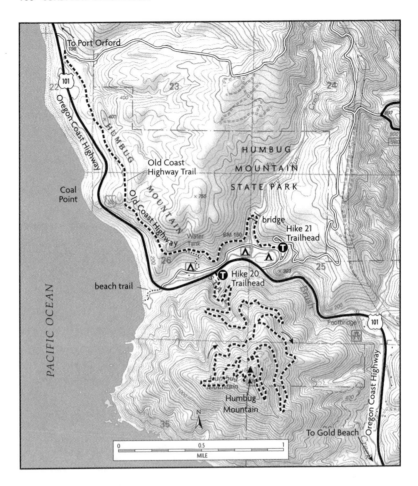

Humbug Mountain Summit trailhead can be reached from a tunnel in the campground between the A and B loops roadways or from the roadside parking lot along US 101.

The 2.9-mile walk to the top of Humbug Mountain (1756 feet) is more a pilgrimage than a hike. One of the most-climbed summits on Oregon's coast, Humbug Mountain proffers a memorable climb through a vigorous coastal forest, along with a feeling of accomplishment when you reach the summit. But don't expect great views. Except for a tunneled glimpse of the coast to the south and a few rare, tree-obscured views to the north in the first mile of hiking, on this trail you mostly see the trees, the forest, a few other hikers, and their dogs.

For dogs, the path provides several crossings of a small unnamed stream, so there are opportunities for canine cooling. But carry water, because there is no water on the upper portion of the mountain, and in summer and fall the streams could be dry or inadequate to keep your dog cool. This is an Oregon state park, so keep dogs leashed at all times. Due to the trail's proximity to the campground, expect children and dogs along the way.

In addition to the featured hike to the top of Humbug Mountain, you can reach the beach at this park, along a trail from the western end of the campground. Parking is hard to find at this short trailhead, but the path provides places to romp in both the surf and the vigorous freshwater flow of Brush Creek where it empties into the Pacific.

From the trailhead, the Summit Trail leads into a forest of big-leaf maple, Douglas fir, and myrtle trees, rising at a rapid-but-hikeable rate, switchbacking past a stream and a number of old-growth Douglas fir that sport scars from a fire that burned much of this coastal area almost a century ago. The first 0.5 mile is the steepest part of the trail—a climb of 420 feet. The trail crosses the stream twice, first at 0.7 mile (at about the 550-foot elevation), and later, on a higher switchback, at 0.9 mile. Wildflowers, including Columbia lily, adorn the trailside along with maidenhair ferns.

Just before the 1-mile marker, the trail splits. Here, you'll also find a bench for planning the next phase of your ascent. Both paths lead to the summit, but take the path to the east (left), which tracks through the drier side of Humbug Mountain and is slightly less steep than the alternative route, to reach the summit in 2 more miles. The path leads through groves of small-diameter tan oak trees. Wild rhododendrons share the forest with an understory of salal and sword ferns. The summit area is

Hikers stroll the forested last stretch of the Humbug Mountain Summit Trail.

a small meadow with several rock outcroppings and a limited view of Cape Sebastian and Gold Beach to the south.

Dogs, even dogs that are in good condition and provided with adequate drinking water, can become overheated on this climb. If your dog asks for a break to cool off, pay attention to her needs—even if you haven't "summited" and the top is tantalizingly close.

To return to the trailhead, take the steeper, west trail down. This path is somewhat rockier than the upbound route. It switchbacks downward, exploring a denser forest on the wetter, western slopes of Humbug Mountain where Douglas fir and Port Orford cedar—including some large second-growth trees and a few old-growth giants—far outnumber tan oak. Rock outcroppings are noticeable along the upper 0.5 mile of the trail. After a quick, steeply switchbacked drop, the western trail hits a saddle and sashays through a brighter forest where salal and vanilla leaf form the understory. The forest here is relatively open for good reason. In 1962, Oregon's infamous Columbus Day storm uprooted and blew down so many trees here that this portion of the trail was closed and did not reopen for more than 20 years. The western loop rejoins the main Summit Trail in 0.9 mile from the summit; return along this path.

21. Humbug Mountain State Park: Coast Trail, Old Coast Highway

Round trip: 4.6 miles
Elevation range: 70–300 feet
Difficulty: Easy
Hiking time: 2 hours
Best canine hiking season: Winter, spring
Regulations: Oregon State Parks parking permit required; dogs must be on leash
Map: USGS Port Orford 7.5' quadrangle
Information: Humbug Mountain State Park, (541) 332-6774 or (800) 551-6949

Humbug Mountain is one of the Oregon Coast's more distinctive features.

Getting there: Take U.S. Highway 101 south of Port Orford for 6 miles to Humbug Mountain State Park. Turn left (north) into the park entrance, and drive 0.25 mile to a trailhead on the right where the Old Coast Highway is gated and before entering a campground. See Hike 20 for the Hike 21 map.

This broad, gentle path follows the abandoned Old Coast Highway from Humbug Mountain north toward Port Orford. For those who are used to hiking in the wilderness, this trail can seem rather civilized—portions of the old road's pavement remain, and the route crosses vintage concrete highway bridges rather than the quaint wooden structures familiar to hikers. Cyclists are attracted by the fact that this trail is a former road, so watch for zippy mountain and road bikes. Yet the route does offer seclusion from crowds, as well as beautiful views of the south-curving reach of shoreline below and Humbug Mountain serving as an exclamation point in the distance.

There is no water along this hike after the first 0.2 mile from the trailhead, so, as always, carry extra for your dog. The stretches of remnant pavement can be very hot on dog paws, so provide opportunities for occasional shady rest stops if you hike this trail on a sunny day.

From the trailhead, the Old Coast Highway heads gently uphill into a cool, leafy tunnel of big-leaf maple, alder, and spruce, passing once-barren road cuts now bristling with mosses and sword ferns. The pavement here is intact, right down to the fading centerline. The path remains at least partly pavement throughout the hike. Gravel appears periodically where erosion or other forces have removed the asphalt. In about 0.5 mile, the old highway crosses a creek on an impressive old bridge. This is the last reliable chance for a doggie dip before the path climbs a bit more steeply through the shade of maples and spruce.

In about 0.7 mile from the start, a spur trail from the campground amphitheater joins the path just as the old highway breaks out of the trees and into the open. At 1 mile, the path rounds a bend and offers a nice beach view complete with a bench to sit on. From here, the route turns north and remains high above the existing highway. You can catch glimpses of the shore through the wind-sculpted fir and spruce.

This path continues for about 2 miles, alternating between open and shady stretches, until it merges with U.S. Highway 101. Watch for poison oak along the edges of the trail where the path is open to the sun. The old road follows a powerline for much of its journey above and parallel to the newer coast highway. The Old Coast Highway Trail ends where it meets the new highway 2.3 miles from the trailhead. Return as you came.

22. John Dellenback Dunes Trail

Round trip: 1-mile paved loop; 6 miles round trip to beach and back
Elevation range: 80–0 feet
Difficulty: Loop trail easy; dunes trek moderate to strenuous
Hiking time: Loop trail 2 hours; dunes trek 4–6 hours
Best canine hiking season: Year-round
Regulations: Northwest Forest Pass required; dogs must be on leash
Map: USGS Florence and Goose Pasture 7.5' quadrangle
Information: Siuslaw National Forest, Waldport Ranger District, (541) 563-8400 or Oregon Dunes National Recreational Area, (541) 271-3611

Getting there: On U.S. Highway 101 along the Oregon Coast, drive 10 miles south of Reedsport. Look for signs for Middle and North Eel Creek

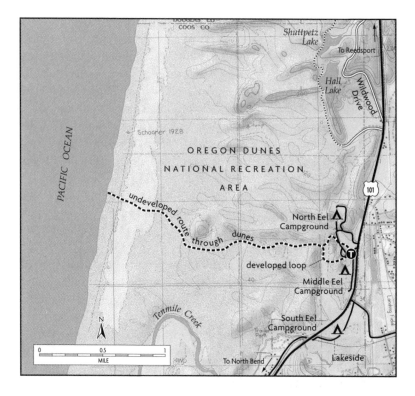

campgrounds. The trailhead parking area is on US 101 approximately 0.25 mile south of this campground entry.

This trail is named for John Dellenback, an environmentally aware Republican congressman who wrote the legislation to establish the Oregon Dunes National Recreation area and served as Peace Corps director from 1975 to 1977.

The hike offers a choice of either a shorter paved loop or a longer wander 2.7 miles through the dunes out to the Pacific—or a combination of the two. There are no off-road vehicles allowed in this area, but there is a lot of wildlife—you'll find deer and deer tracks, and even raccoons. If you go, be sure that (1) you carry plenty of water for you and Fido, and (2) you keep track of landmarks—or GPS locations—so you can find the small, elusive trailheads that are the gateways back to the car. Periodically checking your whereabouts is a good idea. Wind and windblown sand can cover your tracks quickly.

From the trailhead, the path starts in a quiet wooded area, crosses a rustic wooden bridge, and soon offers hikers a choice of entering the main dune area or taking a northern loop. While it's tempting to turn left here and barge into the dunes, prudent hikers should continue straight along the path, which leads through more peaceful wooded dunes and in 0.25 mile crosses an entry road to the campground. Once beyond the paved road, the interpretive loop trail enters a set of classical dunes and fades back into scattered lodgepole pines (*Pinus contorta,* also called shore pines) and native beach grasses for 0.25 mile before emerging into a full-blown, Lawrence of Arabia dunal landscape.

Here, you can continue on the 1-mile interpretive trail paved loop and return through a similar landscape of dunes and rare native grasses. Or, if you are feeling adventurous, you can strike out for the beach, still a very long 1.5 miles ahead.

The dunes are spectacular, and the pathway to the beach is unmarked and much farther than it seems. The walk to the beach is strenuous, as hiking in loose sand is energy-consuming. The big dunes—up to 80

feet in height—are a great place to explore a unique, and starkly beautiful, landscape. Allow plenty of time to explore the dunes and the interspersed small ponds (many are saline) and blowout areas before you return as you came.

For another short dunes hike in the area, you might wish to try Hall–Schuttpelz Lakes (Siuslaw Forest Hike 1357). This 1.5-mile hike is located just west of Tugman State Park, off US 101, 8 miles south of Reedsport and 2 miles north of the John Dellenback Dunes Trail. This hike circumnavigates two small lakes.

Deer tracks lead across huge dunes to sheltered springs and lakes at Dellenback Dunes.

23. Samuel H. Boardman State Scenic Corridor

Round trip: 12 miles
Elevation range: 0–400 feet
Difficulty: Easy to moderate
Hiking time: 7 hours
Best canine hiking season: Year-round
Regulations: Oregon State Parks parking permit required; dogs must be on leash
Maps: USGS Brookings and Carpenterville 7.5' quadrangles
Information: Oregon State Parks, (800) 551-6949

Getting there: From Brookings, drive 4.5 miles north on U.S. Highway 101 to the trailhead at Lone Ranch State Wayside, on the west side of the highway. The unmarked trailhead is at the north end of the picnic area. This is one of the southernmost access points for the Coast Trail.

The Coast Trail is a 300-mile-long, mostly informal network of trails and beach hikes that navigate Oregon's coastline from Astoria to Brookings. One of the network's best—and newest—segments is in southern Oregon. Expect to find relatively tame deer and other wildlife on the grassy slopes of the Lone Ranch Wayside and in park areas farther along the path, so keep dogs leashed. There is no reliable water along this hike, so be sure you carry plenty for your dog.

Begin at the unmarked trailhead at the north end of Lone Ranch State Wayside picnic area. Follow the paved path past the pit toilets, and instead of continuing west (left) to the beach, bear straight ahead along a mowed path that seems to lead into the riparian brush. This is where a dog is especially helpful. Chances are that your four-footed friend can easily find the tunnel through the brush and the ford of Lone Ranch Creek, as well as the path that leads out of the dense thicket on the other side. On my last trip across this creek, an informal bridge constructed with a railroad tie provided a way over the water. In most seasons, this is adequate to allow you to cross the stream with minimal wading.

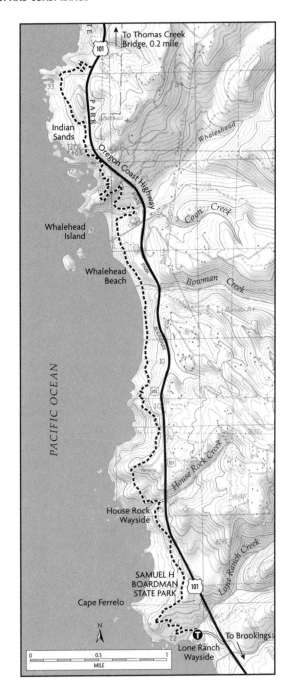

To Thomas Creek Bridge, 0.2 mile

101

Indian Sands

Oregon Coast Highway

PARK

Whalehead Island

Whalehead Beach

Whaleshead

Coon Creek

Bowman Creek

PACIFIC OCEAN

House Rock Creek

House Rock Wayside

Lone Ranch Creek

SAMUEL H BOARDMAN STATE PARK

101

Cape Ferrelo

To Brookings

N

Lone Ranch Wayside

0   0.5   1
MILE

After the creek, the trail bears left through the dense willow thicket, emerging onto a grassy slope and winding uphill across this hummocky and open landscape at the west end of Cape Ferrelo. Numerous trails lead all over the slope—the Coast Trail peters out here like an unraveled rope. Choose trails that mostly head upward, and you will ultimately merge with the main Coast Trail near the top of the slope.

The trail leads through thickets of salal and thimbleberry to a parking area, then plunges into the underbrush again on the north side of the lot. From this point, the trail follows the top of cliffs, balancing between beach and road and ultimately emerging from salal thickets to views of the beach far below. About 0.5 mile from the top of Cape Ferrelo, watch for a spur trail that descends to the beach. This path seems like a difficult route down, but in the end it proves quite dog-worthy and hiker-friendly.

To continue the hike, you'll have to scramble back up to the main trail and follow it through a thickening forest dominated by Sitka spruce. These trees are huge, and their gnarly roots look like something out of *The Wizard of Oz*. This segment of the path emerges into the House Rock Wayside parking area to take a breather before diving back into salal thickets as it continues north.

From the House Rock Wayside parking area, the trail moves closer to the highway, then meanders downslope, reaching Whalehead Beach in

Rascal makes tracks for the surf near Whalehead Cove, along the Samuel Boardman Trail.

about 1.5 miles. From here, it's a 1.5-mile walk along the beach to reach the Whalehead Beach picnic area and entrance road. Follow the entry road back toward US 101, and look for the trail's resumption just before you reach the highway. The path ducks back into Sitka spruce forest, lopes west to a slight hilltop, wobbles briefly back to the highway, and then heads west again to the dunes of Indian Sands about 1.7 miles from the Whalehead Beach picnic area. Watch for wooden signposts for the Coast Trail to be sure you are on the right track here. A spur trail to the right at about 1.9 miles from the picnic area leads to the Indian Sands trailhead and parking.

From Indian Sands, you can continue along the trail to the Thomas Creek Bridge in another mile. This portion of the trail follows the highway shoulder closely for almost 0.3 mile, making the last stretch a less than great place for dogs. Turn around either at Indian Sands or, if your dog is accustomed to traffic, at the Thomas Creek Bridge, which, at 345 feet above Thomas Creek, is the highest span on the Pacific coast north of San Francisco. Return as you came.

24. Francis Shrader Old-Growth Trail

Round trip: 1.5 miles
Elevation range: 1800–2100 feet
Difficulty: Moderate
Hiking time: 1 hour
Best canine hiking season: Summer, fall
Regulations: Northwest Forest Pass required; dogs must be on leash
Map: USGS Signal Buttes 7.5' quadrangle
Information: Siskiyou National Forest, Gold Beach Ranger Station, (541) 247-3600

Getting there: From the town of Gold Beach, drive 0.5 mile south on U.S. Highway 101, cross the Rogue River, and turn left onto Jerrys Flat Road. Continue up the Rogue River 9.8 miles. Turn right onto paved, single-lane Forest Road 090 just before the Lobster Creek Bridge and

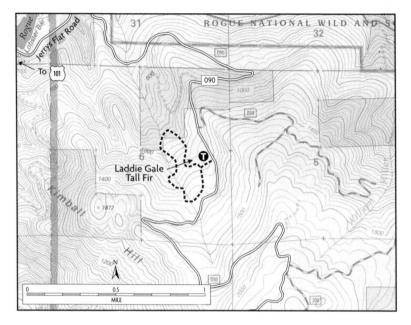

Campground. Drive 2.1 miles to find a parking lot on the left and a trailhead on the right.

This is an interpretive hike through a multistoried old-growth coastal forest where huge cedar and Douglas fir intermingle with deciduous tan oak. Rhododendron form a radiant spring understory. Your drive here will include road signs warning of logging trucks on the road and a clear-cut converted to a plantation of Douglas fir—visual reminders of why there are not many hikes like this left. Yes, it's a short hike. But take time to savor it.

From the road, the looping Francis Shrader Old-Growth Trail dives down into the forest, then splits. Take the path on the left to follow numbered interpretive sites in consecutive order. This is a very moist forest and there are plenty of mosquitoes looking for lunch, so you might want to protect yourself and Fido with insect repellent or long sleeves.

Crossing a small creek five times on sturdy bridges, allowing plenty of soggy doggie dips, the trail loops through an astonishingly complex, multistoried old-growth stand that includes deep forest duff; a huge variety of lichens, ferns, and mosses; and riparian areas that bustle. In spring, the rhododendrons are amazing. Interpreted sites include

Fallen cedars cross the Francis Shrader Old-Growth Trail.

nurse logs, riparian areas, and evidence of a devastating fire about a century ago.

An off-trail picnic area marks the midpoint of the hike. From the midpoint, the path rises to the Laddie Gale Tall Fir, a towering Douglas fir named for the star of the 1939 University of Oregon NCAA champion basketball team, then returns you to your car for only the price of a few donations to the mosquito blood bank.

Five More Great Dogs Hikes on Oregon's Coast and Coast Range

1. Gales Creek, 11 miles round trip; the trail follows the creek through peaceful second-growth forest. Tillamook State Forest, (503) 357-2191.

2. North Fork Smith River, 8 miles round trip; hike along the river to a 100-foot falls. The trail is off Forest Road 23 and has some steep climbs and cliffs. Siuslaw National Forest, Oregon Dunes National Recreation Area, (541) 271-3611.

3. Sweet Creek Trail, 3.5 miles round trip, travels along a creek with 11 waterfalls. Siuslaw National Forest, Mapleton Ranger District, (541) 902-8526.

4. Mount Hebo Pioneer Trail to Mount Hebo summit, 8 miles round trip, takes you to two lakes at the roof of the Coast Range. Siuslaw National Forest, Hebo Ranger District, (503) 392-3161.

5. Horse Creek Trail, Drift Creek Wilderness, 3.5 miles round trip. Siuslaw National Forest, Waldport Ranger District, (541) 563-3211.

CASCADE MOUNTAINS

25. Ramona Falls

Round trip: 7.2 miles via Portage Trail; 6.7 miles returning on Sandy River Trail
Elevation range: 2400–3550 feet
Difficulty: Easy
Hiking time: 4 hours
Best canine hiking season: Summer, fall
Regulations: Northwest Forest Pass required
Map: USGS Bull Run Lake 7.5' quadrangle
Information: Mount Hood National Forest, Zig Zag Ranger District, (503) 622-3191

Getting there: From Zigzag on U.S. Highway 26, turn north onto Forest Road 18, marked for Lolo Pass. Drive 4 miles and bear right onto FR 1825, and in 1.8 miles, just before the Lost Creek Campground, bear left onto Spur Road 1825-100. Continue 0.7 mile to a gigantic parking area and trailhead.

The hike to Ramona Falls is one of the most popular in the Mount Hood area. For dogs, it provides bounteous water and shade as well as the chance to meet other dogs and dog-friendly hikers. The trails are generally broad and gentle. The forest is varied. And there is scarcely a prettier waterfall in Oregon.

Most of the hike—and the drive along narrow forest roads to the huge trailhead parking lot—crosses the deposits of Mount Hood's last major temper tantrum, the eruption of 1781. En route to your Ramona Falls

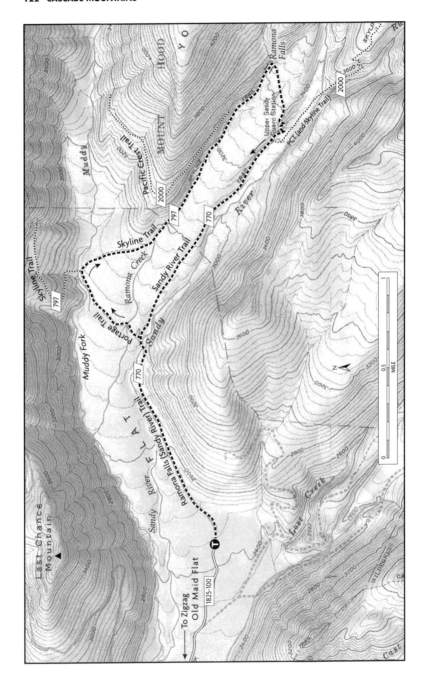

hike, you can pause at Lost Creek Campground and nature trail to view the remains of trees buried by thick debris flows from the 1781 eruption. You will be hiking atop the very same mudflows—which likely contain a forest buried beneath them—on your way to view Ramona Falls.

From the trailhead parking lot, the broad Sandy River Trail follows an abandoned roadway for 1.3 miles to the Sandy River crossing. It is a broad path that winds through the mossy lodgepole pines. These trees specialize in colonizing dry and disturbed sites—including volcanic mudflows and debris flows such as here. Some of these tiny lodgepole pines only 5 or 6 inches in diameter could be 100 years old. They represent the first conifers to colonize this young mudflow.

In 1.3 miles the trail minces across the Sandy River on a small bridge. This structure is placed across the stream in the early summer and taken away by helicopter after the main hiking season closes in the fall to protect it from early spring torrents. From this point, the trail takes you farther into the lodgepole thickets, reaching a trail junction and wilderness registration station in about 0.2 mile.

Both trails lead to Ramona Falls on a loop route, but the best route to Ramona Falls and back for hikers with dogs is the trail to the left, the Portage Trail, which follows Ramona Creek through well-shaded forest, offering plenty of water and cooling opportunities. To the right, the more popular Sandy River Trail is a dry, sunny, sandy path that offers no water and little shade. If you were a dog, which route would you choose?

The path to the left, Portage Trail, fords Ramona Creek in another 0.2 mile, then digresses a bit west toward the Muddy Fork. To reach Ramona Falls, bear right at the trail junction at Muddy Fork, following Ramona Creek on

Tyler and family at a trail junction on the Ramona Falls Loop

the Skyline Trail. Along the trail, huge lichen-covered gray andesite cliffs form a colorful tapestry. Ramona Creek is easily accessible to dogs for much of the hike, and the tawny cliffs offer texture and geology to admire.

A trail, the Pacific Crest Trail, that leads left and upward to connect with the Timberline Trail and Yokum Ridge appears at 3.4 miles—just before Ramona Falls. At 3.6 miles from the trailhead, you reach Ramona Falls, which plummets down a huge, dark, mossy cliff. A sturdy wooden bridge spans the creek at the foot of the cascade, offering a great vantage point as well as a dry-footed creek crossing. Dogs will likely prefer a more watery route.

There are no restrictions on dogs at the falls, but you should keep your canine companion on a leash here and under control, as the falls area is often crowded, or at least shared with picnicking families. You can either return as you came, especially in warm weather, or on cool days follow the Sandy River Trail portion of the loop, which tours the edges of the Sandy River canyon and becomes a feasible option for dogs. It leads without interruption back to the trail junction and the Sandy River crossing in 1.8 miles.

26. Burnt Lake

Round trip: 5.4 miles to Burnt Lake; 7 miles to Zigzag Mountain
Elevation range: 2650–4970 feet
Difficulty: Moderate to Burnt Lake; strenuous to Zigzag Mountain
Hiking time: 5–7 hours
Best canine hiking season: Summer, fall
Regulations: Northwest Forest Pass required
Map: USGS Government Camp 7.5' quadrangle
Information: Mount Hood National Forest Information Center,
(503) 622-7674; Zigzag Ranger District, (503) 622-3191

Getting there: From Zigzag on U.S. Highway 26, turn north onto Forest Road 18 (East Lolo Pass Road), marked for Lolo Pass. Drive 4 miles and bear right onto FR 1825 (Muddy Fork Road), which morphs into FR 1825-109. Continue 3.3 miles to a parking area and trailhead, about 1.5 miles past Lost Creek Campground.

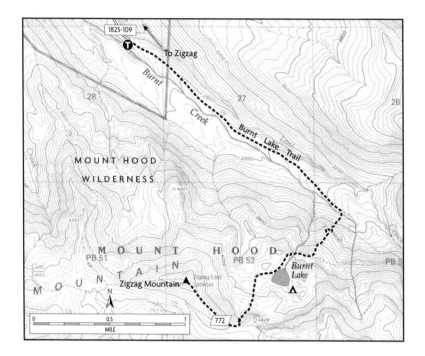

This 3.5-mile walk to Burnt Lake and the summit of Zigzag Mountain provides both water and scenery, as well as a lesson in forest history in an eerie but inviting woodland where the giant, charcoaled stumps of a vanished cedar forest hide among moss-draped younger trees. Although a popular trail, it has fewer hikers than the nearby Ramona Falls Trail (Hike 25). Water is accessible on the first part of the hike, in Burnt Creek and at Burnt Lake.

From the trailhead parking area, the Burnt Lake Trail squeezes through a livestock-restricting gateway and edges along the rim of Burnt Creek's small canyon. You might take a moment to admire the huge cedar trees here and at the edge of the parking lot. These trees all bear large fire scars. They are among the few trees that survived a devastating, human-caused forest fire in 1910 that exterminated much of the old-growth cedar forest here.

In 0.3 mile, just past the wilderness registration ledger, the path enters a darker forest of medium-size Douglas fir and hemlock. Scattered across this relatively flat forest floor for the next 2 miles of the hike are the stumps and cut logs of huge cedars. A close look reveals deep fire scars. Some standing trees have been completely hollowed by fire. Dogs and small children take great delight in climbing over and peering into these charcoal-lined trees. It's worth venturing off the trail and into the open forest here just to explore this burned forest and its fire-sculpted remnants. Burnt Creek is easily accessible just west of the trail.

When this portion of the forest burned, most cedars—a species with relatively thin bark that is not especially fire-resistant—burned. Only tall, charcoaled trunks were left. Believing that these naked tree boles would act as lightning rods, starting yet another fire, the Forest Service sent in crews to cut down the burned trees—and the result is the stumps and cut logs still found here.

After 1.8 miles of a gentle uphill stroll through this altered forest, the trail crosses a small branch of Burnt Creek where a huge hollow cedar greets you, meanders through a marshy area where a number of younger postfire cedars are prospering, and then turns and begins a serious ascent to Burnt Lake. The switchbacking trail rises past some old-growth cedars that survived the fire and are probably the progenitors of the younger trees below.

The trail reaches Burnt Lake in another mile. There are a number of good campsites here—if you arrive early enough. Burnt Lake occupies a small glacial basin. The postfire forest obscures what might be a magnificent view of Mount Hood. To catch a great view of the surrounding landscape, continue past Burnt Lake to the summit of Zigzag Mountain, adding another short mile and about 800 feet in elevation to the hike. The rocky promontory supports salal, huckleberry, and a few rhododendron. Once you've absorbed the view, return as you came.

Meesha and Leigh take a break along the Burnt Lake Trail.

27. Old Salmon River Trail

Round trip: 5.8 miles
Elevation range: 1520–1720 feet
Difficulty: Easy
Hiking time: 4 hours
Best canine hiking season: Year-round
Regulations: Northwest Forest Pass required
Map: USGS Rhododendron 7.5' quadrangle
Information: Mount Hood National Forest, Zigzag Ranger District, (503) 622-3191

Getting there: From Portland, take U.S. Highway 26 east to Welches. About 0.25 mile past the blinking light—and right after the fire station—turn south (right) on Salmon River Road (Forest Road 2618) and continue 2.7 miles to Old Salmon River trailhead sign and parking turnout. **Note:** There are many informal parking spots and turnouts along the 3.9 miles of Salmon River Road that have access to the Lower Salmon River Trail. You may utilize this feature to place a second vehicle along the way and make your walk a one-way stroll or start your hike in a different location.

This easy, scenic trail is understandably crowded on summer weekends, but in shoulder seasons it's possible to hike the entire distance with minimal human contact. Your dog will love this trail for its many fragrances—large nurse logs provide habitat for many small creatures, and the overall soft nature of the ground here holds records of many passing critters. In late summer, even bears utilize the pathway—evidence of their presence may appear as scat or soft logs ripped open to reveal ant-nest snacks.

Megan contemplates taking a dip in the Salmon River at one of many access points along the Old Salmon River Trail.

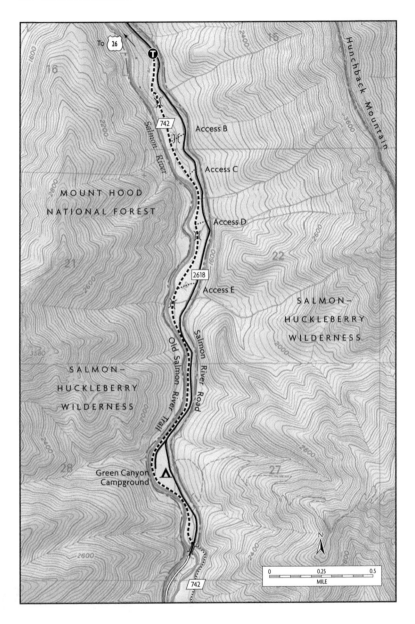

Be aware that the Salmon River is aptly named—runs of salmonids in spring and fall are significant. While it's fascinating to watch the spawning fish, keep in mind that eating even a tiny amount of raw salmon can be lethal for dogs, so keep Fido away from the fish.

The hike begins at a large turnout and follows an early twentieth-century logging road along the river. Old-growth cedar trees line the trail, providing a cathedral-like atmosphere. The broad pathway provides nice wooden bridges across side channels, and many formal and informal short trails lead to the river's edge.

Watch for stairways constructed by the Civilian Conservation Corps on four more developed access points, dubbed Access B (0.3 mile), C (0.5 mile), D (1.0 mile), and E (1.2 miles). There may also be informal camps and campers along the river, so watch for tents and people as you venture to the water's edge. The Salmon River is an inviting place for a doggie dip, especially in summer and fall when its flows are lower. (But keep an eye out for the fish . . .)

At mile 2.0 the trail reaches Green Canyon Campground; it continues past the campground to effectively end at the Salmon River Road Bridge across the river. This is also the starting trailhead for the Upper Salmon River Trail (Hike 28).

28. Salmon-Huckleberry Wilderness: Upper Salmon River Trail

Round trip: 7.8 miles
Elevation range: 1620–2500 feet
Difficulty: Moderate to strenuous
Hiking time: 5–6 hours
Best canine hiking season: Spring, fall
Regulations: Northwest Forest Pass required
Maps: USGS Rhodendron and High Rock 7.5' quadrangles
Information: Mount Hood National Forest, Zigzag Ranger District, (503) 622-3191

Getting there: From Portland, take U.S. Highway 26 to Welches. About 0.25 mile past the blinking light, turn south (right) on Salmon River Road (Forest Road 2618), and follow this narrow paved road 5 miles to a bridge across the Salmon River. Just before the bridge, turn left into trailhead parking area.

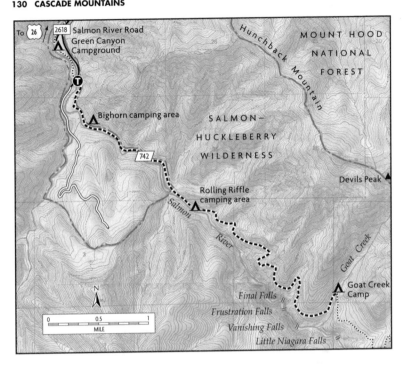

The more rugged Upper Salmon River Trail is less traveled than the lower trail (Hike 27) and provides less access to water or the river, but you'll be able to scramble down to waterside in a few places. Old-growth riparian forest here is spectacular.

The upper trail begins with a dry climb that leads it away from the river and campground and into a quiet forest. However, the trail soon returns to its view of the water, if not riverside. At 0.5 mile, you can access the river for the first doggie dip of the hike. The trail then veers back into woodland and away from the bank as the canyon steepens.

At 1.5 miles into the hike, you'll find the Bighorn camping area, hugging the river's bank. (Campsites here are taken up early on summer weekends.) For the next 0.5 mile to Rolling Riffle camping area, the trail flirts with the river and is relatively flat.

Beyond the Rolling Riffle campground, the trail begins a serious and occasionally steep mile-long climb away from the river. Then it flattens, skirting forested cliffs with the tumbling river and waterfalls far below.

The hike's destination is Goat Creek Camp adjacent to the next reliable water source, at Goat Creek. This stream may run dry late in summer,

At the Upper Salmon River Trailhead—and any trailhead—it's a good idea to have your dog leashed when you approach the parking area.

so it's best to carry plenty of water on this stretch of the hike. Between Rolling Riffle and Goat Creek, you'll cross several small streams (again, unreliable for doggie water late in the summer) and waterfalls that mostly tumble over steep cliffs and valleys below you.

The trail continues beyond Goat Creek Camp, following forested slopes high above the river until the path, which diminishes in quality with distance, reaches the river's headwaters near Clear Lake, some 15 miles farther. However, for most hikers and their canid companions, Goat Camp is an excellent goal and a fine place to turn around.

29. Mount Hood Wilderness: Elk Meadows Trail

Round trip: 4.5 miles
Elevation range: 4500–5200 feet
Difficulty: Moderate
Hiking time: 4 hours
Best canine hiking season: Summer, fall
Regulations: Northest Forest Pass required; register for wilderness entry
Maps: USGS Mount Hood South and Badger Lake 7.5' quadrangles
Information: Mount Hood National Forest, Hood River Ranger District, (541) 352-6002

Getting there: From Hood River, drive 32 miles south of Oregon Route 35. Turn right at the sign for Elk Meadows Trail and drive 0.25 mile to a

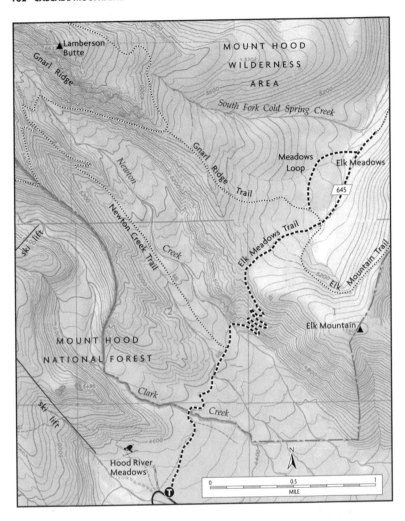

parking area on the right. From Government Camp, drive 2 miles east on U.S. Highway 26, turn north on OR 35 (marked for Hood River), and continue 7 miles to the sign for Elk Meadows Trail. Turn left, and drive 0.25 mile to the parking area on the right.

This trail traverses a variety of landscapes, including two major creeks and volcanic vistas, and provides an outstanding view of Mount Hood's east side along with flowered meadows. It can also be a start for longer hikes to explore more of Mount Hood. Allow time for these extra explorations rather than rushing this hike.

From the trailhead, the path plunges into the diverse cedar-pine-fir forest of Hood's eastside with enthusiasm, providing an easy and flat trail for the first mile. You'll cross two major creeks—first, Clark Creek in about 0.25 mile, followed by the larger Newton Creek at 1.2 miles. Between these two creeks, the Newton Creek Trail, #646, heads to the left (west) before you cross Newton Creek. The more demure Clark Creek still has its bridge and marks your entry into the Mount Hood Wilderness Area. The larger, more powerful Newton Creek has long ago ripped out any bridge that might have dared confine it, and your crossing will be on informal bridges of whatever logs and sticks previous hikers have found. Both crossings offer a cooling opportunity for dogs.

Just beyond Newton Creek, the massive ridge of Elk Mountain–Gnarl Ridge looms. The trail switchbacks up the slopes at a very tolerable pace, and most of the climb on this south-facing slope is shaded.

Once you reach the top, in about 0.5 mile, the trail again flattens, intersecting one spur of the Gnarl Ridge Trail–Elk Mountain Trail at about 1 mile from Newton Creek, and then slopes gently downhill as you approach Elk Meadows. Just before the meadows, the trail splits, with the Meadows Loop to the left and Elk Meadows Trail to right. For the quickest and easiest access to Elk Meadows, turn right. You may also enter the meadow by

The view of Mount Hood from Elk Meadows is stunning, although Meg prefers sniffing flowers and chasing sticks.

following informal trails that provide shortcuts into the open, flowered meadows, the destination for this hike. Return as you came.

If you can invest an entire day in this area, there are many options for extending your time on this portal to Mount Hood. The Gnarl Ridge Trail provides excellent access to and views of Mount Hood after about 1 mile of gradual upslope climbing. The Elk Mountain Trail rises 700 feet and covers 1.5 forested miles to the summit of Elk Mountain, where you have an excellent view of Mount Hood and the adjacent landscape. And finally, the Elk Meadows Trail #645 itself connects in about 7 miles with the Tamanawas Falls Trail (Hike 30).

30. Tamanawas Falls Trail

Round trip: 3.8 miles
Elevation range: 3040–3250 feet
Difficulty: Easy
Hiking time: 2 hours
Best canine hiking season: Spring, summer, fall
Regulations: Northwest Forest Pass required; dogs recommended
    on leash
Map: USGS Dog River 7.5' quadrangle
Information: Mount Hood National Forest, Hood River Ranger
    District, (541) 352-6002

Getting there: From Hood River, follow Oregon Route 35 approximately 24 miles south past Pollalie Trailhead and Campground area to a turnout on the right. If you go past Sherwood Campground, you have gone about 0.5 mile too far.

This easy hike leads to a surprisingly spectacular waterfall. Much of the trail follows scenic Cold Spring Creek, allowing for easy cooling. You can also extend your hike all the way to Elk Meadows.

From the parking area, the trail quickly crosses a broad new footbridge across the East Fork of Hood River—a stream renowned for destructive floods spawned on the slopes of Mount Hood. You then face an intersection. The left fork leads back to Sherwood Campground. Take the right fork, a flat, wooded path that winds among big river rocks and, after 0.5 mile, climbs along bluffs that overlook the river and OR 35 below. Look for an

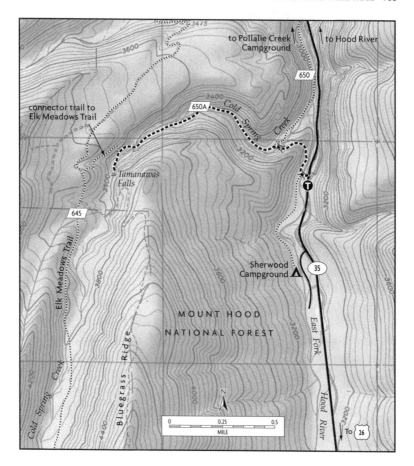

abrupt turn of the trail as it veers away from cliffs above the confluence of East Fork Hood River and Cold Spring Creek. Exuberant dogs would best be leashed or under control here.

Beyond the cliff—which also provides a nice view of gray columned cliffs across the highway—the trail drops back to the creek and splits: Trail 650 continues to the Pollalie Creek Campground 1.5 miles farther north (downriver), and Trail 650A goes to the left. Follow Trail 650A to the left as it crosses on another admirable footbridge and follows the stream for the remaining 1.3 miles of its trip to the falls.

About 0.25 mile before you reach the falls, the trail becomes schizophrenic. A sign and promising trail send you left. But you really want to go to the right (uphill) on the Connector Trail to Trail 645 (Elk Meadows Trail) for another 20 yards or so before turning left on a nice path that

Tamanawas Falls is produced as Cold Springs Creek plunges 150 feet over an ancient lava flow.

leads through a mondo rock slide. This area is now relatively stable, and the path is nicely constructed. Still, large boulders and chunks of outcrop seem poised to take a new plunge, so be wary. Just beyond the rock slide, you round a turn and see the falls; another 0.25 mile of hiking brings you to its foot. Return as you came.

If you and Fido are feeling energetic and adventurous and are carrying plenty of water, your hike can be extended by returning to the junction with Trail 650A and the Connector Trail, then turning left—uphill—on the Elk Meadows Trail, #645, (Hike 29). In about a mile, this trail gains a ridgetop and follows this through forest—and some of the recent (2008) Gnarl Ridge Fire that burned about 3300 acres on the east slopes of Mount Hood. Condition of the trail varies with blowdowns, weather, and maintenance. It reaches Elk Meadows in 4.8 miles.

31. Dog River Trail

Round trip: 7 miles
Elevation range: 2100–3600 feet
Difficulty: Moderate
Hiking time: 4 hours
Best canine hiking season: Spring, summer, fall
Regulations: Northwest Forest Pass required
Maps: USGS Dog River and Fivemile Butte 7.5' quadrangles
Information: Mount Hood National Forest, Hood River Ranger
District, (541) 352-6002

Getting there: From Hood River, drive south on Oregon Route 35 for 18.5 miles. The trailhead is on the left on the highway shoulder.

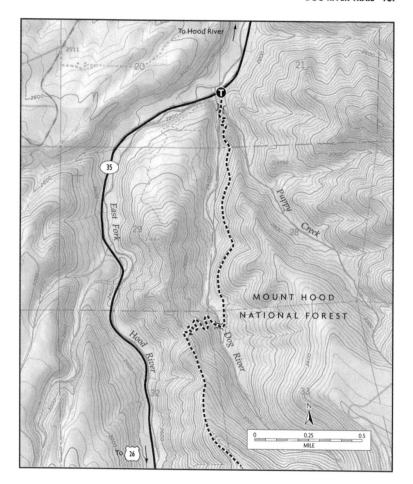

This hike is forested over most of its extent. The trail is open and well maintained partly due to its popularity with mountain bikers. When hiking with dogs, be aware that two-wheelers may be hurtling downhill fast and silently. Keep dogs in control.

A few hundred yards from the trailhead, the path crosses Puppy Creek on a generous footbridge. From here, it switchbacks upward, keeping a tolerable grade and gaining its first 500 feet. The path traverses slopes of second-growth forest, keeping an even pace and crossing a number of side streams that are generally dry by mid-July.

At 2 miles, the trail drops down to Dog River again, providing an opportunity for a quick doggie dip in what is now a small stream and

Dundee cools off in Puppy Creek after a long day on the trail.

crossing on a sturdy bridge. Then the path switchbacks upward again, climbing another 500 feet at a steep pace before reaching a ridge crest at 2.6 miles.

From here to trail's end in another mile, hikers are treated to occasional glimpses of the landscape, including nice views of Mount Hood. The trail saves the best of these for last from the vantage point of a rocky andesite outcrop. Return as you came.

32. Pacific Crest Trail: Twin Lakes

Round trip: 5.8 miles
Elevation range: 4100–4400 feet
Difficulty: Easy to moderate
Hiking time: 3 hours
Best canine hiking season: Spring, summer, fall
Regulations: Northwest Forest Pass required
Maps: USGS Wapanita and Mount Hood South 7.5' quadrangles
Information: Mount Hood National Forest, Barlow–Dufur Ranger District, (541) 467-2291

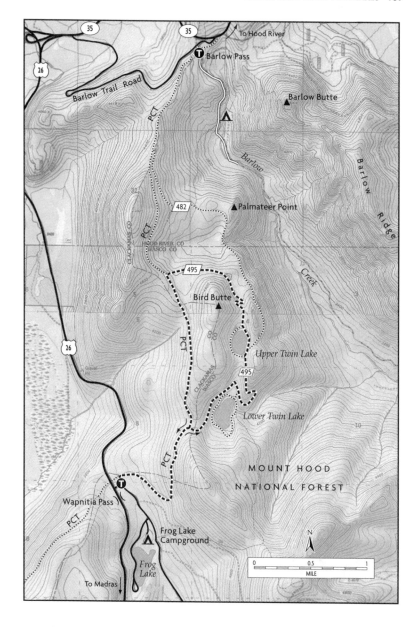

Getting there: Frog Lake PCT trailhead: From Government Camp, drive 10 miles south on U.S. Highway 26. Turn left into the Frog Lake snow-park area. The trailhead is at the northwest side of the parking lot near the restroom structures.

Barlow Trail PCT trailhead: From Government Camp, follow US 26 to the junction with OR Route 35. Follow OR 35 for 3 miles as it winds uphill to Barlow Trail Road on the right. Turn right here, and continue for 0.25 mile to the PCT trailhead and parking. The Pacific Crest Trail to Twin Lakes heads south from here.

The Twin Lakes area is relatively unsung, although with its easy access from popular Frog Lake, it draws a surprisingly large number of hikers—mostly with dogs and/or children—during the summer. It's wise to have Fido close at hand on this hike, as many fellow hikers literally have their hands full as they amble along the trail.

From the Frog Lake trailhead, the broad path enters a fir and cedar forest, follows an almost flat trajectory for the first 0.5 mile, then makes a sweeping turn and gently, deliberately sashays up the slope of Bird Butte. At 0.8 mile, turn east on Trail 495, which heads toward Twin Lakes to the east across a flat saddle before beginning a long, gentle descent that offers tantalizing glimpses of Lower Twin Lake below. In another 0.5 mile, there's a junction with a path to this, the lower of the two lakes. To reach Upper Twin Lake, continue straight and gradually uphill, climbing about 200 feet in another 0.7 mile. The upper lake is slightly smaller and shallower, and its additional remoteness usually offers more privacy.

From Upper Twin Lake, you may return to the Frog Lake trailhead, but for a longer hike that circumnavigates Bird Butte, continue on Trail 495 around Upper Twin Lake, bearing left at the junction with Trail 482 to Palmateer Point, and continue on Trail 495 another 1.2 miles to rejoin the Pacific Crest Trail. At this junction, turn left (south) on the PCT and follow it back to the Frog Lake trailhead. (The Palmateer Trail, #482, also eventually joins the PCT after an additional 1.2 miles of hiking that leads to a nice view of Mount Hood at Palmeteer Point and a mile along another flat section to reach the PCT.)

Meesha and Dundee after a refreshing dip in Lower Twin Lake

You may also access Twin Lakes along the PCT and Trail 495 from the north at the Barlow Pass PCT trailhead. From Barlow Pass, the PCT offers a longer hike of 3 miles one way to reach Upper Twin Lake. The trail is relatively flat, with a slightly greater (500 feet) elevation gain from its lowest to highest points (4150 to 4650 feet).

33. Three Sisters Wilderness: Matthieu Lakes and Collier Cone

Round trip: 14.4 miles
Elevation range: 5310–7020 feet
Difficulty: Moderate
Hiking time: 8 hours or overnight
Best canine hiking season: Summer, early fall
Regulations: Northwest Forest Pass required; register for wilderness entry
Maps: USGS Mount Washington, North Sister, Black Crater, and Trout Creek Butte 7.5' quadrangles
Information: Deschutes National Forest, Sisters Ranger District, (541) 549-7700

Getting there: From the Central Oregon town of Sisters on U.S. Highway 20, drive 14 miles west on Oregon Route 242, the McKenzie Pass Highway, toward McKenzie Pass. Turn left (south) onto a rough red-cinder road marked for Lava Camp. Follow this road 0.3 mile, then bear right and continue 0.1 mile to the far end of this small and relatively undeveloped, waterless campground. The trailhead is at the end of this looped road.

This hike is among the most beautiful in Oregon's high Cascades—a region chock-full of scenic hikes. It visits two lakes, has close encounters with one of the youngest lava flows in the Cascades (including a short stretch of the hike where booties are in order if your dog is tender-footed), and provides an intimate view of one of the Cascades' longest glaciers—or, at least, the moraine-rimmed valley where Collier Glacier used to be. All this in a

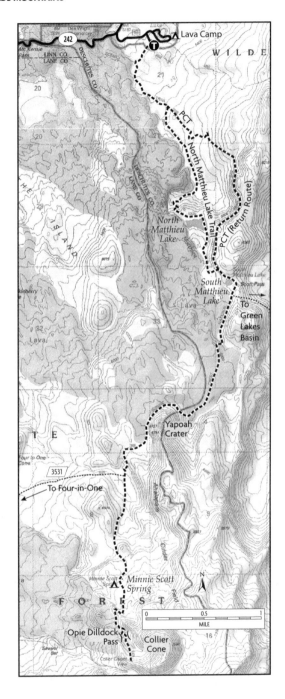

7-mile walk on well-maintained and easy-to-follow trails with no lung-numbing climbs. What hiker and dog could ask for more?

As always, you'll need to take a few aspects of this hike under advisement. Carry extra water for your dog. Although you'll visit two large lakes and a reliable spring, there are long open stretches in the last two-thirds of the hike—some that cross dark cinders or lava—that can be hot, dry going for your canine friends. Not surprisingly, this is a popular route, so expect other hikers, as well as llama trekkers and horseback riders.

The hike to Matthieu Lakes and Collier Cone begins on a short path that leads generally south from the parking area to the Pacific Crest Trail (PCT), which is the main thoroughfare for the hike. Signs point the way to the PCT. At about 0.3 mile the path encounters a dark, crumpled lava flow—and the PCT.

Turn left (south) onto the main PCT. Almost immediately, the path veers away from the rugged lava, entering a cool forest of lichen-draped fir and hemlock. It passes through inviting wetlands—these can be dry in the late summer and fall but usually can provide a good doggie soaking in June and July. At 1 mile from the trailhead, the PCT reaches a well-marked junction. There's a small pond just north of this junction, though it is hard to see among the trees. At the junction, the inviting trail to North Matthieu Lake points straight ahead; the less-traveled PCT turns left to detour around this first lake. If it were up to your dog, chances are she would choose the path straight ahead into darker and wetter woodland.

From atop Collier Cone, you are rewarded with a great view of fast-shrinking Collier Glacier.

This is a good choice. Take the trail to North Matthieu Lake straight ahead. It leads through shady forest, crawling over outcrops and rocks, then tracks along the edge of the lava flow, encountering a tiny forest pond and wetland in 0.5 mile, then switchbacking up to forest-lined North Matthieu Lake 2.2 miles from the beginning of the hike.

The trail tours along the lakeshore, passing a number of designated camping sites. Then it begins a quick, 0.6-mile ascent to South Matthieu Lake. The difference between the settings of the two lakes is stark. North Matthieu Lake, at 5795 feet, is surrounded by forest; the much smaller South Matthieu Lake, elevation 6040, sits in a rock-lined subalpine basin offering a view of North Sister and Collier Cone ahead.

Past South Matthieu Lake, there are few reliable, dog-friendly water sources, especially late in the summer. Be sure you have adequate dog water for the next 4 miles (8 miles round trip) to Collier Cone.

At South Matthieu Lake, a trail leads east to connect with Green Lakes Basin between Broken Top and South Sister. However, for this hike, you should keep straight ahead toward Collier Cone and North Sister on the PCT.

From South Matthieu Lake, the PCT navigates across a lava flow for about 0.7 mile, then steps off into a meadow along the barren side of Yapoah Crater and tiptoes over the top of the very vent that, about twenty-five hundred years ago, produced the lava that today clogs McKenzie Pass. From the vent, the path leads downslope to a verdant meadow and another side trail that leads northwest toward Four-in-One Cone about a mile to the west.

Follow the PCT south. At 6 miles from the trailhead, and 0.5 mile from the Four-in-One intersection, the trail reaches Minnie Scott Spring, usually a reliable source of backpacker water and really no place for a dog. It's fine for Fido to romp and roll in the marshy grass downstream from the spring itself, but keep dogs away from the spot where water emerges and most backpackers dip their (filtered) water bottles. In late summer, this spring may go dry, so plan accordingly.

From the spring, the trail rounds a bend and heads for Collier Cone. About 7 miles into the hike, the PCT climbs to Opie Dilldock Pass on the north flank of Collier Cone. This is an inviting place to explore the varied sculptures that lava and cinders can produce. A short climb to the top or south side of Collier Cone's red cinders provides a view of the rapidly shrinking Collier Glacier and the huge gravel moraines it has left behind.

Return as you came—or, for variety, at South Matthieu Lake continue straight on the PCT rather than dropping to North Matthieu Lake. Here the PCT follows the side of a volcanic cinder cone, providing great views and cooler air (but more sun) than the route past North Matthieu Lake. In 2.1 miles from South Matthieu Lake, the PCT meets the North Matthieu Lake Trail. Continue along the PCT, returning as you came to the trailhead.

34. Metolius River Trail

Round trip: 12 miles
Elevation range: 2730–2880 feet
Difficulty: Easy
Hiking time: 6 hours
Best canine hiking season: Spring, summer, fall
Regulations: Northwest Forest Pass required
Maps: USGS Candle Creek and Prairie Farm Spring 7.5' quadrangles
Information: Deschutes National Forest, Sisters Ranger District, (541) 549-7700

Getting there: From Sisters, drive 9 miles west to milepost 91 on U.S. Highway 20–Oregon Route 126. Turn right (north) onto Forest Road 14 and continue 5 miles, past the Metolius River headwaters parking area, to FR 1420, marked "Campgrounds." Bear left onto FR 1420, following it 2.9 miles to the Canyon Creek Campground entry road, FR 1420-400. Drive 0.8 mile to the trailhead at the far end of the looped road, and park in the designated trailhead parking area. There is no trail connection, unfortunately, to the Metolius River headwaters.

A shady rest stop along the Metolius River Trail

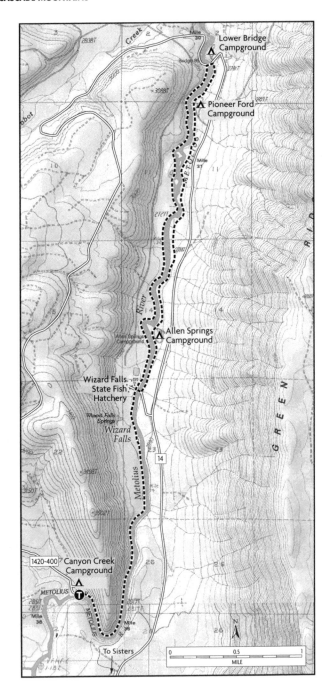

The Metolius River emerges from springs at the base of Black Butte, a symmetrical volcanic cone that is more than a million years in age and one of the oldest mountains of the high Cascades. The riverbank trails here are practically flat by any hiking measure. Mountain bikes, horses, and many other distractions are banned. The trails along the river follow the clear, cold (average temperature is below 50°F), and very swift water, tempting humans and their dogs with its placid appearance. A swim in this frigid, fast river is hazardous, however, so keep Fido out of the water.

The trail starts from the lower part of the Canyon Creek Campground and closely follows the west bank of the Metolius. It parallels the river around a sharp meander. At about 0.5 mile down the path, several highly productive springs gush water into the river on the opposite (west) bank, creating small waterfalls. From here, the well-worn trail threads along the bank through a narrowing gorge, while the stream frolics through a set of riffles and small rapids and rushes past several small islands at 1.7 miles into the hike. The river's histrionics culminate in 3-foot-high Wizard Falls 2.5 miles downstream from the trailhead.

The trail encounters springs and small wetland areas that provide cooling breaks along the stretch just below the falls where the river is not very accessible. In another 0.2 mile, the path enters the Wizard Falls State Fish Hatchery parking area. While the hatchery offers an interesting tour, it is better to continue your hike, returning to tour when you don't have to take the dog along.

For a short hike, you can turn around here. To continue, cross the river at the hatchery to follow the east bank trail for another 3.2 miles. The east trail also follows the river closely, though vine maple and small conifers often obscure the stream—a quick plunge through the vegetation will generally bring you to streamside for a scenic break. At 3.5 miles from its start, the east trail moves away from the river to veer around a piece of private property and across the neck of a meander loop. In another 0.5 mile, the path returns to the riverbank.

At Lower Bridge, 3.2 miles from the Wizard Falls Hatchery, cross the river back to the west side and return along the west bank. The landscape is more open on this trail, and the ponderosa pines are perhaps more in their element of flat-sloped, dry-footed, and sunny ground. Back at Wizard Falls, continue as you came to the trailhead where your vehicle awaits.

35. South Breitenbush River Gorge National Recreation Trail

One-way trip: 4.5 miles
Elevation range: 2440–3080 feet
Difficulty: Easy
Hiking time: 2.5 hours
Best canine hiking season: Summer, fall
Regulations: Northwest Forest Pass required
Map: USGS Breitenbush Hot Springs 7.5' quadrangle
Information: Willamette National Forest, Detroit Ranger District, (503) 854-3366

Getting there: From Salem, follow Oregon Route 22 about 35 miles east to Detroit. Turn left (north) on Breitenbush Road (Forest Road 46). Drive 10.7 miles, and turn right onto FR 4685. Drive 0.5 mile to a small trailhead parking area on the right.

To reach the upper trailhead and leave a shuttle vehicle there, continue 4.5 miles on FR 4685 to a large parking area on the right. The trailhead for the South Breitenbush River Gorge National Recreation Trail (Trail 3366), marked by a sign, is on the west side of the parking area.

This stroll through old-growth Douglas fir has a few cedar and hemlock to add diversity. Look for towering Douglas fir that are more than 5 feet in diameter. The path plows past gigantic, blown-down trees felled by a 1990 windstorm—a reminder that Mother Nature can be a bit heavy-handed at times. In June the rhododendrons along the trail put on a spectacular show. In August, ripe huckleberries are a trail favorite.

From the roadside trailhead, the path travels about 100 yards south to connect with the main trail, informally called the South Breitenbush River NRT, especially on signs. To the right is a 1-mile walk to Breitenbush Hot Springs—but the better dog hike is to the left. In about 0.6 mile, the blown-down trees are conveniently cut for your passage. At 1.5 miles, a well-marked side trail to the left follows a wooden walkway to a slippery

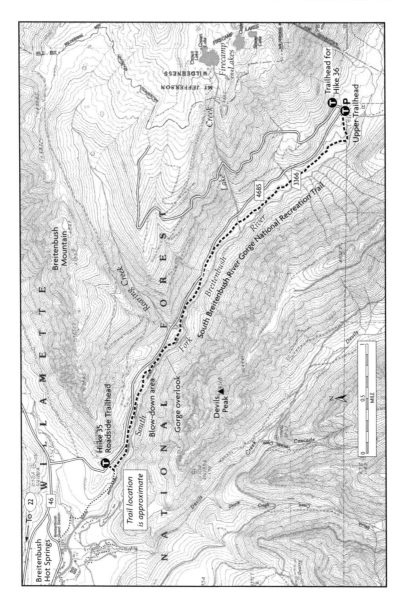

overlook of the South Breitenbush's tempestuous gorge. Return to the main trail to continue the hike.

The remainder of the hike weaves through scenic old-growth forest. At 2.4 miles, a path to the left leads back to FR 4685 at an intermediate

Steps were hewn into giant logs on the South Breitenbush River Trail.

trailhead, but this longer one-way hike continues on the less-traveled but well-maintained trail. Although the trail is never far from the road, it seems remote and provides several informal side paths for access to the river. Alternatively, creek crossings at 2.5 miles and 3.8 miles provide doggie water. Even in late summer, seeps and springs along the path provide additional doggie cooling spots. At 4.5 miles you reach the upper trailhead.

36. South Breitenbush Trail: Jefferson Park

Round trip: 13 miles
Elevation range: 3200–6040 feet
Difficulty: Strenuous
Hiking time: 10 hours
Best canine hiking season: Summer, fall
Regulations: Northwest Forest Pass required; campsites are regulated in this very popular area—call ahead to determine whether entry permits are required
Maps: USGS Mount Bruno and Mount Jefferson 7.5' quadrangles
Information: Willamette National Forest, Detroit Ranger District, (503) 854-3366

Getting there: From Salem, follow Oregon Route 22 about 35 miles east to Detroit. Turn left (north) on Breitenbush Road (Forest Road 46). Drive 10.7 miles, and turn right on FR 4685. Drive 4.5 miles and turn right into the huge trailhead parking area. To find the beginning of the hike to Jefferson Park, walk 0.2 mile farther (east) along FR 4685 to the South Breitenbush Trail (Trail 3375).

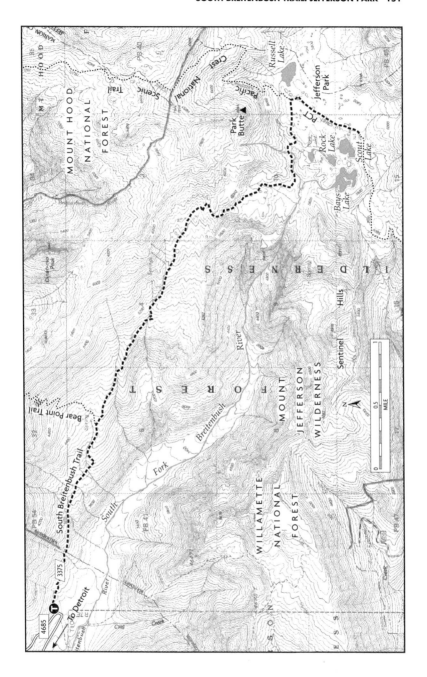

The hike to Jefferson Park, one of the high Cascades' most scenic spots, is deservedly popular. Lakes and water abound in the alpine landscape. Expect to meet other hikers and dogs, even in nonpeak times. Much of the area is in recovery from past overuse, and campfires are banned. So here, especially, go lightly on the land.

From the trailhead, the South Breitenbush Trail (Trail 3375) begins an unrepentant but even-gaited climb. The forest is mostly 50- to 100-year-old Douglas fir and hemlock, replacements for the Douglas fir–cedar forest that was consumed in a forest fire here almost a century ago. Charcoal-encrusted snags still loom along the trail. In the first 3 miles, the path encounters four small streams that provide cool water for warm paws. In addition, the trail crosses several smaller seasonal streams and seeps, but late in the season these smaller water sources may dry up.

At 1.6 miles, the Bear Point Trail turns left. This path provides a tempting climb along a less popular trail. It leads to Bear Lake in another 1.6 miles of uphill. It makes a tempting side trip in cooler weather. However, the lack of shade and water for most of the climb advises against it on hot days, especially for dogs not in great condition.

To reach the alpine lakes of Jefferson Park, bear right on the South Breitenbush Trail at its junction with the Bear Point Trail. Look for western white pine along with azalea and rhododendron as the forest opens. The path leads through a mile of young trees growing where the older forest was burned away several decades ago. You can catch glimpses of Mount

From the South Breitenbush Trail, Mount Jefferson rises above Jefferson Park.

Jefferson from the trail, or saunter a few hundred feet off the trail to better viewpoints along the rim of Breitenbush Canyon. As you reach 5000 feet near the base of Park Butte, the forest closes in again. Look for young western red cedar trees in trailside wetlands.

The trail makes a quick plunge into a small, forested basin and tiny lake, then climbs out again to find the Pacific Crest Trail (PCT) and Russell Lake at the base of Mount Jefferson 5.5 miles from the trailhead. This is the portal to Jefferson Park. Subalpine firs grow on rock-clad islands amid spongy alpine meadows. Fido will exult in the soft footing but may not fully appreciate the views of Whitewater Glacier and Jefferson's craggy summit. Turn right at the PCT and follow it about 0.5 mile to Scout Lake at the south edge of Jefferson Park. Return as you came.

37. Devils Lake to Moraine Lake Loop

Round trip: 6.8 miles
Elevation range: 5460–7200 feet
Difficulty: Strenuous
Hiking time: 6 hours
Best canine hiking season: Summer, fall
Regulations: Northwest Forest Pass required; register for wilderness entry; dogs must be on leash; avoid hiking on fragile areas as signed
Map: USGS South Sister 7.5' quadrangle
Information: Deschutes-Ochoco National Forest, Bend–Fort Rock Ranger District, (541) 383-4000

Getting there: On U.S. Highway 97 (Bend Parkway), take the Cascades Lakes Highway–Century Drive exit and turn west on Colorado Avenue (Oregon Route 372). This road traverses a business district and engages several roundabouts, then is renamed Century Drive at 2 miles, and then, at the Bend city limits, morphs into Cascade Lakes Highway (Forest Road 46). The Devils Lake trailhead parking is on the left, about 27 miles west of Bend and about 1 mile west of the western end of Sparks Lake.

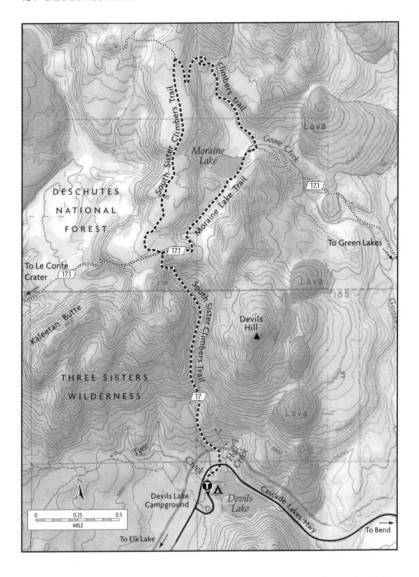

The trip to Moraine Lake is a day hike into a high Cascades truly alpine setting. The lake, at the foot of South Sister, provides great views, and should you choose to test your alpine chops, there's easy access to the challenging, steep trail to South Sister's 10,363-foot summit.

From the parking area, the trail wanders into the woods, crosses Tyee Creek, and then crosses the highway for the real hike. (You'll notice that some people who have done this hike before have parked on the highway shoulder where the trail crosses.)

After a short walk and a second creek crossing of Hell Creek, the path climbs easily for the first mile, with a few abrupt "steps" to galumph up. There's a lot of Douglas fir forest to admire and, in early summer, moist, soft substrate for dog paws. The path reaches a large rock outcropping on the right—the rock is andesite, erupted beneath glacial ice perhaps twenty-five thousand years ago—and then

South Sister dominates the landscape along the Moraine Lake Trail.

it steepens and begins a short 0.5 mile of switchbacks before topping out. In 100 yards from the "top," you'll find a four-way intersection.

Turn right, on the path marked Moraine Lake Trail. The trail wiggles through a broad canyon and then advances across the flat bottom of Lewis Glacier's old valley, reaching the far (east) side of Moraine Lake in 0.8 mile.

Moraine Lake is a favorite camping spot for those who are trudging up South Sister. Here, you have an option to continue east on the trail to Green Lakes—a 4-mile hike one way. For the loop hike around Moraine Lake, from the lake follow the climbers trail(s) on the east side. Several informal but well-used trails all head for the steep outcrops at the head of Moraine Lake, merging into one trail that then connects with the South Sister climbers trail in 1.3 miles.

At the unmarked junction with the South Sister climbers trail, turn left to return to the Devils Lake trailhead. You may extend your hike, of course, by following the South Sister trail up as far as you wish (the summit is 3.2 miles and 3200 vertical feet from here, with some tough hiking and rough rocks for dog paws—carry water for Rover if you decide to do this). For the loop hike, return to the four-way intersection; here, for an easier extended hike than the South Sister summit, turn right for a relatively flat, easy hike 2 miles to Le Conte Crater, a cinder cone, and Rock Mesa, a twelve-hundred-year-old volcanic dome. When you're done exploring, return along the South Sister climbers trail to the Devils Lake trailhead.

38. Three Sisters Wilderness: Sisters Mirror Lake

Round trip: 12 miles
Elevation range: 5400–6200 feet
Difficulty: Moderate
Hiking time: 6 hours
Best canine hiking season: Summer, early fall
Regulations: Northwest Forest Pass required
Map: USGS South Sister 7.5' quadrangle
Information: Deschutes National Forest, Bend–Fort Rock Ranger
   District, (541) 383-4000

Getting there: From Bend, drive 30 miles west on Cascade Lakes Highway (Forest Road 46). Turn right (north) into a small parking area marked as the Mirror Lake trailhead.

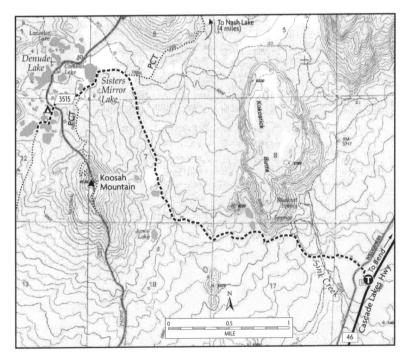

The name of this trail and its destination, Sisters Mirror Lake, conjures visions of high alpine splendor. Instead, what you get is a rather level hike through lodgepole pines, a fleeting glimpse of higher peaks, and a satisfactory romp in a huge heather-filled meadow along the shore of a placid little pond. There are other lakes in the vicinity, and most of the day can be spent sampling each one for size.

From the trailhead, the path plunges into lodgepole pines, dropping in 0.5 mile into a small valley of fir and spruce with springs and bogs along Sink Creek. Here, the trail crosses a broader trail—part of a road to Rock Mesa crafted when a mining company threatened to turn Rock Mesa into kitty litter in the 1960s. Continue straight across this broad, tempting path. The trail to Sisters Mirror Lake climbs out of the small valley, sideswipes a small forest pond at the top of the grade, and then circumnavigates several large rock outcroppings. These make inviting play areas for dogs, and a climb to the top offers a view of Kokostick Butte and a rare glimpse of South Sister peeking over the pine-fringed landscape.

From the rock outcroppings, the trail ambles 3 miles through a lodgepole stand. There is no dog water here, and it can be a long stretch on hot days, so carry dog water for this portion of the hike.

At 3.8 miles from the trailhead, the path intersects the Pacific Crest Trail. If you veer right, the path circles around the lake basin and leads about 4 miles through still more lodgepoles, meandering downslope through firs to Sphinx Creek and Nash Lake (4920 feet). To reach Sisters

Meesha contemplates a plunge into the water along the trail to Sisters Mirror Lake, Three Sisters Wilderness.

Mirror Lake (6200 feet) and a welter of other small alpine lakes and ponds, turn left here onto the Pacific Crest Trail. The path leads across a heather-floored meadow—a former lake bottom—to reach the shore of Sisters Mirror Lake in 0.6 mile.

The view of South Sister is disappointing here, but it improves slightly as you travel farther south and west along the trail. Once at Sisters Mirror Lake, the trail (which can be a challenge to find among the heather and sedges) splits. One branch leads northwest away from the lake; the other heads southwest along the lakeshore. Other lakes in this basin to explore include Denude Lake 0.6 mile along a trail to the northwest and a cluster of slightly smaller, unnamed lakes along the trail about 1 mile to the southwest. Return to the trailhead as you came.

39. Todd Lake

Round trip: 5.6 miles
Elevation range: 6120–6840 feet
Difficulty: Moderate
Hiking time: 4 hours
Best canine hiking season: Summer, early fall
Regulations: Northwest Forest Pass required
Map: USGS Broken Top 7.5' quadrangle
Information: Deschutes National Forest, Bend–Fort Rock Ranger District, (541) 383-4000

Getting there: From Bend, drive 27 miles west on Cascade Lakes Highway (Forest Road 46). Just past Sparks Lake, turn right (north) onto FR 370, marked for Todd Lake. Drive 0.6 mile to the trailhead and campground parking area.

This hike tours a varied landscape, rising from a large lake lined with fir and hemlock into a subalpine environment with less than 1000 feet of climb. Most of the hike is forested; open meadowlands offer streams or marshes. The first half of this almost 6-mile hike follows well-maintained Forest Service trails; the second portion tracks along roads, most of which are abandoned or gated off. They are really nothing more than luxuriously wide hiking paths,

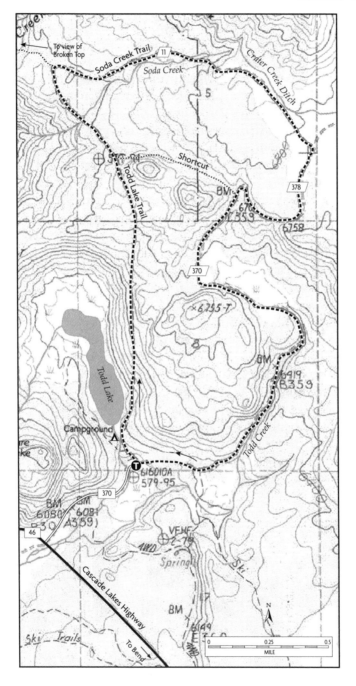

though there is occasional use by vehicles on the last 0.5 mile, so as you return be vigilant for the sound of approaching engines and keep dogs close.

From the trailhead, the broad path to Todd Lake and its walk-in campground is well marked and offers an easy stroll to the popular lake's well-trampled beach. For dogs, this is a good spot for a wetting before heading out. The likely proximity of campers and picnickers during the peak summer season recommends that dogs remain on leashes here.

The Todd Lake Trail leaves to the left along the east side of the lake, climbing quickly and steadily away from the water and into dense Douglas fir forest, leaving the lake only a blue glimmer through the trees. After gaining about 300 feet in the first 0.5 mile, the path moderates its climb.

At 1.2 miles, a trail leads to the right. If you wish to make this a shorter hike than the 4-hour route outlined here, you can turn right (east) here, reaching a two-track gravel road in 0.5 mile, where you turn right, followed by boggy subalpine meadows and a small stream in about 1 mile, and continuing on the road 2.6 miles back to the trailhead for a 4-mile loop. This option forgoes the best views of Broken Top, however.

To continue on the main hike, go straight at the intersection, heading northwest. At 1.7 miles, the trail intersects the Soda Creek Trail. For a good view of Broken Top, a mountain that owes its craggy countenance to glaciers rather than explosive eruptions, turn left onto the Soda Creek Trail and continue for 0.5 mile to alpine meadows and the headwaters of Soda Creek before turning around and retracing your steps to the intersection.

Broken Top, an extinct, glaciated Cascade volcano, rises above the trails from Todd Lake and Green Lakes.

To return to the Todd Lake trailhead, head east (right) on the Soda Creek Trail. This path intercepts the Crater Creek Ditch in 0.9 mile, then about 1 mile from the intersection with the Todd Lake Trail merges with abandoned Spur Road 378; turn right onto this old road. In 0.5 mile, the two-track path leads past boggy meadows, then merges into a more traveled road—Spur Road 370. Like Spur Road 378, this road is not maintained for vehicular traffic and is gated most of the year. However, use caution when hiking with dogs, as it is open at times during the fall, and mountain bikers occasionally use these roads.

In 1 mile, Spur Road 370 joins the upper reaches of Todd Creek, a small stream that leads you, your dog, and the old road 1.5 miles back to the Todd Lake trailhead.

40. Bend: Deschutes River Trail

One-way trip: 8.5 miles
Elevation range: 3850–4290 feet
Difficulty: Easy
Hiking time: 5 hours
Best canine hiking season: Spring, summer, fall
Regulations: Northwest Forest Pass required; dogs must be on leash
Maps: USGS Benham Falls and Shevlin Park 7.5' quadrangles
Information: Deschutes National Forest, Bend–Fort Rock Ranger
    District, (541) 383-4000

Getting there: To reach the start of this hike at the Benham Falls trailhead, drive west from Bend on Century Drive, which becomes the Cascade Lakes Highway and then Forest Road 46. Approximately 6 miles from downtown Bend, turn left (south) onto FR 4600-100. Continue past the Meadow Picnic Area on FR 4600-100 for another 2 miles toward Mount Bachelor. Turn left (south) onto FR 41, marked for Benham Falls. Drive 2.6 miles, then turn left (east) onto FR 4120 and continue for 0.5 mile. Bear right onto FR 4120-100 and follow the washboarded gravel road 3.1 miles to a parking area and the trailhead.

The Benham Falls trailhead can also be reached from U.S. Highway 97. To use this route, drive 9 miles south from Bend on US 97. Turn right (west) at Lava Butte and then almost immediately turn left onto FR 9702,

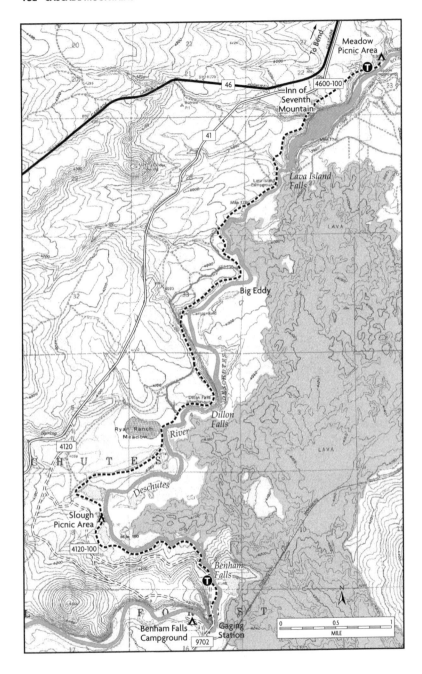

marked for Benham Falls. Drive 4 miles (crossing a set of railroad tracks at 3.2 miles) to a picnic area and parking. Cross the Deschutes River on the bridge at the west end of the picnic area, and follow alongside the well-developed riverside trail 0.7 mile to Benham Falls and a connection with the Deschutes River Trail 0.2 mile past the falls.

To leave a second vehicle at Meadow Picnic Area, where this hike ends, exit the Benham Falls trailhead and return along FR 4120-100, FR 4120, and FR 41 to FR 4600-100. You will reach the trailhead at Meadow Picnic Area in about 2.1 miles. There also is trail access at five other points along the Deschutes, all of them reachable from FR 41.

The trail along the Deschutes River is really three trails—one that is dedicated to horses, another that is dedicated to mountain bikers, and a third, the one closest to the river, for hikers. The three paths often overlap, however. Generally, as long as you follow the river, it's hard to get lost. This is a popular trail, so watch for other hikers and dogs, as well as mountain bikes. Bend is a mecca for mountain bikers, the Deschutes River Trail is a favorite ride, and some riders stray from the mountain bike route. In the spring, you are likely to find deer—especially does and young fawns near the trail—or if you don't, your dog will. Forest Service regulations require that dogs be leashed, and it's best to heed the rules here.

The hike begins at the Benham Falls trailhead, a manicured, civilized path replete with handrails, mesh fences, and wooden benches. The trail switchbacks down to an overlook of the falls and the narrow canyon that the unruly river has chopped through a lava flow belched out of Lava Butte about sixty-two hundred years ago. The river plays tag with the flow for most of the hike. It was this eruption that pushed the river channel west to its present location. The Deschutes is only now fighting its way back to its former channel closer to Lava Butte.

From the overlook area, a gravel path leads down to the river and the start of the 8.5-mile Deschutes River Trail. The path is broad for virtually all of its length as it weaves from the river's edge for views of desolate lava flows and back into forest dominated by ponderosa pine. Shooting stars and lupine color the early summer forest floor. Bitterbrush and rabbitbrush fringe the rocks at the river's edge.

The first segment of the trail, Benham Falls to the slough (a sluggish, abandoned river meander), is 1.5 miles long. It hugs the water's edge, rising and falling gently along an undulating forest floor, allowing

Megan, Dundee, and Meesha pause for a rest along the Deschutes River Trail to view the side channel of the river—and the lava flow that blocked the river's main channel about seven thousand years ago.

relatively easy river access at numerous places with a short scramble. This segment, like most of the trail, is popular for fishing, so be wary of lost hooks and other gear, as well as discarded fish. (Trout can carry the same parasites that produce salmon poisoning.)

At 1.5 miles, the trail moves away from the riverbank, crossing the Slough Picnic Area (accessible by car from FR 41), then tours the edge of a large, lily-filled pond and wetland (the slough). This is a fine place to practice good canine citizenship and avoid disruption of the wetland and slough while dogs cool off.

In about 0.3 mile, the path returns to the Deschutes, again following a low bank with easy access to water before it swings away from the river to shortcut through bunchgrass meadows.

At Dillon Falls, 3.8 miles downstream from Benham Falls, is another automotive access point. Here, the river enters a deeper, narrower gorge, remaining inaccessible for about the next 1.2 miles. Be sure to carry extra dog water for this segment on hot days. The trail occasionally teeters toward the gorge rimrock, then meanders back under cover of ponderosa pine. The path is relatively level here and provides views of the lava field across the river. At 4.3 miles from the trailhead, a side trail leads to a nice view of Dillon Falls, a 15-foot-high cataract, and the class IV rapids below it.

From Dillon Falls, the trail generally parallels the river, but the stream remains inaccessible for another mile. Where the water becomes more accessible in a few places, access requires some adroit climbing over rocks. At 5.7 miles from Benham Falls, the path reaches the flat terrain of Big Eddy access point, a calm river stretch where lodgepole pines, bitterbrush, and bunchgrass are the dominant vegetation.

Beyond Big Eddy, the path returns to more familiar ponderosa pine and tracks along low, friendly riverbanks for about a mile before winding through more rocky terrain above the canyon that encloses Lava Island Falls. Six-thousand-year-old human artifacts have been found in small caves near this small cataract, indicating probable human occupation of the area within several hundred years of Lava Butte's eruption.

At Lava Island Falls, the trail detours away from the river for the last 1.2 miles before reaching the Meadows Picnic Area and your shuttle car waiting at the end of the trail.

41. Shevlin Park: Tumalo Creek Trail

Round trip: 5.8 miles
Elevation range: 3630–3810 feet
Difficulty: Easy
Hiking time: 3 hours
Best canine hiking season: Spring, summer, fall
Regulations: Parking permit required; dogs (and all domestic animals) must be on leash at all times (so bring a leash for the cat and pet duck, too . . .)
Maps: USGS Bend and Shevlin Park 7.5' quadrangles
Information: City of Bend Parks and Recreation, (541) 389-7275

Getting there: To reach Shevlin Park, drive west on Newport Avenue in Bend. This street transitions to Shevlin Park Road and in 3 miles from this transition reaches the park, at 18920 Shevlin Park Road. To access the best trails, turn left at Aspen Hall entry and follow the short paved roadway to shaded parking. A good bet for hiking with Fido is the Tumalo Creek Trail, a footpath that runs through the most shade-rich parts of the park. This path is accessed by following signs and bearing left just before the first covered bridge near the park's Aspen Hall entry.

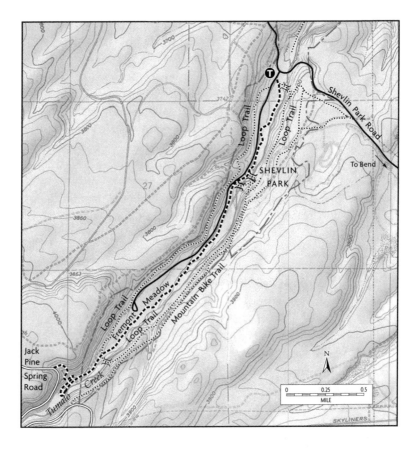

Shevlin Park is 600 acres of undeveloped forest and grassland, with miles of trails. It is a popular place to hike and walk, with access to adjacent Forest Service public lands. This park has multiple parallel trails, and it is easy to loop back and forth between them for an extended walk. The roadway provides a nice path for a stroll, leading you deeper into the wooded valley of Tumalo Creek. While a fire charred the surrounding uplands in 1990, Tumalo Creek was spared, and large ponderosa pines provide welcome shade and shelter here.

From the start near the Aspen Hall entry, the broad Tumalo Creek Trail weaves among tall pines and manzanita, providing close proximity to the creek in the first 0.5 mile. At about 1 mile, the trail intersects two covered bridges that provide access to the rim trail on the other side of Tumalo Creek; this is a good opportunity to make a short loop hike.

Trails in Shevlin Park are generally flat and quite civilized.

Beyond the bridges, the trail runs close to a paved roadway, then turns back into pines, reaching a grassy opening (and restroom) at Fremont Meadow about 2 miles from the park entry.

From here, the Tumalo Creek Trail morphs into a Forest Service trail that skirts the creek and climbs slightly away from its banks. At about 2.5 miles, the trail makes a turn out of a nicely shaded riparian area, climbing uphill past an impressive basaltic outcrop and intersecting Jack Pine Spring Road—a graveled Forest Service road at 3 miles from the trail's start. To avoid traffic, this is a good turnaround spot. You may wish to explore some of the adjacent and parallel trails as you return to the trailhead.

42. La Pine State Park: Fall River Loop

Round trip: 4.75 miles
Elevation range: 4190–4220 feet
Difficulty: Easy
Hiking time: 3 hours
Best canine hiking season: Spring, summer, fall
Regulations: Oregon State Parks parking permit required; dogs must be on 6-foot leash
Map: USGS Pistol Butte 7.5' quadrangle
Information: Oregon State Parks and Recreation, La Pine State Park, (541) 536-2071

Getting there: This park is just west of Newberry National Volcanic Monument. To get there, follow U.S. Highway 97 south from Bend about

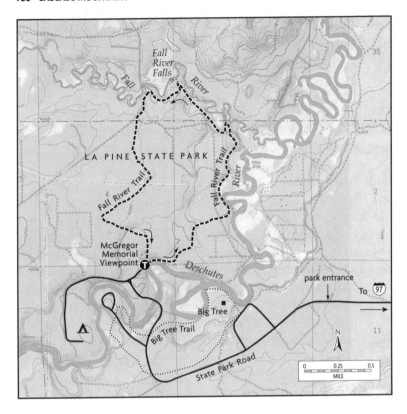

25 miles. Watch for signs to La Pine State Park near milepost 160. Turn right (west) on State Park Road (also known as Fall River Road). Follow this road 5.5 miles and bear right on State Recreation Road to the park entry. Trails start at McGregor Memorial Viewpoint (an overview of a pretty meander on the Deschutes River), an additional 0.5 mile along park roadways. To get to the Big Tree, turn right on a well-marked spur road just beyond the park entry.

La Pine State Park is a quiet, underappreciated location with easy hiking and great access to serene rivers and giant trees. Oregon's biggest ponderosa pine—28.9 feet in circumference and, at last count, 162 feet tall—makes its home here. "Big Tree's" age is an estimated five hundred years. The Big Tree Trail ambles for 1.3 miles through lodgepole and pine woodland. There are multiple trails, all well marked and easy to hike, so you can devote an entire day to trekking at least 10 deliciously flat and semi-shady miles if you wish. Or combine hikes here with a visit to nearby Newberry National Volcanic Monument for a weekend of dog hikes. The park includes a campground, cabins, and yurts. La Pine State Park provides "pet friendly" cabins for overnight stays.

The longest and most inspiring trail is a loop that leads to Fall River Falls. Start at McGregor Memorial Viewpoint and head north on the Fall River Trail. The path explores a flat lodgepole and ponderosa pine forest, with a few large "yellow-bellies" occasionally interspersed with the smaller, darker, dominant lodgepoles and subalpine firs. Much of the trails here, including the Fall River Trail, encounter a

Chad and his dogs, Remy and PrAna, head out on a hike from Big Tree at La Pine State Park.

patchwork of open forest and clearings, where downed logs are a part of the landscape. The trail is well defined, and portions follow older two-track roads that are now simply broad hiking trails. In 0.8 mile, the nearly flat path provides another glimpse of the Deschutes River, which is more accessible here than at McGregor Viewpoint. The Deschutes is deceptively swift, and deep, so keep watch of Rover if she goes for a swim.

In another mile, the trail finds the banks of the Fall River. Like the Deschutes, it's cold, clear, flat, and almost mirrorlike. And like the Deschutes, it has more water and *faster* water than it might seem. Access here requires scrambling down steep embankments. As you continue, the trail skirts Fall River; in about 0.5 mile keep watch for a side trail and a small, unprepossessing sign that just says "To Falls." The path leads to Fall River Falls in about 0.25 mile—a pretty (and noisy) stretch of white water that is somewhere between a very steep, major riffle and a very horizontal waterfall. This cascade of water empties into a quiet pool that often attracts fly-fishermen and fly-fisherwomen.

From the falls, the Fall River Trail engages the river once more in about 0.25 mile and then takes to the open lodgepole forest seriously, reaching the loop trailhead in about 1.8 miles.

43. Newberry National Volcanic Monument: Peter Skene Ogden Trail

One-way trip: 9.5 miles
Elevation range: 4300–6350 feet
Difficulty: Moderate
Hiking time: 6 hours
Best canine hiking season: Early summer, early fall
Regulations: Northwest Forest Pass required
Maps: USGS Paulina Peak and Finley Butte 7.5' quadrangles
Information: Deschutes National Forest, Bend–Fort Rock Ranger
District, (541) 383-4000

Getting there: Reach the beginning of this hike by following U.S.
Highway 97 south 23.5 miles from Bend. Turn left (east) onto Forest
Road 211, which is the main entrance road to Newberry National Vol-
canic Monument. Drive 2.8 miles to FR 2120, then turn left (north) into
Ogden Group Camp.

To leave a second vehicle at the far end of this one-way hike, continue
east on FR 21 for 12 miles past the entrance to Ogden Group Camp. Turn
left into a service road marked "Paulina Lake Lodge."

This hike on the Peter Skene Ogden National Scenic Trail follows Paulina
Creek for 9.5 miles to Paulina Lake. En route to the lake, the trail passes
several waterfalls and provides a tour of how a forest changes with increasing altitude. Mountain bikers ride this trail uphill, but their downhill
run is supposed to be on the road or a separate path. Horses, however,
share the trail both uphill and down, though there is a separate parallel
trail just for them.

From the trailhead in a large parking lot just before Ogden Group Camp,
the trail points upstream along Paulina Creek. In 0.25 mile it crosses the
creek on a sturdy bridge, then moves across grassy meadows and into
lodgepole pine stands with an understory of bitterbrush and manzanita.
These trees are well adapted to Newberry's ash-rich soils and to the

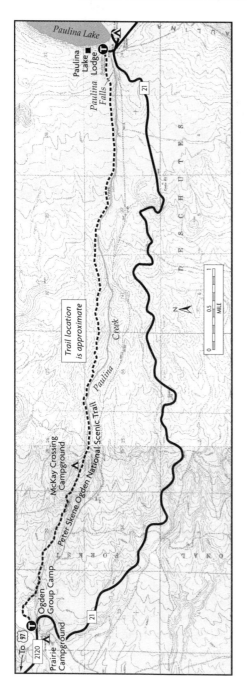

eruptions and disturbance cycles of volcanoes.

The trail jogs right at 0.7 mile then left at 0.9 mile, crosses another wooden footbridge, and then emerges onto a narrow-gauge railroad grade well above the creek. At 2.5 miles, Paulina Creek begins a retreat into its gorge, making creek access next to impossible for the next 0.5 mile until the campground at McKay Crossing. Here, a pretty 15-foot waterfall marks Paulina Creek's renewed accessibility.

The path uphill for the next 5.7 miles is uninterrupted by campgrounds or other distractions. This forest includes occasional old-growth ponderosa pines and an understory of kinnikinnick—a low manzanita. This segment of the trail is rocky in places, and Paulina Creek is not always accessible, especially in the stretch between mile 4.6 and mile 5.2, where the creek cuts through another gorge just downstream from an unnamed 10-foot falls. From this falls to Paulina Falls is another 3 miles of trekking through a fragrant lodgepole forest, interspersed

Hot dogs. Dundee and Meesha on the Peter Skene Ogden Trail at Newberry National Volcanic Monument

with more ponderosa pine and eventually Douglas fir as the trail moves higher. The path moves away from the stream at 7.9 miles into the hike, remaining safely atop the rims of a deepening gorge—the entry to Paulina Falls. Where the path encounters the falls at 8.5 miles, it offers only a rudimentary glimpse of the rushing water from the north side of the stream. For a better view, visit the developed interpretive trails on the south bank at the conclusion of your hike.

The trail continues 0.3 mile past Paulina Falls to the entrance road to Paulina Lake Lodge. To reach the main Paulina picnic area, cross the bridge and follow a path along the highway guardrail 0.3 mile to the west.

NORTH UMPQUA TRAIL

Built over an 18-year period from 1978 to 1996, the North Umpqua Trail (NUT) is one of the newest pathways along Oregon's scenic rivers. It extends for 79 miles from just east of Glide on Oregon Route 138 upstream to Maidu Lake, the North Umpqua River headwaters. The trail is divided into nine easily accessible segments that follow the river, offering a variety of hiking environments with old-growth cedar and spruce forest and high-altitude hikes amid lodgepole pine and subalpine fir. Trailheads are easily accessible, but the trail itself is remote from traffic, even on the segments that follow the Umpqua along the main highway—the trail is across the river from the road and well screened by forest. The entire North Umpqua Trail is excellent for hiking with dogs, though this book covers just four segments of it. The trail is also increasingly popular with mountain bikers, so watch for them hurtling silently downhill.

Because of the frequent access points, three of the hikes along the North Umpqua Trail are described as one-way trips. Hikers can use a two-vehicle shuttle system to hike the trail in only one direction. An alternate way to enjoy these hikes is to walk the whole distance to the next trailhead and return, or walk part of the distance from one trailhead, return, and then hike from the next trailhead.

44. North Umpqua Trail: Tioga Segment, Miles 1–16

One-way trip: 15.7 miles
Elevation range: 770–1800 feet
Difficulty: Moderate
Hiking time: 8 hours
Best canine hiking season: Fall
Regulations: Northwest Forest Pass required
Maps: USGS Old Fairview and Mace Mountain 7.5' quadrangles (this trail is too new to appear on maps)
Information: Umpqua National Forest, North Umpqua Ranger District, (541) 496-3532; Bureau of Land Management, Coos Bay–Umpqua Office, (541) 756-0100

Getting there: To reach the west trailhead where this hike begins, start at the North Umpqua Ranger Station at Glide and head east for 2 miles on Oregon Route 138. At the Swiftwater Bridge, turn right (south) across the bridge, marked for the North Umpqua Trail, Tioga segment. Turn left into the trailhead parking area.

To reach the east trailhead, where you can leave a shuttle car to make this a one-way hike, return to OR 138. Drive 18 miles east on OR 138 to Forest Road 4711 (Wright Creek Road). Turn right onto FR 4711 and drive across the bridge. The trailhead is almost immediately across the bridge.

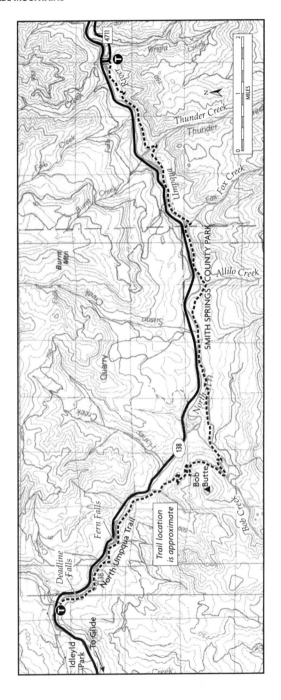

The Tioga segment of the North Umpqua Trail (NUT) is the lowest-elevation portion of the trail and lies closest to Roseburg and other towns. Ironically, this popular and most accessible segment, mostly on land operated by the Bureau of Land Management and Douglas County Parks, is also one of the NUT's longest and most rigorous. It climbs over Bob Butte, one of the few strenuous uphill stretches in the 79-mile trail. Watch for poison oak in sunny or open places. The North Umpqua is a big and powerful river along this segment, so exercise caution when you take Fido for a dip. You also might encounter inexperienced hikers whose destination is the river overlook along a handicapped-accessible interpretive trail to Deadline Falls, so be sure to keep dogs on a leash.

From the west trailhead (Tioga, also the start of the 79-mile trek to Maidu Lake on the north flank of Mount Theilsen), the path follows the river and in 0.1 mile offers a short interpretive side trail to an overlook of a riparian wetland and Deadline Falls—a 6-foot cataract jumped by migrating salmon and steelhead in the fall. From this side trail, the main route turns back into the forest, following the river at a respectful and generally inaccessible distance. Periodic encounters with small side creeks provide adequate doggie dunkings in spring and early summer. Douglas fir, Alaska yellow cedar, and big-leaf maple form most of the forest canopy along the Tioga trail segment. Maidenhair and sword ferns

The North Umpqua River plunges over numerous small falls and rapids near the North Umpqua Trail's Tioga segment.

and manzanita form most of the low understory. Watch for kingfishers, with their clicking, ratchety call along the river.

At 1.8 miles, the path provides an overlook of Fern Falls, a misty curtain of water that plummets off a rock outcrop and scampers into a deep blue hole in the adjacent North Umpqua. Beyond this falls, the trail maintains some distance between itself and the river, though with a little perseverance you can scamper down the slopes (sometimes steep) to find the shore. After maintaining its distance from the river, the path begins a climb up the west shoulder of Bob Butte at about 3.5 miles into the hike. It climbs about 900 feet in a switchbacking ascent through mostly Douglas fir forest. Look for pileated woodpeckers here. In summer, the call of hermit thrush sounds like a distant flute.

The ascent of the northern shoulder of Bob Butte is the only real climb on this segment of the trail, but there is no water along it, so carry extra for your dog and be prepared to take a break on hot days. Westbound mountain bikers relish the downhill challenge, so keep your dog under close control here and be ready for hurtling two-wheelers.

The trail reaches its summit at 1800 feet (Bob Butte's northern shoulder) and begins a much straighter descent to Bob Creek. The creek provides an adequate doggie dip to compensate for the long, hot climb. There's still another 10 miles ahead before reaching the next trailhead.

Once across the creek, the trail ducks beneath a powerline and then joins an old two-track road. It follows this road for about 2 miles, including a stint through the south side of Smith Springs County Park. At the end of this road near the riverbank, the NUT resumes its more familiar form as a single-track trail. At 10 miles into the hike, a side trail invites you up a canyon with a small creek. This trail leads to a very pretty 45-foot waterfall. It's best explored in spring and early summer, though the stream, Allilo Creek, is perennial. For the next 5.7 miles, the trail continues through a diverse fir and cedar forest, generally keeping away from the riverbank and at times perching on steep slopes above the water. It crosses 10 more creeks, so even if you cannot access the North Umpqua River, there are enough doggie dips to keep even Labrador retrievers happy.

At its end, the Tioga segment of the North Umpqua Trail emerges from a dark, sheltered forest at the small trailhead area on Forest Road 4711 near the small community of Steamboat.

45. North Umpqua Trail: Hot Springs Segment, Miles 47–54

One-way trip: 6.2 miles
Elevation range: 2512–3135 feet
Difficulty: Moderate
Hiking time: 4 hours
Best canine hiking season: Summer, fall
Regulations: Northwest Forest Pass required
Maps: USGS Potter Mountain and Toketee Falls 7.5' quadrangles
Information: Umpqua National Forest, Diamond Lake Ranger Station, (541) 498-2531

Getting there: To reach the start of the hike, from Interstate 5 at Roseburg drive 59 miles east on Oregon Route 138. Turn left (north) onto Forest Road 34, the Toketee Lake turnoff. Continue 2 miles on FR 34, past a noisy generator plant and Toketee Campground, and bear right onto FR 3401, marked Hot Springs. Park at a small trailhead parking turnout on the right on FR 3401, about 0.6 mile beyond the turnoff from FR 34, just after a bridge across the river.

To reach the Thorn Prairie trailhead, where you can leave a shuttle car to make this a one-way hike, return to FR 3401. Drive an additional 4.6 miles on FR 3401 and turn left (north) onto Spur Road 700, marked North Umpqua Trail. Drive 0.5 mile on Spur Road 700, then bear left onto Spur Road 710 and drive another 0.5 mile to the Thorn Prairie trailhead parking area.

The Hot Springs segment of the North Umpqua Trail (NUT) starts in a Douglas fir and Alaska yellow cedar forest, then encounters a thinned forest segment where there is more daylight. Here, an understory of thorny ceanothus is struggling. This plant has such robust thorns that Forest Service planters who had to work here dubbed the ceanothus-covered ridge to the east "Dread and Terror Ridge." The remaining trees provide

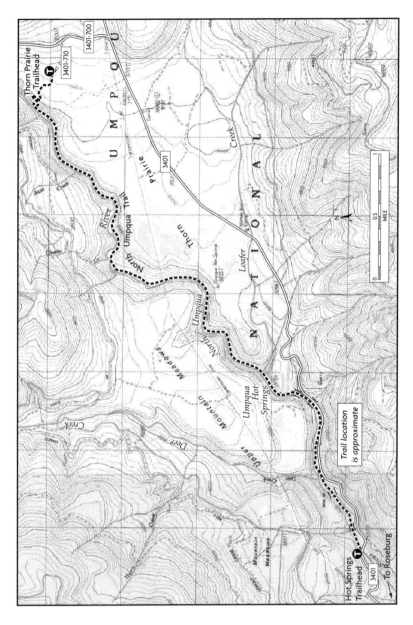

too little shade for this plant to flourish, but the thorns here will likely keep Fido pretty close to the trail. Sunlight has its upside, though. Look for huckleberry bushes among the thorns.

From the Hot Springs trailhead, the NUT sets off briskly, winding past one of many springs on this segment, then crosses Deer Creek, a broad tributary stream, on a narrow log bridge at 0.7 mile. In spring, this creek roars. In summer and fall, it's an ideal place for a dog to play. In about 1 mile, the trail meets the path to Umpqua Hot Springs. Venturesome soakers will turn left, uphill, to relax in the warm waters. The hot spring water is far too warm for dogs, however, so it's best to save your luxurious soak for a time when your dog doesn't have to wait. Follow the main trail right (northeast) across a sturdy bridge to resume the hike at the north end of a parking lot.

Just past this crossing, the trail crosses a copious spring, then in 0.2 mile dips into a small riverside meadow and passes a moist and mossy outcrop of columnar basalt along the river's edge. This rock is a harbinger of the higher country, an outlying flow of the young lavas of the high Cascades.

Beyond this outcrop, the spring-saturated trail follows the river closely. In 0.3 mile it passes a fern-fringed waterfall and crosses a footbridge across Loafer Creek, offering another nice view of the river. For the remaining 3 miles, the path splashes across more springs and wetlands, traversing a Douglas fir, cedar, and hemlock forest. At 5.6 miles from the trailhead, a

Shouldn't we be wading through the stream instead of going up here on the bridge? Meesha crosses a log bridge on the North Umpqua Trail, Hot Springs segment.

spur trail from the right leads steeply to the Thorn Prairie trailhead. This path climbs about 350 feet in 0.6 mile of rough, switchbacked trail. The trailhead area, marked with sharp, spiky white ceanothus, is aptly named.

46. North Umpqua Trail: Dread and Terror Segment, Miles 54–63

One-way trip: 8.1 miles
Elevation range: 3020–4025 feet
Difficulty: Moderate
Hiking time: 4 hours
Best canine hiking season: Spring, summer, fall
Regulations: Northwest Forest Pass required
Maps: USGS Potter Mountain and Lemolo Lake 7.5' quadrangles
Information: Umpqua National Forest, Diamond Lake Ranger Station, (541) 498-2531

Getting there: To find the west trailhead at Thorn Prairie where this hike begins, from Interstate 5 at Roseburg drive 59 miles east on Oregon Route 138. Turn left (north) onto Forest Road 34, the Toketee Lake turnoff. Continue 2 miles on FR 34, past a noisy generator plant and Toketee Campground, and bear right onto FR 3401, marked Hot Springs. Drive an additional 4.6 miles on FR 3401 and turn left (north) onto Spur Road 700, marked for the North Umpqua Trail. Drive 0.5 mile on Spur Road 710 to the trailhead.

To reach the trailhead where you can leave a shuttle car to make this a one-way hike, return to OR 138. Turn left (north) onto FR 2610, marked for Lemolo Lake. Drive 6 miles, crossing Lemolo Lake dam, and turn left (west) 0.2 mile past the dam and continue 0.6 mile on gravel road to the trailhead.

This segment of the NUT hugs the riverbank, rising and falling gently to cross several small drainages. The path offers a variety of springs and seeps—more than enough to keep dogs happy. A road to a power

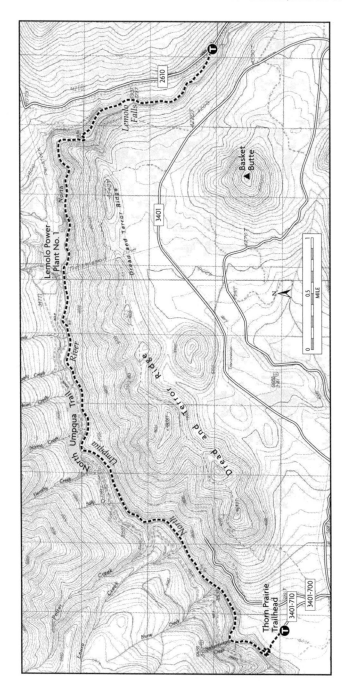

plant occupies the opposite (north) shore, and occasionally you can hear a pickup rumbling along it.

From the Thorn Prairie trailhead, an access path plunges 0.3 mile downward into Douglas fir, yellow pine, and Alaska cedar forest along the river. Once at the main North Umpqua Trail (NUT), the path follows the North Umpqua River religiously. At 4.7 miles into the hike, the hum of the plant can be discerned, and it makes a fleeting appearance, along with a set of transmission lines, at 5 miles into the walk. The annoying contact with civilization subsides quickly as you enter a deeper and steeper canyon and head for scenic Lemolo Falls.

About 1 mile from the power plant, the trail rounds a sharp river bend and heads purposefully for Lemolo Falls, crossing the stream on a solid wooden bridge at 1.5 miles from the plant and then angling steadily uphill. The trail levels 0.5 mile before the falls, following the precipitous cliffs above the North Umpqua, now raging far below. Dogs should be on leashes along this segment.

Lemolo Falls can be better heard than seen from this trail. The roar of the 108-foot waterfall (*lemolo* is an Umpqua word thought to mean "untamed") lures hikers closer and closer to the edges of cliffs and outcrops for a view that never quite materializes. The best views can be had from the path just before it passes the falls, about 2.5 miles from the power station, or about 1 mile before the Lemolo Falls NUT trailhead.

The trail rejoins the river just beyond the falls. The waters within a few hundred yards of the falls' dangerous brim are deceptively smooth and placid. They look like a perfect place to cool overheated dogs. However,

the water is exceptionally swift here. Continue at least another 0.1 mile up the trail before allowing dogs to cool off in the water.

Above the falls, the North Umpqua flows over a superb sequence of lesser falls, like a gymnast

Lemolo Falls, where the North Umpqua River plunges more than 100 feet, appears near the north end of the North Umpqua Trail's Dread and Terror segment.

practicing routines before attempting a death-defying leap. The sound of the big falls fades rapidly, leaving you with the songs of many other beautiful and more accessible waterfalls. Watch for dippers (water ouzels) along this upper segment where the trail is close to the stream. These gentle upper falls are beautiful and pleasantly soothing after the disconcerting plunge and cliffs at Lemolo Falls.

The trail rises gradually through old-growth Douglas fir and ponderosa pine for another mile, seeming to linger along the stream before emerging at the Lemolo trailhead 8.1 miles from the segment's beginning.

From this point, the NUT follows forests above the north shore of Lemolo Lake. The Lemolo segment, miles 63–69, offers no water along its length and no access to the lake, either. Its only redeeming virtue is that it connects the Dread and Terror segment with the final segment, Maidu.

47. North Umpqua Trail: Maidu Lake Segment, Miles 69–79

Round trip: 18 miles
Elevation range: 4245–5990 feet
Difficulty: Moderate
Hiking time: 9 hours
Best canine hiking season: Summer, early fall
Regulations: Northwest Forest Pass required
Map: USGS Tolo Mountain 7.5' quadrangle
Information: Umpqua National Forest, Diamond Lake Ranger Station, (541) 498-2531

Getting there: From Interstate 5 at Roseburg, drive 73.5 miles east on Oregon Route 138. Turn left (north) onto Windigo Pass Road (Forest Road 60). Drive 4.5 miles on FR 60 to its crossing of the North Umpqua River. Just before a bridge across the North Umpqua, park in the small parking area on the left (west) side of the road. The trailhead is on the right.

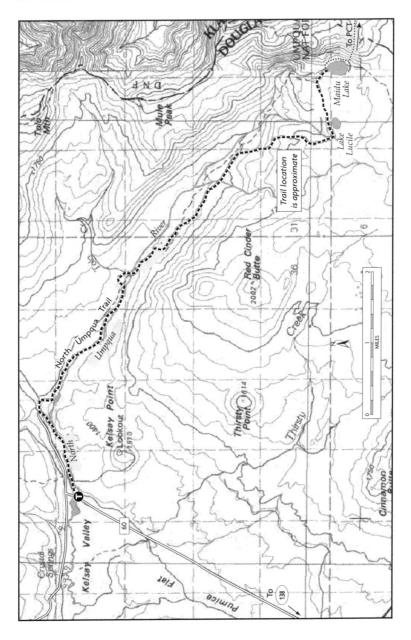

At this uppermost trailhead on the North Umpqua Trail (NUT), the North Umpqua River is just another pretty alpine stream, serene and placid

The North Umpqua River is just a pretty alpine stream along the Maidu Lake segment of the North Umpqua Trail.

as it winds through alpine meadows and marshes. The landscape here owes its gentle flatness to Mount Mazama. Much of the valley at the trailhead is filled with pumice and ash from the cataclysmic eruption sixty-five hundred years ago. The river is only now beginning to cut its way downward again. The lower portions of the trail explore peaceful meadows and stands of lodgepole pine and subalpine fir. But as the trail rises, the North Umpqua retreats into a steep-sided canyon. The path climbs out of the canyon to find two lakes—petite Lake Lucile and then Maidu Lake a mile farther: the end of this hike and the headwaters of the North Umpqua River.

From the trailhead, the NUT saunters into the lodgepole pines, heading northeast along the crystal-clear stream. It seems the perfect river for a dog—just enough depth to allow a swim, but not too much speed and few rocks. The banks here are low and lined with huckleberries in August. Dogs who have learned to pick and eat them might need a reminder to keep up. The river meanders through ashy sand. Lodgepoles provide sporadic shade through the first third of the hike before denser forest appears. Watch for kingfishers along the open meadows. At 1.8 miles, the trail crosses an off-road vehicle trail. Watch for mountain bikers here as well. In the open lodgepole woodland, pine squirrels scold both dogs and hikers.

From this point, the NUT swings away from the river, occasionally crossing wetlands and fragile meadows via sturdy boardwalks. The path maintains an easy grade as it enters denser forests with grand fir and subalpine fir and fewer lodgepole pines about 4 miles into the hike. Though the path has abandoned the river, now several hundred yards to the north, there is ample water for canine cooling at 5.3 miles into the hike where the trail encounters wetlands and crosses an unnamed creek.

At 6.5 miles, the trail's gradient steepens noticeably and the vegetation shifts to dense fir. This marks the approach to Lake Lucile, 1.5 miles farther and 1000 feet higher. This relatively small lake squats in a fir-lined basin. The trail circumvents the lake and heads back into the trees to find the true headwater lake—Maidu Lake, an easy and short 1-mile hike farther.

Maidu Lake, a bit larger than Lucile, is entrenched in forest at the north base of Mount Thielsen—there are spectacular views of the needle-shaped peak from the wooded shore. The NUT intersects the Pacific Crest Trail on the far (south) side of the small lake, offering an opportunity to climb the peak in another day's hike. The 5-mile approach to Mount Thielsen is definitely hikeable with a dog, but the final mile-long trail to the summit is extremely narrow with abrupt cliffs, so it is not recommended for dogs.

Maidu Lake offers a number of camping sites along its shore and outlet—the beginning of the North Umpqua. Return as you came.

THE UPPER ROGUE RIVER TRAIL

The Upper Rogue River Trail is 48 miles long, popular, and exquisitely maintained. Divided into seven segments, it provides easy to moderately easy hiking over its entire length. The river is close at hand in most segments. Leashes are required or recommended on all trail segments. The most northern segment is the least dog-friendly, but even it has adequate cooling water and enough shade to make it a comfortable stroll for most dogs. The trail is best hiked in spring, early summer, or fall to avoid the warmest weather. Southern portions of the Upper Rogue River Trail can be accessed in winter. Mountain bikers share the trail, though they are few in number as of this writing. An OHV trail parallels the hiking path in some segments as well.

Because of the frequent access points, two of the hikes along the Upper Rogue River Trail are described as one-way trips. Hikers can use a two-vehicle shuttle system to limit the hike to one direction. An alternate way to enjoy these hikes is to walk half the distance desired, then turn around and return to your vehicle the way you came.

48. Upper Rogue River Trail: Takelma Gorge Segment, Miles 6–10

One-way trip: 4 miles
Elevation range: 2815–2960 feet
Difficulty: Moderate
Hiking time: 2 hours
Best canine hiking season: Spring, fall
Regulations: Northwest Forest Pass required; dogs must be on leash
Maps: USGS Whetstone Point and North Prospect 7.5' quadrangles
Information: Rogue River National Forest, Prospect Ranger District, (541) 560-3400

Getting there: To reach the start of this hike, from Medford drive north and east on Oregon Route 62 until you reach milepost 49. Turn right (west) onto Forest Road 6210, marked for River Bridge Campground. Drive 0.5 mile to the trailhead.

To reach the Woodruff Bridge trailhead where this hike ends, return to OR 62 and head north to milepost 68 (0.75 mile north of the Mammoth Pines Picnic Area). Turn left (west) onto FR 68, marked for Woodruff Bridge Picnic Area. Drive 1.75 miles on this paved road—it can seem as though you will never reach the river, but eventually the picnic area appears on the right, the bridge and river are straight ahead, and trailhead parking is on the left.

The Takelma Gorge segment of the Upper Rogue River Trail is scenic and dog-worthy. The river is an affable companion almost the entire way—although for a mile or so the stream runs through narrow and steep-walled Takelma Gorge while the trail follows along the top, making water inaccessible for this section only. You will also encounter buildings and likely some people at the Rogue Baptist Camp, so keep dogs on leash or under close control here.

From the River Bridge trailhead, the path follows a broad, calm, almost quiescent river. The river is only resting, however, from its

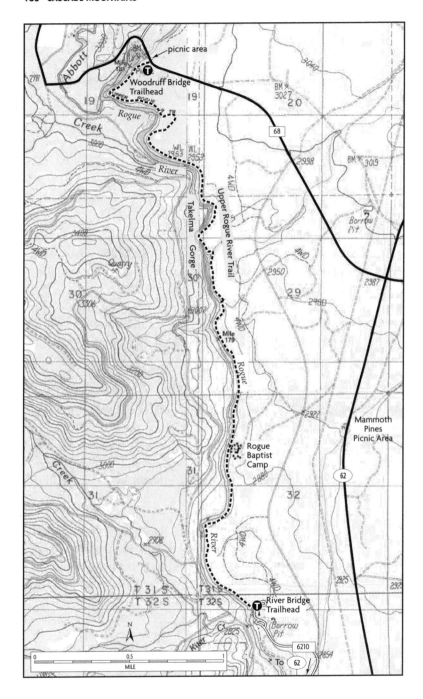

The Rogue River carves steep-sided Takelma Gorge through soft volcanic debris flows.

labors upstream where it has notched a 100-foot-deep canyon through young lava and mudflows that blocked its way about a million years ago. Many of the boulders along the stream here were quarried from the gorge walls. Their angular shapes indicate that they have not been carried far by the bouncing, rolling, and rounding power of high-energy river water.

Along the pumice-strewn flats near the trailhead, huge ponderosa pine and sugar pine vie for sky space, dwarfing fir and an understory of vine maple and alder. This portion of the trail glows with fluorescent reds, oranges, and yellows when frost kindles fall colors in October.

For the first mile, the trail hugs the riverbank, allowing easy dog access. This trail segment is also a favorite place to fish, so while your dog explores the riverbank, be wary of possible fishhooks and even possible dead or discarded fish. Most of the time, the worst-case scenario is a doggie roll in dead and pungent fish—an odor that your dog will relish, but you might be less enthusiastic about—but see the section on first aid in this book's introduction for information on salmon poisoning and other riverside risks.

At the end of the first mile of nearly level hiking, you'll catch a glimpse of low-slung buildings ahead through the thinned forest. The trail hugs the river but still cruises close to the Rogue Baptist Camp—an unoccupied facility for much of the year. Keep dogs leashed and under control as you approach and continue past the facility.

Beyond the camp, the trail enters a section that appears wild and pristine, although it is never far from the gravel entry roads that lead to the camp. The river's pace quickens a bit, the forest closes its canopy, and the trail picks up its pace, steepening ever so slightly though it remains essentially flat by most hiking standards.

About 0.7 mile beyond the Rogue Baptist Camp, the trail moves away from the river as the stream recedes into Takelma Gorge. This channel was cut by the Rogue River through a relatively young lava flow—one that is less than one million years in age. The gorge is about 100 feet deep and 1 mile in length. The path along its rim offers occasional glimpses into the chasm. You will have to leave the trail for the best views—keeping an eye and a grip on Rover. The gorge walls reveal a sequence of rubbly basalt flows, as well as more fragile mudflows. Because the relatively thin lava flows were underlain by soft and unconsolidated mudflow deposits, the river was able to erode its channel easily once it had worn its way through the harder basalts.

Near the north end of the hike along the gorge, the trail steps over ropy, pahoehoe basalt—now relatively subtle after a million years of rain and organic acids—and 20 years of human feet—have weathered it.

After exploring the rim of Takelma Gorge, the trail remains remote from the river for another 0.5 mile, then plays tag with the stream, dropping to a wetland area in 3 miles from the River Bridge trailhead and reaching the Woodruff Bridge trailhead in 4 miles from the start of the hike.

49. Upper Rogue River Trail: Knob Falls Segment, Miles 10–14

One-way trip: 3.5 miles
Elevation range: 2960–3200 feet
Difficulty: Easy
Hiking time: 2 hours
Best canine hiking season: Fall
Regulations: Northwest Forest Pass required; dogs must be leashed on interpretive trail
Maps: USGS Whetstone Point, Prospect North, Abbott Butte, and Union Creek 7.5' quadrangles
Information: Rogue River National Forest, Prospect Ranger District, (541) 560-3400

Getting there: To find the beginning of the hike, take Oregon Route 62 from Medford to milepost 68 (0.75 mile north of the Mammoth Pines Picnic Area). Turn right (west) onto Forest Road 68, marked for Woodruff Bridge Picnic Area. Drive 1.75 miles on this paved road—it seems as though you will never get to the river, but eventually the picnic area appears on the right, the bridge and river are straight ahead, and the trailhead parking is on the left.

To reach the end of this hike, where you can leave a shuttle car, return to OR 62 and drive to milepost 52. Turn left (west) at the sign for the Natural Bridge Campground. Drive west 0.4 mile and bear left (south) into a parking area for the Natural Bridge Interpretive Trail. The paved interpretive trail leads toward a bridge across the Rogue. The southbound Upper Rogue River Trail is unpaved trail, ducking into the forest about 200 feet before the snazzy, arching footbridge across the river.

This relatively short segment of the Upper Rogue River Trail is one of the easiest and prettiest touring some of the Upper Rogue River's most spectacular gymnastics. Most of the river is accessible for doggie dips, with the sole exception being the slightly daunting stretch at Knob Falls and another point where the river makes a sharp curve about 0.5 mile south of the Natural Bridge trailhead. Leashes are required along the

A black-tailed pine squirrel bears watching along the Knob Falls segment of the Upper Rogue River Trail.

paved interpretive trail at the northern end of this hike. Expect to find many people on the paved trail, but very few venture onto the wilder, unpaved Upper Rogue River Trail—or even know it is there.

This forest is adapted to slightly colder and wetter conditions than the forest at the lowest trailhead near the town of Prospect. Manzanitas disappear at about 3000 feet and above. But the amazing multiplicity of tree species still provides surprises galore. Look for mixed forests that include three different pines—sugar pine, western white pine, and ponderosa pine—that often grow adjacent to one another, as well as incense cedar, western hemlock, and Douglas fir. Huckleberries appear along portions of this trail.

From Woodruff Bridge Picnic Area, the path that heads upstream follows a calm and pretty stretch of the Upper Rogue River. The path is nearly flat for the first mile, weaving through an open forest and swinging to meet the stream at 0.4 mile into the hike. For the next mile, the trail follows the Rogue's bidding, never departing from the stream. Look for many wet-dog opportunities along this mile. For aquaphilic dogs, the easygoing stream is irresistible here.

At 1.4 miles into the hike, the Rogue begins to prove it is not just a placid stream. The gradient picks up, rocks become numerous, the banks are steeper, and water roils over stony cataracts. This is all in preparation for Knob Falls, where the river performs a brief disappearing act. At 1.5 miles, the trail pulls away from the river, climbing upward about 100 feet. Here, a torrent of water funnels through a remnant lava tube and then emerges with a roar. A short, steep side trail provides an overview of the river's brief vanishing act—a practiced and common magic for this portion of the Rogue. If you indulge your dog's penchant for wading before you reach Knob Falls, she will be less likely to think this might be a good place for a swim. It's not. A trail leads out onto the promontory above Knob Falls, but the view is disappointing. Take the side trail just a bit before the trail climbs to the oxbow's "summit" for a better view.

Once past Knob Falls, the trail rejoins the river. The forest is rich in Douglas fir and ponderosa pine. Tree trunks are charcoaled, hinting at past fires that cleared the understory but left large trees standing. The path climbs one more overlook of a river bend before connecting with the paved trail and parking area at Natural Bridge, a huge lava tube that briefly swallows the Rogue River. Be sure to keep dogs leashed while on the paved interpretive trail.

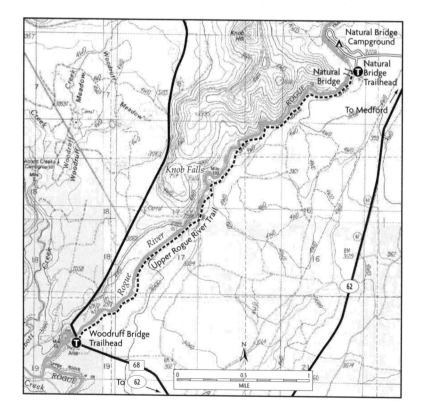

50. Upper Rogue River Trail: Natural Bridge to Big Bend Segment, Miles 14–21

One-way trip: 6.8 miles
Elevation range: 3200–3740 feet
Difficulty: Moderate
Hiking time: 5 hours
Best canine hiking season: Summer, early fall
Regulations: Northwest Forest Pass required; dogs must be leashed on interpretive trails
Map: USGS Union Creek 7.5' quadrangle
Information: Rogue River–Siskiyou National Forest, High Cascades Ranger District, (541) 560-3400

Getting there: To reach the Natural Bridge trailhead where this hike begins, from Medford take Oregon Route 62 east to milepost 52. Turn left (west) at the sign for Natural Bridge Campground. Bear left into the parking area. To reach the northbound Rogue River trailhead from the interpretive trail, follow the paved trails northward along the east bank of the Rogue, bypassing the Natural Bridge Campground and keeping to the riverbank behind the campsites. Dogs should be leashed for this 0.4-mile stretch, and it's best to keep them leashed until you cross the footbridge to the west bank of the Rogue about 1 mile from the start of the interpretive trail.

To reach the end of this hike where you can leave a shuttle, return to OR 62 and drive northeast to the junction with OR 230 in 2.6 miles. Follow OR 230 north 0.9 mile, then turn left (west) onto Forest Road 6510, marked for Big Bend. Cross the Rogue on this road and drive 0.6 mile to a well-marked Big Bend–Upper Rogue River Trail trailhead.

One of the best things about the superbly designed Upper Rogue River Trail is that even amid the crowds at tourist attractions, such as Natural Bridge and the popular campground at Union Creek, you and your dog can find solitude along the trail. At Natural Bridge and the Rogue Gorge interpretive site to the north, the Rogue River Trail accomplishes this

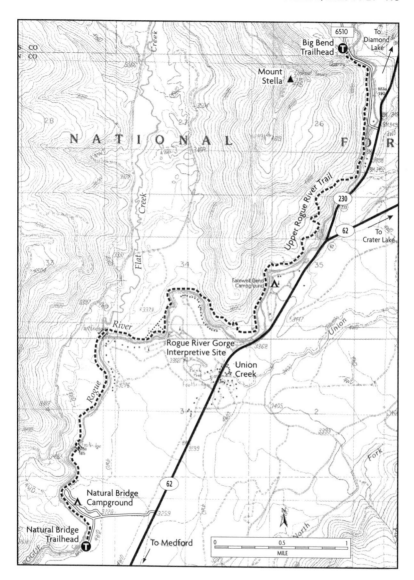

miracle by taking refuge on the west side of the river—a position it occupies for most of this hike.

Both these interpretive sites are well worth touring, however, with your dog on a leash. If you charge through them en route to the next trailhead, don't forget to return for a more leisurely examination. The name Natural Bridge evokes a mental image of red sandstone arches such as those found in Utah's Arches National Park. But there is no sandstone within 100 miles or so of this spot. Instead, this "natural bridge" is a lava tube that swallows the Rogue River whole, and then disgorges it 100 yards or so downstream. The Rogue Gorge is a former lava tube that probably contained the river underground until the top of the lava tube gradually collapsed, leaving the river visible and confined to a narrow but rather deep channel where the water is incredibly swift.

Here, the Upper Rogue River Trail achieves its solitude at a cost—especially for canine hikers. This stretch of the trail abandons the riverbank for a substantial portion of its length. The trail climbs about 300 feet above the riverbed at its highest deviation on this trail segment. But to hikers who have gotten used to an almost flat, watery route, the sudden imposition of this climb comes as a rude reminder that this is Oregon and there are hills here. Furthermore, the hilly segment of the hike has no reliable water along the way, so be sure to carry ample dog water, especially in hot weather. The trail does have shade by early afternoon, however, mitigating canine temperature concerns somewhat.

From the Natural Bridge trailhead, once you and your pup are on the west side of the river and away from the chatter of campers, the trail follows the river quite faithfully for 1.5 miles. There are plenty of opportunities for doggie dunks along this stretch of the trail. The west trail

bypasses a set of cabins and yurts along the river's east bank—part of Union Creek and the Union Creek Campground. The hike here moves through stately yellow and sugar pines, crosses a footbridge over Flat Creek, and follows a river bend to the east. You will have to endure another mile of hiking along the west bank with views of cabins and campers as the river bends north and then east.

The Rogue River enters a system of topless lava tubes as it nears its narrow gorge and Natural Bridge.

At 2.8 miles from the trailhead, the trail begins to climb up the bank to avoid steep shores along the river and the Rogue Gorge. This first digression from the river rises about 100 feet in a gradual switchback. The trail then winds back to the river in another 0.3 mile. This segment of the river is swift and uninviting as the Rogue begins to settle into its fast trip through the short gorge. You might want to leash your dog here should the river pose a temptation.

After a fleeting glimpse of the water, the trail moves away again, and then upslope, this time climbing well above the river into a forest dominated by Douglas fir along fairly steep slopes. This part of the trip is cool, even on hot summer days. There are springs along this uphill stretch in spring and early summer, but it is a good idea to carry dog water as there is no reliable stream or spring for the last 3.7 miles of this 6.8-mile hike. The upper trailhead appears at the end of a downhill stretch, when the trail finds Forest Road 6510.

51. Union Creek Trail

Round trip: 7.5 miles; 3.7 miles one way
Elevation range: 3330–3767 feet
Difficulty: Easy
Hiking time: 4 hours; 2 hours one way
Best canine hiking season: Fall
Regulations: Northwest Forest Pass required
Map: USGS Union Creek 7.5' quadrangle
Information: Rogue River–Siskiyou National Forest, High Cascades Ranger District, (541) 560-3400

Getting there: From Medford, take Oregon Route 62 to Prospect, then continue 10 miles to Union Creek Campground at the community of Union Creek. Turn left (west) at the campground entrance and find the parking area just before you enter the campground. The trail begins at the opposite (east) side of the highway just south of the small bridge. Alternatively, to avoid crossing the highway, there is a small parking area on the east (right) side of OR 62 near the trailhead. Parking is very limited here. The Union Creek Store is on the north side of Union Creek here, and permission is needed to park in its parking lot.

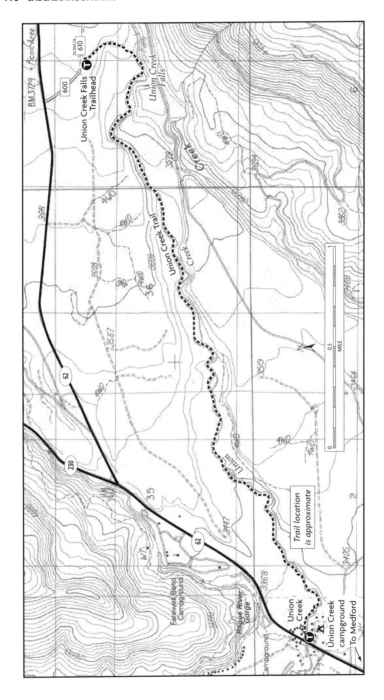

To reach the trailhead at Union Creek Falls, continue 3 miles past the community of Union Creek on OR 62 and turn right (south) onto Forest Road 600, marked for Union Creek Falls. Follow FR 600 for 0.25 mile, then bear left onto FR 610 for another 0.1 mile to the trailhead parking area.

This hike follows closely along Union Creek, a stream that starts 15 miles away and 3000 feet higher on the western flanks of Union Peak in Crater Lake National Park. The portion of the waterway covered by this hike traverses a bit of the Rogue River's famously diverse forest. The path is broad and flat and offers dogs the opportunity to take frequent dips in an inviting and accessible stream. For those (dogs) who like to wade in mud up to their elbows, there are several opportunities here.

From the Union Creek trailhead, the Union Creek Trail moves into the open forest, crossing a solid bridge 100 yards or so from the highway, then moving past a wetland area before turning upstream. Look for kingfishers, red-tailed hawks, and water ouzels. Beaver have left chiseled stumps along the creek. Incense cedar, Douglas fir, hemlock, big-leaf maple, and alder comprise a diverse forest along the creek's banks. Sugar pine and ponderosa pine appear on higher slopes or on drier sites. Look for the huge, curving sugar pine cones along the trail. The old-growth trees are huge, and many show scars from fires here early in the 20th century.

At about 1.5 miles, the creek burrows a bit deeper into the landscape, and the forest closes in. Mountain hemlock and western white pine are your hiking companions now. Black-tailed pine squirrels scold, warning their families that there are dogs on the trail. In the fall, dogs might encounter squirrels so intent on sequestering their supply of pine nuts and other succulent snacks underground that they forget to watch for predators.

Taking a break on the bridge across Union Creek

A cornered squirrel can give a nasty bite, so hikers and dogs should be wary and also take steps to ensure the safety of squirrels and all wildlife.

The trail rises at almost a flat grade but becomes a little narrower and less used with every step beyond about 1.5 miles. The hike follows Union Creek closely, even where the canyon becomes notably narrower at about mile 2. From here to the falls, wet areas make the path a bit mushy in spring and early summer. The moisture is welcome on dogs' feet, but chances are that they'll already be blissfully wet and cool.

At about 2.5 miles, both the creek and trail quicken their pace. The creek tumbles more urgently over rocks; the path rises at a steeper grade— though still an easy pace by almost any measure. Alder, cedar, Douglas fir, and a few stalwart pine occupy the canyon bottom and south-facing slopes. Look for a few huckleberry bushes upslope from the trail here.

At 3.5 miles from the trailhead, the trail leads to a small, 20-foot waterfall. The cataract is impressive in early summer, but by fall it is reduced to a lacy curtain of water. The pool beneath the falls is refreshingly deep for doggie dips and a swim.

At Union Creek Falls, the trail turns upslope abruptly, rising at an earnest pace and reaching the Union Creek Falls trailhead parking area in 0.3 mile and a climb of about 100 feet. End your hike here if you parked a shuttle car, or return the way you came.

Five More Great Dog Hikes in the Cascade Mountains

1. Elk Lake Creek, 9 miles, forested, with abundant water. Mount Hood National Forest, Estacada Ranger Station, (503) 630-6861.

2. East Fork McKenzie River Trail, Three Sisters Wilderness, 10 miles, follows the upper river from Cougar Reservoir almost to its headwaters. Willamette National Forest, McKenzie River Ranger District, (541) 822-3381.

3. McKenzie River Trail, Three Sisters Wilderness, 26 miles; follows the river from above McKenzie Bridge to Clear Lake. Willamette National Forest, McKenzie River Ranger District, (541) 822-3381.

4. Lower South Fork Trail, 20 miles, follows the South Fork of the Rogue River through pine-rich forest. Rogue River National Forest, Butte Falls Ranger District, (541) 865-2700.

5. Six Lakes Trail, Doris Lake to Mink Lake, 18 miles. Take the Cascade Lakes Highway 0.75 mile south of Elk Lake to the trailhead for Trail 3526. Many lakes are ideal for swimming. Deschutes National Forest, Bend–Fort Rock District, (541) 383-4000.

KLAMATH MOUNTAINS

52. Summit Lake

Round trip: 4 miles
Elevation range: 3080–4730 feet
Difficulty: Strenuous
Hiking time: 3–4 hours
Best canine hiking season: Spring, summer, fall
Regulations: Northwest Forest Pass required
Map: USGS Squaw Lakes 7.5' quadrangle
Information: Rogue River–Siskiyou National Forest, Siskiyou
   Mountains Ranger District, (541) 899-3800

Getting there: From Interstate 5 at Medford, take exit 30, Jacksonville and Oregon Route 238. Follow OR 238 for 14 miles through Jacksonville to Ruch. At Ruch, turn left (south) onto Upper Applegate Road and drive 14.5 miles to Applegate Dam. Turn left onto Forest Road 1075 to cross the dam, and continue on this road for 8.5 miles to Squaw Lakes. The last 5 miles of FR 1075 is a narrow single-track gravel road. Watch for traffic, including occasional logging trucks. Keep to your right as you navigate the many cars at the entry to popular Squaw Lakes. The trailhead is on the right in the upper parking lot.

Summit Lake is a grassy, wetland depression rimmed by beautiful old-growth pine. It is somewhat boggy in the spring when the snow melts, but it's a nice soft place to rest after a hard 2-mile climb in the summer. In early July the "lake" surface shimmers with delicate violet blooms.

From the Squaw Lakes trailhead, the Summit Lake Trail climbs evenly at an easy grade for the first 0.5 mile, crossing a wooden bridge and

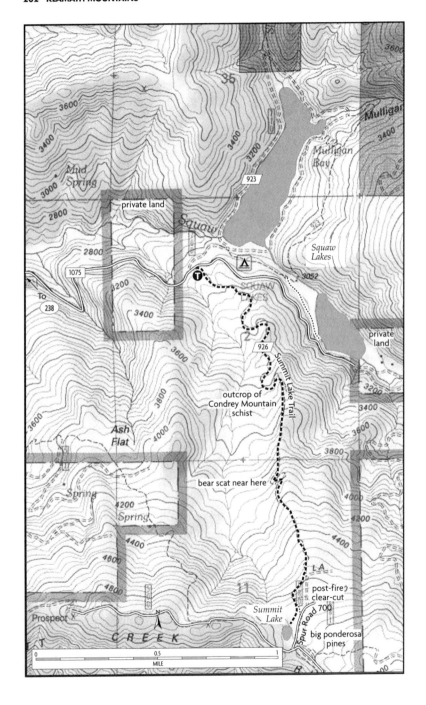

3600

35

Mulligan

3600

3400

3400

Mud
Spring

3000

3600

3400

3200

3200

923

Mulligan
Bay

private land

2800

Squaw

3400

Squaw
Lakes

1075

2800

3200

3052

To
238

3400

2

926

3600

Summit Lake Trail

private
land

3800

3200

outcrop of
Condrey Mountain
schist

3400

Ash
Flat

4000

3600

3800

3600

3800

bear scat near here

4000

Spring

4200

4200

Spring

4400

4400

4600

11

post-fire
clear-cut

4800

Summit
Lake

700

Prospect

big ponderosa
pines

Spur Road

CREEK

0   0.5   1
MILE

A tree-fringed grassy meadow takes the place of boggy Summit Lake in late summer.

switchbacking gently uphill. There is no water here—at least not in late summer—so carry plenty for Fido. Look for an osprey nest in a tall pine snag just a few hundred yards up the trail. After the second bend, the trail begins to climb in earnest.

At about 1 mile, the trail ducks behind a slope, tempers its rise, and lets you explore a natural schist outcropping. Here, you enter bear country— look for signs including droppings, dead trees that have been ripped open in search of ants and grubs, and large rocks rolled over in similar hunts for food. The diverse forest along the way includes madrone, Douglas fir, ponderosa pine, sugar pine, and cedar.

At 1.7 miles, the trail skirts a huge clearing—the result of a 1980 forest fire that was subsequently logged so as not to "waste" wood. (Today we know that the number of birds increases in a burned area as new species including flickers, nuthatches, and pileated woodpeckers harvest the insects that come to feed on damaged or dead trees.) Only one or two lonely snags remain standing. At the upper end of the clearing, the trail zigzags and then joins Spur Road 700. Just before the junction with the Forest Service road, an unmarked trail leads gently downslope 100 yards to a clearing—Summit Lake. There are nice views of the Siskiyous from the logged-over fire area and an opportunity to explore the old-growth pine grove that encloses Summit Lake. Return as you came.

53. French Gulch–Payette Trail: Applegate Lake

Round trip: 4.5 miles
Elevation range: 1950–2460 feet
Difficulty: Moderate
Hiking time: 3 hours
Best canine hiking season: Spring, early summer, fall
Regulations: Northwest Forest Pass required
Map: USGS Squaw Lakes 7.5' quadrangle
Information: Rogue River–Siskiyou National Forest, Siskiyou
    Mountains Ranger District, (541) 899-3800

Getting there: From Interstate 5 at Medford, take exit 30, Jacksonville and Oregon Route 238. Follow OR 238 for 14 miles through Jacksonville to Ruch. At Ruch, turn left (south) onto Upper Applegate Road and drive 14.5 miles to Applegate Dam. Turn left onto Forest Road 1075 to cross the dam and drive 1.1 miles to French Gulch Campground. The trailhead is at the east end of the parking area.

The Payette Trail is popular with mountain bikers, so keep an eye out for them throughout the hike. Wild blackberries line the trail here and appear in other locations along the way. They are ready to eat in mid- to late July. Poison oak also festoons the trail edge periodically, but it is easily avoided, at least by humans. This hike leads along the shores of Applegate Lake, ensuring ample access to water. In spring, it also ensures ample mosquitoes, so bring bug repellent for yourself and your dog. After touring the lakeshore, the trail climbs away from the lake to a hilltop, then returns to the French Gulch trailhead.

To find the trail, park at the French Gulch trailhead area and follow the Payette Trail, which leaves from the far end of the campground. Keep dogs under control for the first few hundred yards as the trail bisects the campground. Beyond the campground, the forest above the trail has been commercially thinned using helicopter logging. These more open woods, with abundant snags and second-growth and some old-growth trees, are habitat for pileated woodpeckers.

About 0.3 mile into the hike, watch for an accessible beach at the Latgawa Cove boat-in campground. From here, the trail heads uphill 0.2 mile to a junction with two other trails. For an interesting side jaunt, take the short side trail to the right marked Viewpoint. It rises through a moss- and lichen-festooned woodland of oak, manzanita, madrone, pine, and Douglas fir. The lichens, light green and diaphanous, are nitrogen fixers—they pull moisture and nitrogen from the air, and when they die and fall from the trees, they enrich the soils with nitrogen. This short side trail ends at what I like to call "Corps of Engineers Hubris Viewpoint." It offers a view of the dam, its water-intake structure, and the campground and boat launch across the lake.

The other trail at the junction (Calish Trail, #971) will be your return path as you complete this loop hike.

Meesha, on an overlook of Applegate Lake along the trail

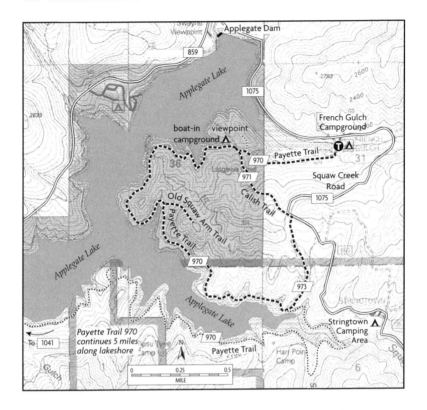

Continue right on the Payette Trail. It offers a number of opportunities to visit the lakeshore—usually on points that jut out into the water. At 1.7 miles, the Payette Trail drops to the right toward the lake, while a broader path marked Old Squaw Arm Trail (an old mining road) goes straight. Follow the Payette Trail down to the lakeshore here. The trail finds coves and beaches for the next mile. Then at 3 miles from the trailhead, it meets a trail on the left.

Turn left here onto Trail 973. Watch for poison oak along the path as it rises through oak-strewn forest. There is no dog water for the next 1.5 miles of hiking, so be sure you have adequate water with you.

This trail winds through a mixed forest. It is not well maintained, and poison oak can be thick in places, but it makes a nice climb of 500 feet in 0.5 mile to meet a paved Forest Service road. A short, 100-yard walk along the road leads to the Calish Trail and its oversize parking lot. At the trailhead, turn left and go down the Calish Trail to intersect with the

Payette Trail in 0.7 mile. Turn right to follow the Payette Trail another 0.3 mile back to the French Gulch trailhead.

54. Little Falls Trail

Round trip: 3 miles
Elevation range: 1360–1320 feet
Difficulty: Easy
Hiking time: 1–2 hours
Best canine hiking season: Spring
Regulations: Northwest Forest Pass required
Maps: USGS Eight Dollar Mountain and Kerby 7.5' quadrangles
Information: Rogue River–Siskiyou National Forest, Wild Rivers
  Ranger District, (541) 592-4000

Getting there: From U.S. Highway 199, 5 miles north of Cave Junction or 3.5 miles south of Selma, turn west on Eight Dollar Road (also Forest Road 5240) marked for Eight Dollar loop and Howell Botanical Drive. Follow this road 2 miles to a parking area and very small camping area on the left.

The Little Falls Trail is just one of several short but impressive hikes that can be accessed from the T. J. Howell Botanical Loop. There are three short hikes here. In addition to the Little Falls Trail, the Contact Trail (1.8 miles) and Jeffrey Pine Trail (1.5 miles) are also accessed from Eight Dollar Road. The area abuts some of the most severe burns of the 500,000-acre 2002 Biscuit Fire that torched much of the Kalmiopsis Wilderness. However, the hikes here traverse landscapes that escaped the flames.

At Little Falls the Illinois River makes a rocky ten-foot plunge.

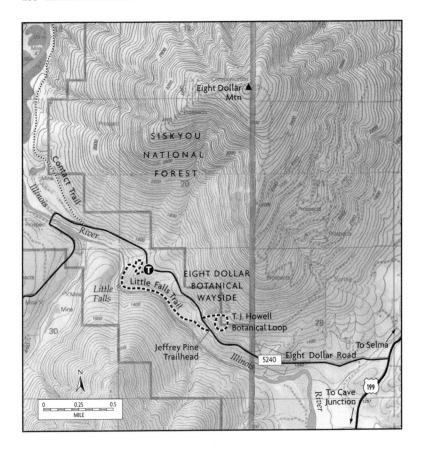

From the trailhead, the Little Falls Trail heads downhill and curves to the right, entering a small valley and then angling for the Illinois River. It reaches the river in about 0.5 mile. The river here provides a beach, a great place for a doggy dip. As you follow the trail upstream, it encounters rockier substrate, eventually leading to a short but rugged and powerful waterfall—Little Falls. The river's azure colors here are startlingly beautiful, and there are ample places for doggie dips along the way.

The Little Falls Trail continues upstream along the Illinois River, but return as you came. The Little Falls Trail is planned to connect with the Jeffrey Pine Trail in 2011, providing a lovely 3-mile out-and-back trail along the river. Or if you wish, you may return to the roadway and explore the Eight Dollar Botanical Wayside—a boardwalk through pitcher plants—before you return the way you came.

55. Cook and Green Trail

Round trip: 16 miles
Elevation range: 2280–4765 feet
Difficulty: Moderate
Hiking time: 8 hours
Best canine hiking season: Spring
Regulations: Northwest Forest Pass required
Map: USGS Kangaroo Mountain 7.5' quadrangle
Information: Rogue River–Siskiyou National Forest, Siskiyou
 Mountains Ranger District, (541) 899-3800

Getting there: From Interstate 5 at Medford, take exit 30, Jacksonville and Oregon Route 238. Follow OR 238 for 14 miles through Jacksonville to Ruch. At Ruch, turn left (south) onto Upper Applegate Road. Continue 19 miles to a T intersection at the upper end of Applegate Lake. Turn left and follow Forest Road 1040 for 1.3 miles to a large open area where FR 1040 turns sharply right downhill. Follow FR 1040—a good but narrow single-lane gravel road—along the Middle Fork of the Applegate River for 4 miles. The parking area, on the left (east) side of the road, is easy to find, and the trail leads into the forest here.

Beagles Tasha and Taz are still ready to go after a hike along the Cook and Green Trail.

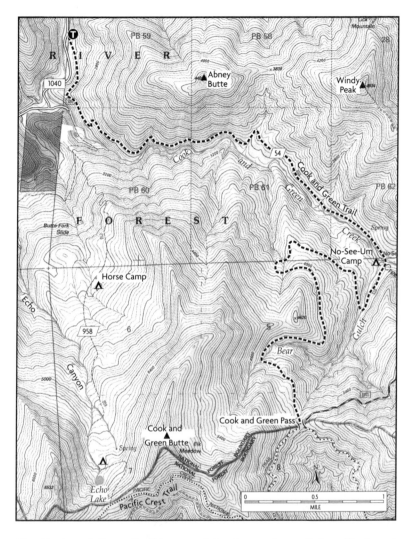

The Cook and Green Trail is named for three miners, Robert Cook and the Green brothers, who used it between 1860 and 1870. Technically, this hike is in California, but its only access is from the Oregon side. The trail climbs through old-growth sugar pine and Douglas fir. It offers minimal dog water along the way, so on hot days offer your dog the opportunity for a drink at the car and a cooling dunk before starting. An informal trail leads from the trailhead parking area to the stream.

The trail begins through a shaded forest of oak, big-leaf maple, and madrone that soon becomes more conifer-dominant. About 0.25 mile into the hike, the trail encounters a huge old-growth Douglas fir and crosses an old placer ditch. Here, the path begins a series of switchbacks that weave across a seasonal stream and carry you up about 500 feet in elevation. As the trail straightens, the forest changes to a typically dry, south-facing slope assemblage of madrone, fir, and sugar pine. The trail is more open and sunnier here, and on warm days occasional stops for water from your pack will help your dog endure the long hike to the end. A good place for a break is at No-See-Um Camp about 3.5 miles into the hike.

Above this point, the trail encounters a more diverse conifer forest that includes old-growth Douglas fir, sugar pine, and ponderosa pine. A few Brewer's spruce and noble fir also can be spotted from the trail. There is another small but usually reliable spring just before reaching Cook and Green Pass and a junction with the Pacific Crest Trail (PCT). From here, you can further explore the Red Butte Wilderness along the PCT, eventually returning to the trailhead as you came.

56. Middle Fork Applegate River

Round trip: 6 miles
Elevation range: 2660–3670 feet
Difficulty: Moderate
Hiking time: 3 hours
Best canine hiking season: Spring, early summer
Regulations: Northwest Forest Pass required
Map: USGS Kangaroo Mountain 7.5' quadrangle
Information: Siskiyou Mountains Ranger District, Starr Ranger
   Station, Jacksonville, (541) 899-3800

Getting there: From Interstate 5 at Medford, take exit 30, Jacksonville and Oregon Route 238. Follow OR 238 for 14 miles through Jacksonville to Ruch. At Ruch, turn left (south) onto Upper Applegate Road. Continue 19 miles to a T intersection at the upper end of Applegate Lake. Turn left and follow Forest Road 1040 for 1.3 miles to a large open area where it turns sharply right downhill. Follow FR 1040—a good but narrow, single-lane gravel road—along the Upper Applegate 5.8 miles to a junction with FR 1035. FR 1035 goes straight while FR 1040 turns left and crosses a bridge. Continue straight on FR 1035 for 0.2 mile to a curve. The trailhead is a subtly marked path at this curve.

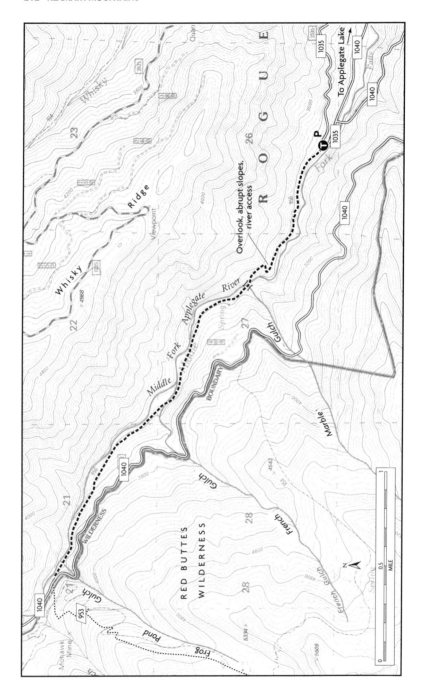

Overlook, abrupt slopes, river access

To Applegate Lake

ROGUE

Middle Fork Applegate River

Whisky Ridge

Viewpoint

Spring

BOUNDARY

Marble Gulch

Gulch

French Gulch

Spring

RED BUTTES WILDERNESS

Frog Pond

Mohawk Mine

953

N

MILE

This Middle Fork Applegate River Trail, located in California but accessible only from Oregon, is an ideal summer hike with dogs. It begins as a broad mining road, then narrows to a well-maintained single track that periodically veers away from the Middle Fork of the Applegate River to bypass narrow chasms but always returns to the river.

From the trailhead, the broad path heads purposefully along a bank above the river. In about 0.5 mile a tempting trail bears left downhill and toward the river. This unnamed, unmarked spur dead-ends at the riverbank, though, so if you take it you'll have to backtrack. The real trail goes straight, suddenly narrowing to a single-track path. It curves into a shady dell, where a side stream offers a second opportunity for a cooling dog bath, and continues well above the river for another 0.2 mile. Here, a steep side trail plunges to a deep swimming hole; however, a better option is to continue along the trail, which begins a gradual descent to stream level and offers multiple opportunities for safer dog swims.

This forest is a mix of old-growth and younger Douglas fir. Madrones arch upward where light permits and are more abundant on south-facing upper slopes. Vine maple and manzanita populate the understory. A few white oaks and big-leaf maple struggle to grow on upper slopes. At 1.1 miles, the trail crosses the river on a bridge hewn from a single huge log. The bridge has a rickety handrail for humans and is broad enough for dogs to cross with ease—though they likely will splash across the stream instead.

The best part of the trail lies ahead. It is more rugged, but the trees are spectacular. Jeffrey pines 3 to 4 feet in diameter begin to appear. Douglas firs exceed 4 feet with such regularity that big trees begin to seem normal. The trail swings away from the stream periodically. In this segment, the forest canopy permits occasional glimpses of the rugged slopes

Oh, PLEEEEEEEEZE throw the stick! Meesha and friends along the Middle Fork Applegate River

and rock cliffs in the Applegate canyon. The Applegate River remains accessible periodically. At 1.8 miles the path scoots through wetland areas and crosses a stream at French Gulch. A mile farther, just before it reaches FR 1040, the path crosses another side stream at Frog Pond Gulch. The intersection with the road marks the end of this hike, although the trail jogs up the road and continues steeply upward for another 2 miles without any trailside water to Frog Camp. Return as you came.

57. Wagner Butte Trail

Round trip: 10 miles
Elevation range: 4900–7100 feet
Difficulty: Strenuous
Hiking time: 7 hours
Best canine hiking season: Spring, summer, fall
Regulations: Northwest Forest Pass required
Maps: USGS Talent and Mount Ashland 7.5' quadrangles
Information: Rogue River–Siskiyou National Forest, Siskiyou
   Mountains Ranger Station, Ashland, (541) 552-2900

Getting there: From Interstate 5 south of Medford, take the Talent exit and drive to the center of town on West Valley View Drive. Turn right on Talent Avenue, then make an immediate left on Main Street. Follow Main Street, which morphs into Wagner Creek Road. In about 5 miles the road becomes a gravel road, Forest Road 22. Look for trailhead parking on the left 2 miles from the start of the gravel.

This is a strenuous trail, but the reward is a stunning view of almost the entire world from the concrete base of a dismantled Forest Service fire lookout perched on granitic (granitelike) bedrock. The creek crossings and springs along the way may be minimal to nonexistent as the summer wears on. It's a great hike to test your mettle, and it's also a relatively little-used trail, so you can escape from the crowds here.

This trail begins by letting you know who's boss right away, with a climb through pine and Douglas fir forest for the first 0.5 mile or so. Then it flattens, luring you along for 0.3 mile before returning to character with a steep 0.5-mile pull uphill along the valley of Sheep Creek (to your

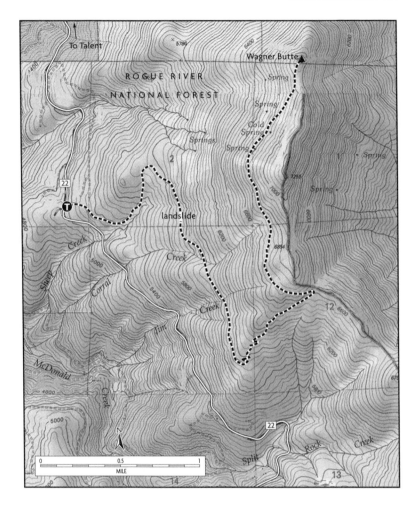

right) to an opening that provides a glimpse of Wagner Butte's summit ridge ahead and the valley below.

From this first respite, the trail makes a sweeping turn to the south and then contours uphill for 1.5 miles. You cross Corral Creek in 0.25 mile and Jim Creek in another 0.5 mile. At 1.2 miles from the beginning, the trail navigates across the open and still-sodden Sheep Creek Landslide that occurred in 1983 when the forested slope, saturated by heavy rain, failed abruptly, causing an avalanche of trees, debris, and soil that slid rapidly all the way to the Applegate River, eradicating the forest in its path.

The trail continues on an easy upward pace into the forest. Enjoy this "flat" stretch while it lasts because at 3 miles from the start, the trail enters a nice, sage-filled clearing and then blasts up a ridge, using minimal switchbacks to climb 1100 feet in about 0.75 mile. Then it heaves to, rounds an abrupt curve, and continues at a much more reasonable pace of 500 feet in 1.5 miles to reach the old lookout. The scramble over rocks to reach the flat pad of the dismantled lookout is worthwhile. From the perch on the concrete pad, views of Shasta and the Applegate Valley are impressive enough to even make your dog admire them. Return as you came.

58. Pacific Crest Trail: Mount Ashland to Siskiyou Gap

Round trip: 12 miles (16 miles from the picnic area)
Elevation range: 5880–7080 feet
Difficulty: Strenuous
Hiking time: 10 hours
Best canine hiking season: Early summer, fall
Regulations: Northwest Forest Pass required
Maps: USGS Mount Ashland and Siskiyou Peak 7.5' quadrangles
Information: Rogue River–Siskiyou National Forest, Siskiyou
   Mountains Ranger Station, Ashland, (541) 552-2900

Getting there: Traveling on Interstate 5 south from Ashland or north from Yreka, take the Mount Ashland exit (exit 6) and follow the signs along the 8-mile paved access road leading to the Mount Ashland Ski Area. At the end of the paved parking lot, Forest Road 40S15 takes off south, and the Mount Ashland Botanical Area is 0.25 mile down this road; the Pacific Crest Trail can be accessed at the east end of the Botanical Area.

Or you can begin your hike from Grouse Gap: Just past the ski area parking lot, the pavement ends and the access road becomes the gravel Forest Road 20. This road continues west through the length of the Botanical Area. The road intersects the PCT 1.2 miles past the parking

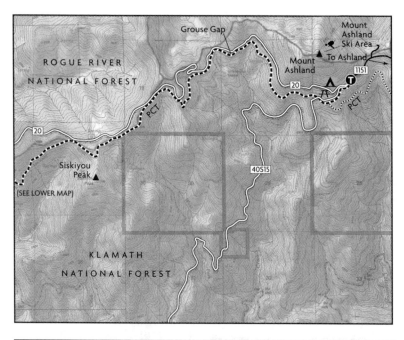

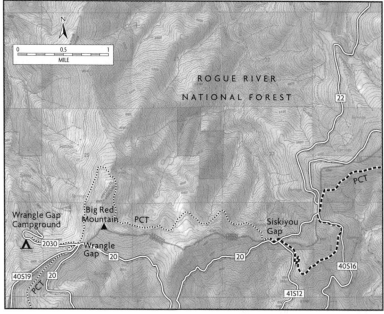

area. (Or you can just hike from the parking area to Grouse Gap and back . . .)

On the torrid summer days that are legend in southern Oregon, this hike will take you and Rover up and above all the heat for a refreshing exploration of Siskiyou Mountain Range ridge crests and a variety of plants and geology. Views from high points are inspiring. The trail is easily accessed, and you can make the hike as long or short a hike as you wish. Water is present in springs along or near the trail in spring and early summer, but by July and August many springs are dry, so carry water, and/or stash some along Forest Road 20—which is never far from the trail—before you set out. You may also make this a one-way hike if you leave a second vehicle at your end point. FR 20 is suitable for high- or higher-clearance vehicles (yes, the Outback should be okay) with 10-ply tires.

The hike begins at the Mount Ashland Ski Area parking lot's extreme west end. Follow the connecting gravel road (FR 40S15) as it drops 200 feet in 0.25 mile to a picnic table, where a path leads west and downhill, contouring across open slopes and patches of subalpine fir

and connecting with the Pacific Crest Trail (PCT) in another 0.25 mile. Here, the PCT crosses open meadows and glades, small headwater streams, and wetlands. This is part of the Mount Ashland Botanical Area, an 800-acre reserve that showcases the diverse flora of the Siskiyou Mountains. Here, at the crossroads of the Cascade and Klamath ranges, alpine meadows and lower forests boast the greatest botanical biodiversity in North America. While Rover may not appreciate the pretty flowers, his nose will detect the plethora of

The Mount Ashland/PCT hike offers many views of Mount Shasta and the Shasta Valley.

scents they produce. The U.S. Forest Service website for the Mount Ashland Botanical Area–Oak Knoll Ranger District notes:

"On the top and western ridge of Mount Ashland, you can see Mount Ashland lupine, which is found nowhere else in the world. The open ridges and sandy soils are also habitat for the rare Henderson's horkelia and Howell's tauschia. Engelmann spruce and subalpine fir, rare this far south in Oregon, can be found in small isolated patches. The slopes below the ridgetop are a mix of wet and dry meadows with an abundance of several species of lupine, monkshood, phacelia, larkspur, and exceptional stands of native grasses. The shrub fields are dominated by mountain sagebrush and greenleaf manzanita. The rocky areas are good places to find small mounding perennials such as Jaynes Canyon buckwheat, coyote mint, and several species of penstemon. Four species of anemone can be found in the different habitats, and western pasqueflower (*Anemone occidentalis*) is at its showiest as the snowbanks melt."

From the junction with the PCT, you have views of Mount Ashland's granitic summit, replete with NOAA weather stations, a microwave relay, and other electronic gear sticking up like a rocker's spiked hair. On the ground, you'll find granite boulders and a lot of sand. The going here is easy. There are wet meadows in spring and early summer—and the ravenous mosquitoes that go with them. At 1.5 miles, you intersect FR 20 at Grouse Gap. The Grouse Gap shelter makes a nice picnic spot (or turnaround for a shorter hike).

Beyond Grouse Gap, the trail enters a more serious and very diverse forest of subalpine fir, Engelmann spruce, Jeffrey pine, and Douglas fir. You are never far from the road, but it is a road less traveled, and its company is rarely intrusive. For the first 0.75 mile beyond Grouse Gap, the trail is nearly flat, but then it surges up and across a ridge and then becomes almost conjoined with the road for the next 1.7 miles. (About a mile from the ridgetop, a spur trail leads about 0.25 mile south, downhill, to access springs that provide early and midsummer water.)

At about 4 miles the PCT reaches another flat, open ridge crest: Siskiyou Butte (aka Siskiyou Peak), which rises another 300 feet in elevation just to the south, is designated as another Botanical Area. An off-trail exploration here affords excellent views and diverse wildflowers. Then the path angles downhill, touching FR 20 and fading into forest again, along the south slope of the ridge crest. You'll find a few seeps and springs along the way before intersecting FR 20 again in 1.8 miles. Here, for 0.25 mile the trail briefly follows FR 40S16, which branches to the left. Then the PCT diverges to the right, back into shade. It rejoins FR 20 in a mile and follows the road to Siskiyou Gap. This is the beginning of another ridge-crest botanical area (Red Mountain Botanical Area) that was developed on the magnesium-rich peridotite bedrock of Big Red Mountain.

For the adventurous, the PCT continues to a backpacker's campground 2 miles farther on the west side of Big Red Mountain. To get there, follow the PCT on a rugged and open stretch on the north side of Big Red Mountain. The path crawls past jagged peridotite boulders (not as bad as it sounds...) and skirts beneath red peridotite cliffs, making a wide excursion to the north to contour along a scenic ridge before returning to the main ridge crest, where it intersects with FR 20, FR 40S19, and, importantly, FR 2030—and the path (really a rugged roadway) to the campground. To reach the Wrangle Gap camp, turn right on FR 2030 here and proceed downslope about 0.5 mile.

You may explore farther before returning to Mount Ashland, either following FR 20 or the PCT.

59. Rogue River Trail: Illahee to Paradise Bar

Round trip: 21 miles
Elevation range: 240–350 feet
Difficulty: Moderate
Hiking time: 2–3 days
Best canine hiking season: Winter, spring
Regulations: Northwest Forest Pass required; register for wilderness entry
Maps: USGS Illahee and Marial 7.5' quadrangles
Information: Siskiyou National Forest, Gold Beach Ranger District, (541) 247-3600; Paradise Lodge, (800) 525-2161; Clay Hill Lodge, (503) 859-3772

Getting there: From Gold Beach on the southern Oregon coast, turn east onto Jerrys Flat Road (Forest Road 33) at the south end of the Rogue River Bridge. Drive 30 miles to County Road 375, marked for the Illahee and Rogue River trails. Follow this road 3 miles to a large, grassy parking area and the trailhead.

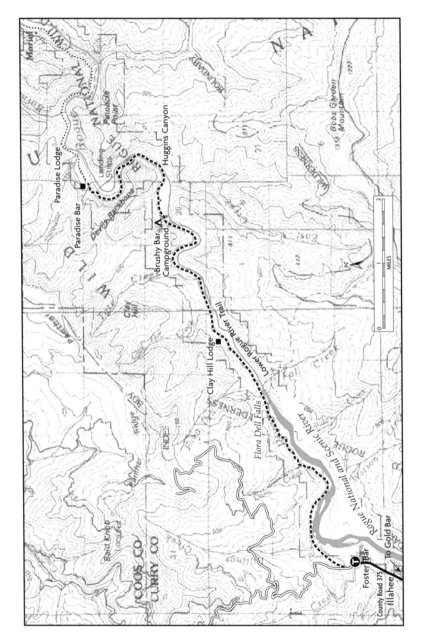

A refreshing waterfall greets hikers at Flora Dell Creek along the Lower Rogue River Trail.

The Rogue River Trail is a 40-mile adventure that follows the river from Illahee to Grave Creek. This hike tours the lower part of this trail, as an out-and-back trip of 21 miles, beginning on a gentle path through shady forests. As the trail travels upstream, shade becomes rarer. Most of the hike travels along rocky, bare, and poison oak–infested riverbank, with the Rogue River not easily accessible. The lower part of this trail, described here, is the best for dogs, as the openness of much of the trail beyond Paradise Lodge is downright uninviting for pooches, especially on hot summer days. That said, the lower portion of the trail, especially the first 8 miles, is doggie heaven, with shade, soft trail surfaces, and a lot of small streams to dabble in even when the main channel of the Rogue is far below the path or a long distance through the forest.

The trail leads from the east side of the expansive parking area at Foster Bar, where the Rogue, a broad and relatively tame river here, makes a gracious meander. For the first mile, the trail swings away from the river through a forest of largely deciduous trees—big-leaf maple, oak, and alder. You'll want to carry water here, as there are limited side creeks for several miles.

In about a mile, the river comes into view, but well below the trail. The trail closes on the river at 1.5 miles and then strays away. Look for doggie cooling water at Flora Dell Falls, a 30-foot cascade 3.5 miles into the hike. The trail continues through a mixed plant community that includes manzanita, sugar pine, and yellow pine. The river is fairly accessible for the next 2 miles beyond the falls. Then at 5.5 miles into the hike, the path ducks into deeper forest and encounters a small settlement and overnight lodge, known as Clay Hill Lodge. Expect people, cabins, and loose dogs here. You can arrange accommodations and obtain food here. (The next lodge offering overnight accommodations to hikers and rafters is 7 miles ahead.)

Once past this stray outpost of civilization, the trail again hugs the river, seeking the boundary between forest and rocky shoreline, so that shade is never really absent—but seldom fully present either. At 7.5 miles from the trailhead, after touring river bends with rugged banks and rocky shores, the trail ducks back under forest cover at Brushy Bar Campground. There are good campsites here along almost 0.5 mile of flat, sandy ground, with two creeks for water.

Beyond Brushy Bar, the trail enters the steep-walled gorge of Huggins Canyon and becomes markedly more rugged and less shaded. In 1.5 miles, it emerges and reaches Paradise Bar 10.5 miles from the trailhead. Paradise Bar is aptly named. This is a pretty site with a historic lodge established in 1903. Paradise Lodge can provide food and lodging if you reserve space ahead of time.

The Rogue River Trail continues to Graves Creek some 30 miles beyond Paradise Bar. For dogs, however, the rest of the trail is unpleasant in many places—rough, with minimal shade and abundant poison oak. It's fine in cool weather, but on hot sunny days it's a difficult trek for Fido. For most hikers, Paradise Lodge makes a great destination and turnaround spot.

60. Vulcan Lake

Round trip: 3.5 miles
Elevation range: 3740–4180 feet
Difficulty: Moderate
Hiking time: 4 hours
Best canine hiking season: Spring, summer
Regulations: Northwest Forest Pass required
Map: USGS Chetco Peak 7.5' quadrangle
Information: Rogue River–Siskiyou National Forest, Gold Beach
Ranger District, (541) 247-3600

Getting there: From Brookings, drive east on the North Bank Road up
the Chetco River. In 10 miles, at Little Redwood Campground, the paved
county road morphs into gravel Forest Road 1376. At 16 miles, the road
crosses the Chetco River on a high bridge. Turn right at a T intersection
just across the bridge and follow FR 1909 for 21 miles to an intersection
marked for Chetco Lake Trail to the right and Vulcan Lake Trail to the left.
To reach Vulcan Lake, turn left to follow a very narrow, rough, single-lane
road. It's driveable, but use caution and take your time. The trailhead,
with room for parking and turning around, is at the end of the road 1.8
miles from the intersection.

From the Vulcan Lake trailhead, the path travels along a road that once
led to chrome mines near here; then, in 0.25 mile, it begins a 0.5-mile
climb up a slope of tawny talus and outcrops, the dunnage of a collision
between the North American continent with the Klamath microcontinent
and seafloor about 130 million years ago. The peculiar orange-colored
rock found here is called peridotite. It once was part of the earth's mantle.
Geology is of little interest to your dog, however, who is probably more
focused on the golden-mantled ground squirrels that make their homes
in rock crevices. Look for Jeffrey pines along the ridgetops—these variants
of three-needle yellow pines are well adapted to eking a living from the
magnesium-rich soils that stifle most other plants here.

At the ridge crest, you gain a view of the Chetco River watershed and the
Pacific coast to the west, the rugged interior of the Kalmiopsis Wilderness
and Big Craggies Botanical Area to the north, and Vulcan Lake, a teal-colored

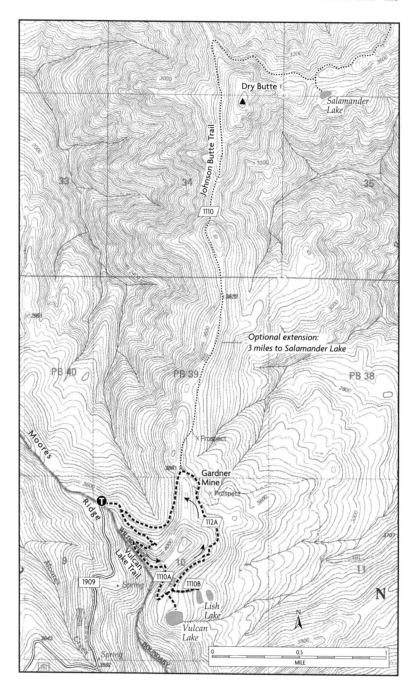

The trail to Vulcan Lake provides an overview of the Chetco River's basin and the Pacific Ocean.

pool 300 feet below. From this vantage, you can also see a vast area (500,000 acres, or almost 800 square miles) burned by the Biscuit Fire of 2002. Flames reached Vulcan Lake, and a number of trees in this basin were killed. However, because this site has such a high percentage of bedrock and was not a thick forest to begin with, fire damage here was minimal. But gray "ghost" trees span much of the landscape here to the horizon.

From the crest, the Vulcan Lake Trail drops, reaching Vulcan Lake in about 0.75 mile. You can work your way around the small lake, which was carved out by very localized glacial action during the Pleistocene Ice Age.

From Vulcan Lake, retrace your steps to the main trail. The path continues downslope toward Lish Lake. This lake is also reached by side paths. Lish Lake, also known as Little Vulcan Lake, sustains a substantial population of pitcher plants. Take care that dogs do not disturb these rare, wetland-loving carnivorous plants.

Retrace your path to the rather diaphanous main trail, Trail 112A, and follow it upslope through a forest of huge-coned sugar pine and Jeffrey pine. Cairns help you find your way where the path is elusive. After about 0.5 mile, the trail merges with an abandoned road and leads to the Gardner Mine. This was once a chrome mine, and you can still find shiny, black-spotted chrome ore here in places.

From the mine, the road leads to the ridgetop. Return to the trailhead by following the road to the left (south) back to your vehicle. Or you can turn right and follow the road and Johnson Butte Trail, #1110, north toward Dry Butte for 10 miles. If you choose to venture toward Dry Butte, be sure you have extra water for your dog, as there's none along the trail for the next 5 miles until you reach Salamander Lake—which may be dry. Shade is not abundant along this ridgetop either, so on hot days it's best to forego this extension of your hike.

Another nearby hike explores similar open country to Chetco Lake, a small lake also tucked into the Kalmiopsis Wilderness. It is a 10-mile round-trip hike so, as with Vulcan Lake, carry plenty of dog water. To reach the trailhead, follow directions for Vulcan lake, but at the junction for Chetco and Vulcan lakes, on Forest Road 1909, turn right and drive about 0.8 mile to the trailhead. (See "Five More Great Dog Hikes in the Klamath Mountains.")

61. Sourdough Trail #1114

Round trip: 7.5 miles
Elevation range: 1100–2500 feet
Difficulty: Moderate to strenuous
Hiking time: 6 hours
Best canine hiking season: Spring, summer, fall
Regulations: None
Maps: USGS Fourth of July Creek and Biscuit Hill 7.5' quadrangles
Information: Rogue River–Siskiyou National Forest, Gold Beach
　　Ranger District, (541) 247-3600

Getting there: The trail is located 26 miles east of Brookings. From U.S. Highway 101 about a mile north of the California border, take paved County Road 896 (Winchuck River Road) east 11 miles to the trailhead. This paved road morphs into graveled Forest Road 1107 and in 6 miles, find Spur Road 1107-220, which leads 0.5 mile to the trailhead. The spur road was flirting with a serious erosion issue in 2010, and while the Forest Service intends to repair this access road, use caution when driving it.

This trail has minimal water along the way, but its variety of landscapes, geology, and botany, as well as historical importance as a route for miners, make it a good walk with your dog. If you plan your walk in cooler weather, it will be more enjoyable for you and Fido.

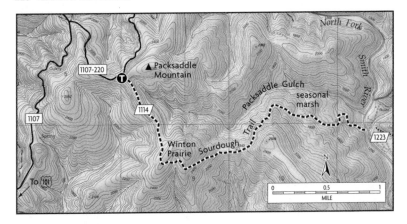

The trail begins where the roadway is gated and follows the ridgeline through an old burn. In spring and midsummer, the way is lined with blossoming wild rhododendron and azaleas. Other plants include lusty-leaved chinquapin and Douglas fir. Where you can peer over the bushes or a clearing provides a view, the southern Klamaths (Trinity Alps) and coast are inspiring. After a relatively level 0.5 mile, the path enters a forest. The small-diameter trees provide a full canopy and welcome shade. Then, after a mile, the trail crosses a small ravine and climbs to a clearing.

Known as Winton Prairie, this spot makes a change to a different kind of bedrock (peridotite) and a new plant community. From here on, the trail is more open, and Jeffrey pine predominates, with cedars more abundant as the trail approaches the river. In wet areas, look for Darlingtonia (pitcher) plants as well as many vegetative and soil changes. Spring is a good time to view serpentinite-associated plant species: lilies and odd-colored paintbrush. Just as you enter the clearing, look for a commemorative sign. At this place in 1934 (the height of the Great Depression), a 64-year-old miner named Al Harzicker froze to death. There are no other details, and his biography is a mystery, but the sign—and a few scattered remnants of early twentieth-century equipment, are fertile grounds for the imagination.

From this summit glade, the path leads brazenly across the rest of Winton Prairie's grassy flat space, then begins a descent across a landscape of odd, orangey-red peridotite bedrock (the stuff of which the Earth's mantle is made) to the North Fork of the Smith River, 2 miles ahead and 1400 feet below. The river is a wonderful respite, with rugged riffles, soothing pools, and shade. (Watch for poison oak and ivy here!) Return as you came.

The very adventurous may wish to ford the river, if water flow permits it, and explore the continuing trail on the east side. Here, it's the North Fork Smith River Trail, #1223. This trail ascends back to the summit of the Klamaths, following a ridge crest through the Klamaths for another 12 miles. There is minimal water on this trail, and because it travels through areas burned intensely in the 2002 Biscuit Fire, it may be plagued by fallen trees.

The second half of the Sourdough Trail leads through generally open country with views of the Klamaths.

Five More Great Dog Hikes in the Klamath Mountains

Note that many trails, especially those in the Kalmiopsis Wilderness, were affected by the cataclysmic Biscuit Fire of 2002. As of this writing, burned, dead, and newly downed trees make travel on many trails very difficult. The trails below are chosen to avoid the Biscuit Fire area.

1. Fish Lake Trail, #1013, 5 miles round trip, is a relatively civilized stroll that takes you to young lava flows from Brown Mountain; this trail connects the Cascades' and the Klamaths' ecosystems. Siskiyou Mountains Ranger District, Ashland, (541) 552-2900.

2. Mount Bolivar Trail, 3 miles round trip, is short and steep but has a great view. Powers Ranger District, (541) 439-6200.

3. Stein Butte Trail, #929, 9 miles round trip, climbs from Applegate Lake to Elliot Ridge and Stein Butte. Siskiyou Mountains Ranger District, (541) 899-3800.

4. Chetco Lake, 10 miles round trip. Begins near Vulcan Lake (Hike 60) and leads to a small lake across open country. Gold Beach Ranger District, (541) 247-3600.

5. Frog Pond, Red Buttes Wilderness, 8 miles round trip, features alpine meadows and small ponds. Siskiyou Mountains Ranger District, (541) 899-3800.

BLUE MOUNTAINS, WALLOWA MOUNTAINS, AND EASTERN OREGON

62. Deschutes River: Scout Camp Trail

Round trip: 2.5 miles
Elevation range: 2700–2150 feet
Difficulty: Strenuous
Hiking time: 3 hours
Best canine hiking season: Fall, winter, spring
Regulations: None
Map: USGS Steelhead Falls 7.5' quadrangle
Information: Bureau of Land Management, Prineville Office,
(541) 416-6700

Getting there: From just north of Terrebonne on U.S. Highway 97 in central Oregon, turn west onto Lower Bridge Road. In 2 miles, turn right

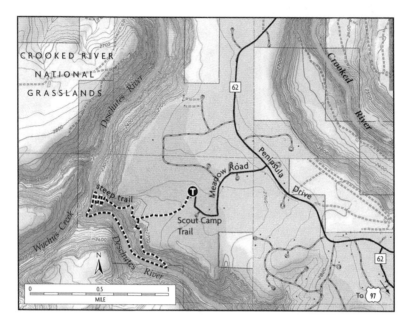

on 43rd Street. Then in 1.7 miles turn left on Chinook Drive. In 2.3 miles, turn left on Mustang Drive, then right on Shad Road after 1.1 miles, then right on Peninsula Drive (Forest Road 62) in 1.4 miles, and left on Meadow Road after 3.2 miles. About 0.5 mile down Meadow Road, turn right on Scout Camp Trail. The parking area is 0.2 mile ahead.

This rugged new trail is part of the Bureau of Land Management's efforts to make the Crooked River and Deschutes River more accessible for recreation. This area will be very hot in the summer, but it's a great place for fall, winter, and spring hikes. In any season, carry water. In warm weather, be alert for snakes.

The path from the parking lot drops slowly into the canyon of the Deschutes Wild and Scenic River. It affords views of lava flows that emanated from Newberry Volcano south of Bend between 1 and 2 million years ago. It also offers good views of the canyon.

As you descend into the canyon, the trail forks. This is a loop, and no matter which way you go, you won't miss anything. However, the path to the right seems the steepest of the two routes, so its recommended that you bear right and head to the river, which you reach in about 0.7 mile. This downhill part of the trail requires some scrambles over rocks, and navigates a steep slope above the river. The trail along the river, like the

Dundee tops out above the Deschutes River on the Scout Camp Trail.

rest of the path, is rocky and very open, but it does permit a few stops for splashing in the water on warmer days. (Fido may not really care much about the temperature . . .)

After the milelong tour of the riverbanks, the loop trail turns upward, making steady and stalwart progress toward the top on a straight grade. At the junction, turn right to return to the trailhead.

63. Crooked River National Grasslands: Cole Loop Trail

Round trip: 6.6 miles
Elevation range: 2900–4200 feet
Difficulty: Easy to strenuous
Hiking time: 4–5 hours
Best canine hiking season: Spring, fall
Regulations: No leash requirements
Map: USGS Gray Butte 7.5' quadrangle
Information: Ochoco National Forest, Crooked River National
Grasslands, Madras, (541) 475-9272

Getting there: From Terrebonne (north of Redmond on U.S. Highway 97), drive north on US 97 for 4 miles and turn right (east) on SW Park Road. Follow the paved road about 1.5 miles, where it crosses an irrigation

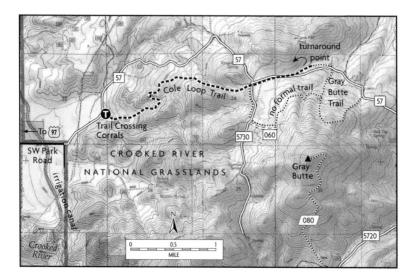

canal and then becomes a gravel road as it enters public lands. Continue straight on the road, now Sherwood Drive (Forest Road 57) for 0.5 mile. At a set of large wooden corrals (Trail Crossing Corrals) on the right, pull into the broad parking area. The Cole Loop Trail heads east through the green gate here. Please be sure you close and secure the gate after you pass through.

The Cole Loop Trail (25 miles total) and the nearby shorter Warner Loop (10 miles total) are trail systems initially designed for horseback riders. However, the trails have proven more popular with hikers, and the open country of the Crooked River National Grasslands here inspires freedom to explore, with multiple short trails and roads less traveled. The hike described here covers only the first 5 miles of the Cole Loop Trail—the most inviting for canid hikers. There is no water along the trail, so it's best hiked in cooler weather, and be sure you take ample water with you. Juniper trees provide shade, although juniper-clearing projects may remove many trees in the future.

The hike begins on an old road, but Cole Loop Trail branches northward in about 0.25 mile. The path clambers up juniper-clad slopes at an easy pace, providing views of Gray Butte to the south and Haystack and Juniper buttes to the north. Because the trail covers uneven ground and winds through small valleys and ridges to keep an even grade and pace, it's an interesting place to walk, revealing new micro-landscapes at every turn.

In about 1.2 miles, the trail crests a ridge and wanders down to meet a seldom-traveled gravel road (FR 57) at 2.2 miles, which it follows for another mile before again asserting its independence. This spot, at 3.3 miles from the trailhead, makes a good turnaround spot.

If you are feeling more adventurous, you can continue on BLM Road 57 another 0.25 mile to the trailhead for the Gray Butte Trail. The developed part of the Gray Butte Trail avoids the summit and instead skirts the north and west sides of the butte, ultimately connecting with ridges above Smith Rock. A good plan here would be to hike part of the trail on the east side, and then follow an informal path that connects with USFS Spur Road 060 and then FR 5730, where you turn right to return easily to the Cole Loop Trail at the junction of FR 5730 and FR 57, from where you can retrace the Cole Loop Trail to return to your beginning point.

Dundee and Meesha take a breather under an old-growth juniper on the Cole Loop Trail.

64. Lookout Mountain Trail

Round trip: 15 miles
Elevation range: 4030–6926 feet
Difficulty: Moderate
Hiking time: 8 hours
Best canine hiking season: Spring, summer, fall
Regulations: Northwest Forest Pass required
Maps: USGS Gerow Butte and Lookout Mountain 7.5' quadrangles
Information: Ochoco National Forest, Lookout Mountain Ranger
District, (541) 416-6500

Getting there: From Prineville in the middle of Oregon, drive 14.7 miles
east on U.S. Highway 26 and bear right (east) onto County Road 23 (Lookout Mountain Road). Continue 8 miles to Ochoco Ranger Station. The
trailhead is on the right (south) side of the road just past the ranger station.

The hike to Lookout Mountain's flat, windblown summit travels through
a diverse landscape with spectacular groves of ancient ponderosa pine
and south-facing, sun-blasted stands of mountain mahogany. Along the
way you might encounter wild horses (they are more wary than truly
wild). Signs suggest that cougar sightings are not uncommon here. It's
also habitat for bears and other forest denizens. Take water and a camera.
And, of course, your dog.

From the roadside trailhead, the Lookout Mountain Trail winds upslope
through a Douglas fir forest. This is not a straight-up climb but more of a
shambling up-and-down affair, rising and dropping over the small hills
along Lookout Mountain's generous northern slope. As the trail rounds the
first summit about 1 mile into the hike, it offers a view of nearby Round
Mountain to the east. Then it curves back down a moist forest slope—look
for wild iris here and along the rest of the trail in midsummer. At 1.7 miles,
the trail finds a beautiful stand of ponderosa pine, along with a grassy,
iris-lined meadow. Wild horses like to hang out here in the spring. They
might have foals, so keep dogs close at hand here.

The trail turns and climbs again, leaving the ponderosas behind. It
reaches Crooked Tree Spring—the only reliable water along the entire
hike—at 2.3 miles from the trailhead. The spring is located just downhill

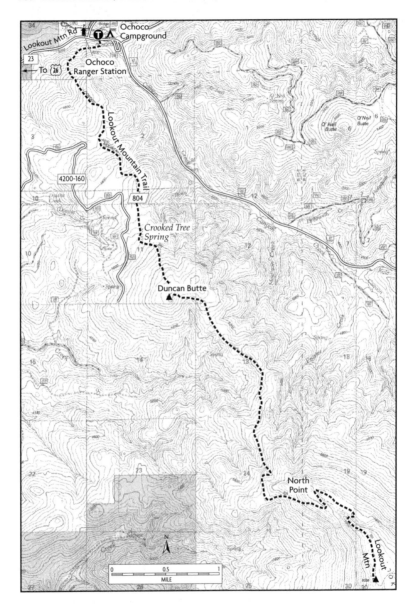

from the trail. An informal trail leads to the spring and a set of water troughs.

The path tops Duncan Butte at 3 miles. You can scramble west through the forest here for a few hundred yards for a preview of the Cascades.

Dundee and Megan practice "off trail," and wait for Meesha and Ellen to catch up.

From the butte, the trail plunges down through thicker forest to a saddle. Mountain mahogany grows on this warm and rocky site.

Beyond the saddle, the trail climbs toward the top of Lookout Mountain, bypassing the rocky basalt outcrops at North Point. To reach the summit, the trail switchbacks along a narrow ridge, finally topping out on the mountain's broad plateau at about 7 miles from the trailhead. Take time to explore this top area—red-tailed hawks and other raptors ride the thermals to hunt ground squirrels that live in this summit grassland. Return as you came.

65. Round Mountain Trail

Round trip: 8.4 miles
Elevation range: 5350–6785 feet
Difficulty: Moderate
Hiking time: 4 hours
Best canine hiking season: Spring, fall
Regulations: Northwest Forest Pass required
Map: USGS Ochoco Butte 7.5' quadrangle
Information: Ochoco National Forest, Lookout Mountain Ranger District, (541) 416-6500

Getting there: From Prineville, drive 14.7 miles east on U.S. Highway 26 and bear right (east) onto County Road 23 (Lookout Mountain Road).

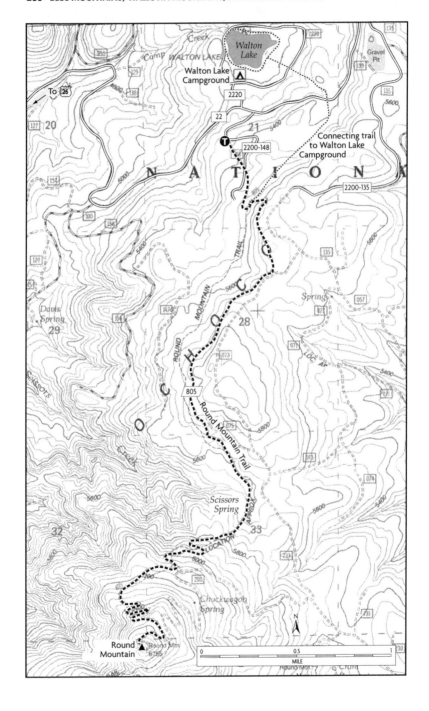

Continue 8 miles to Ochoco Ranger Station, and bear left onto Forest Road 22, marked for Walton Lake. Continue 6.5 miles to the Walton Lake Campground entrance. The road to the trailhead is a right turn just past the campground entrance. Follow this road 0.2 mile to the trailhead.

This hike explores a part-wooded, part-open landscape and climbs to the summit of Round Mountain for panoramic views of Big Summit Prairie and distant Cascade peaks. There's not much water for dogs on the hike, but there's plenty of opportunity for pre- and post-hike swims in Walton Lake just across the road from the trailhead.

Meesha checks out the route to Round Mountain.

From the trailhead, the path toward Round Mountain heads through a grassy meadow and then enters a forest dominated by Douglas fir. The woods here are an example of "forest health problems"—the forest is replete with snags, many of which bear the telltale huge holes left by pileated woodpeckers. For most of its length, the trail plays tag with a Forest Service road—the trail is the straighter route to the summit.

After switchbacking up a ridge, the trail crosses an open, rocky meadow with views of Round Mountain's antennae-cluttered summit, distant Cascade peaks, and Big Summit Prairie to the south. From here, the path heads toward a forested saddle and reaches Scissors Spring—the only water on the trail—at 2.4 miles from the trailhead. This spring may be dry in the mid to late summer

Beyond the spring, the trail again enters open grassland, then begins a switchbacking ascent of Round Mountain's north slope. A few juniper trees, undernourished yellow pine, and scruffy Douglas fir provide little shade on the upper half of this milelong, 1000-foot climb, so let dogs take their time here. The path joins the gravel road just below the summit and reaches Round Mountain summit at 4.2 miles from the trailhead. Though the summit bristles with communication towers, it offers a great view. Return as you came.

66. Elkhorn Crest Trail to Anthony Lake

Round trip: 8 miles
Elevation range: 7130–8180 feet
Difficulty: Moderate
Hiking time: 5 hours
Best canine hiking season: Summer
Regulations: Northwest Forest Pass required
Map: USGS Anthony Lakes 7.5' quadrangle
Information: Wallowa-Whitman National Forest, Whitman
   Ranger District, (541) 523-4476

Getting there: From Interstate 84, 25 miles south of La Grande, take exit 285 at North Powder. Drive west on County Road 101 marked for Anthony Lakes. In 3.5 miles, turn left (south) at a four-way intersection, drive 0.6 mile, and turn right (west) onto the Elkhorn Scenic Byway. This road becomes Forest Road 73 when it crosses into the Wallowa-Whitman National Forest. At about 19.2 miles from I-84, turn left (south) into a Forest Service parking area marked for Elkhorn Crest Trail. If you reach the Anthony Lake Campground, you've gone about 0.8 mile too far.

This loop hike takes you into truly alpine landscapes—the realm of mountain goats, whitebark pine, and Clark's nutcrackers. A few springs provide minor stops for cooling in midsummer, and you are likely to find lingering snow if you hike this trail before the Fourth of July. Overall, however, there's not much shade or water on the trail, so carry extra water for your pooch.

   The trail begins at a parking area about 0.8 mile east of the Anthony Lake Campground. This trailhead is the main point of departure for horseback riders touring the Elkhorn Crest Trail, so in midsummer you might meet horses on the path.

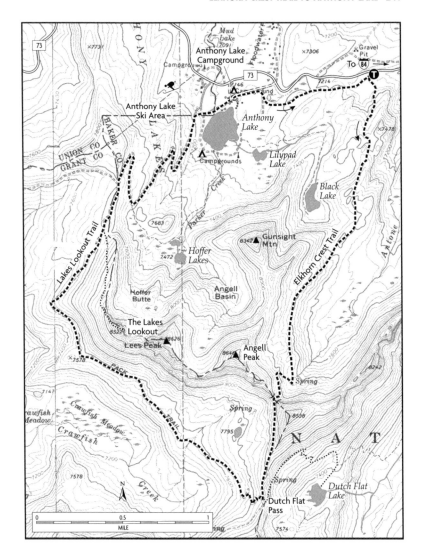

The Elkhorn Crest Trail leads unabashedly upslope, climbing through a lodgepole and subalpine fir forest into whitebark pine. It passes a small spring at about 2 miles en route to an unnamed pass (8180 feet) just east of Angell Peak in 3 miles of steady going. This highly scenic route has clear views of the Wallowa Mountains to the east and Baker Valley below.

Beyond the pass, the trail ducks behind a small peak, then emerges to provide a view of the valley of Dutch Flat Creek—a forested, U-shaped

Erika and Wolf, a nine-year-old Alaskan malamute, stroll along the trail around Anthony Lake.

valley that sprawls to the east. At 3.7 miles into the hike, you reach a four-way intersection at Dutch Flat Pass. Dutch Flat Lake lies temptingly below. The trail to the east leads to the lake, 600 feet below you, in about 1 mile.

The loop route turns west onto the Lakes Lookout Trail here, following signs to the Lakes Lookout. The trail contours along a slope of granitic boulders and craggy outcrops where subalpine fir and whitebark pine provide the major vegetation. At 4.3 miles, the trail crosses a boggy area, part of the headwaters of Crawfish Lake far below.

The trail continues along this south-facing slope—a place that, despite its 7500-foot altitude, can become quite warm on hot days. Paintbrush and buckwheat vegetate the barren alpine landscape. At 6.2 miles into the hike, the path reaches another saddle—this provides an overlook of Hoffer and Anthony lakes. Here, a two-track gravel road switchbacks down to Anthony Lake, allowing an easy descent. At the bottom of the grade, follow the lakeshore path into the campground. The connecting trail to the Elkhorn Crest trailhead is located at the east end of the campground. From here, the trail leads back to the trailhead in 0.8 mile.

67. Hoffer Lakes

Round trip: 2 miles
Elevation range: 7150–7430 feet
Difficulty: Easy
Hiking time: 1 hour
Best canine hiking season: Summer
Regulations: Northwest Forest Pass required
Map: USGS Anthony Lakes 7.5' quadrangle
Information: Wallowa-Whitman National Forest, Whitman
   Ranger District, (541) 523-4476

Getting there: From Interstate 84, take exit 285 at North Powder. Drive west on County Road 101 marked for Anthony Lakes. In 3.5 miles, turn left (south) at a four-way intersection. Drive 0.6 mile from the intersection and turn right (west) onto the Elkhorn Scenic Byway. This road becomes Forest Road 73 when it crosses into the Wallowa-Whitman National Forest. Follow FR 73 to the Anthony Lake Campground 20 miles from the exit off I-84. At the main campground intersection, turn right past a gazebo into the day-use area. Continue 0.3 mile to the road's end. Follow the path past campsites 0.1 mile to a trailhead on the right.

This short, popular hike leads from Anthony Lake to scenic Hoffer Lakes, which seem quite wild and very alpine. Expect dogs and children here. It's a great hike for both. The soft alpine meadows blaze with wildflowers in early summer, including dogtooth violet, shooting star, and paintbrush; trout dart through the alpine streams, tempting dogs to make futile leaps to catch them.

From the trailhead parking lot, follow the broad path that leads east around Anthony Lake. In about 100 yards, a side trail marked for Hoffer Lakes heads to the left (south). The path marches quite purposefully upslope, passing huge boulders as it parallels Parker Creek, which it crosses on several bridges. In 0.5 mile the path emerges from the lodgepole pine forest at the bank of Hoffer Lake. Informal trails travel left around the lake and right to marshy meadows with views of this small but serene lake basin.

To continue the loop hike, when you reach the lake bear right along a well-worn path that follows the shoreline. In 0.3 mile the trail emerges

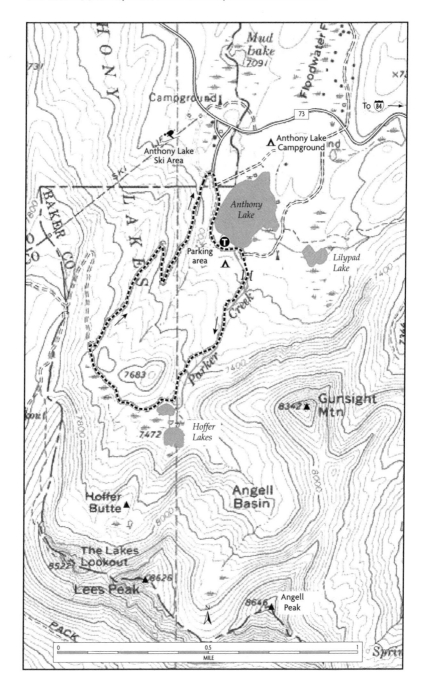

Small streams and creeks make the basin around Hoffer Lakes a perfect early-summer hike.

from the lodgepole pines and subalpine fir into alpine meadows; at 0.6 mile it joins a gravel roadway that turns right and leads back to the Anthony Lake picnic areas in another 0.4 mile. At the picnic area and gazebo, turn right again and follow the road to the parking area and trailhead.

68. Crawfish Lake

Round trip: 2.5 miles
Elevation range: 7160–6840 feet
Difficulty: Moderate
Hiking time: 2 hours
Best canine hiking season: Summer
Regulations: Northwest Forest Pass required
Map: USGS Crawfish Lake 7.5' quadrangle
Information: Wallowa-Whitman National Forest, Whitman
     Ranger District, (541) 523-4476

Getting there: From Interstate 84, take exit 285 at North Powder. Drive west on County Road 101 marked for Anthony Lakes. In 3.5 miles, turn left (south) at a four-way intersection. Drive 0.6 mile from the intersection and turn right (west) onto the Elkhorn Scenic Byway. This road becomes Forest Road 73 when it crosses into the Wallowa-Whitman National Forest. Follow FR 73 for 20 miles from the I-84 exit past Anthony Lakes

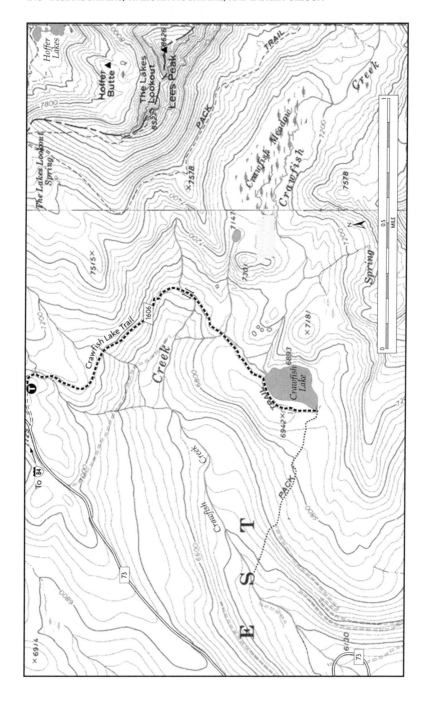

Ski Resort (7500 feet) to a Forest Service spur road on the left marked for Crawfish Lake. Drive 0.2 mile to the parking area.

This hike is simply a short walk to a picturesque lake tucked in a glacial basin. The Sloan Ridge Fire burned the pine and fir forest upslope from here in 1996, while a 1962 fire, the Anthony Lakes Burn, affected ridges along the north fringe of the hike. There has been little regrowth and forest recovery at this higher elevation, even after decades. Pearly everlasting, horsemint, wild delphinium, lupine, and paintbrush are the masters of these open meadows now, and the flowers are at their best in mid-July.

The Crawfish Lake Trail (Trail 1606) departs enthusiastically downhill, but it quickly tempers its plunge, moderating to a more gradual descent across open slopes with gaunt, charcoal-girdled snags. After a 0.5-mile tour of the fire zone, the trail retreats to forest and levels off for the remainder of its trip to Crawfish Lake. This small, glacier-carved lake is sequestered in lodgepole pine and fir forest, with granitic outcrops above its scenic eastern shore. There is plenty of room for a 0.5-mile hike around the lake on informal trails, and the easy clamber up the granite rocks is fun for both dogs and people. Watch for fishing debris that might snare a dog.

A second trail to Crawfish Lake, also Trail 1606, leaves from the opposite shore, descending steeply at first toward the drainage of Crawfish Creek, then leveling off to an easier grade before it plunges back into denser cover to arrive at a second Crawfish Lake trailhead on FR 73. Trying to make this a loop hike by returning on this trail is not a good idea because the only option for connecting the two trailheads is a long, 3.5-mile walk uphill along the busy, paved, shadeless roadway. Instead, from Crawfish Lake return to the start of the hike the way you came.

Belgian Malois pups cool off in Crawfish Lake.

69. Baldy Creek Trail

Round trip: 12 miles
Elevation range: 5600–7100 feet
Difficulty: Moderate
Hiking time: 8 hours
Best canine hiking season: Summer
Regulations: Northwest Forest Pass required
Maps: USGS Crawfish Lake and Mount Ireland 7.5' quadrangles
Information: Wallowa-Whitman National Forest, Whitman
   Ranger District, (541) 523-4476

Getting there: From Interstate 84, take exit 285 at North Powder. Drive west on County Road 101 marked for Anthony Lakes. In 3.5 miles, turn left (south) at a four-way intersection. Drive 0.6 mile from the intersection and turn right (west) onto the Elkhorn Scenic Byway. This road becomes Forest Road 73 when it crosses into the Wallowa-Whitman National Forest. Follow FR 73 for 20 miles from the I-84 exit to Anthony Lakes, then continue 11.5 miles to a Forest Service spur road marked for Baldy Creek trailhead. The trailhead is at the end of this 0.2-mile road.

This hike is a gentle excursion along a clear stream through quite wild country. It leads to a tree-rimmed alpine lake below a clean granite peak. This is a calm, wild, secluded place to camp. Wildlife abounds. You might encounter elk and deer here, and in the early summer be aware that vulnerable calves and fawns are present. A family of goshawks is resident in an old-growth Douglas fir on the edge of the stand-replacement burn. Gray jays, hermit thrushes, and flickers enliven the forest. You also will hear the serious percussion of pileated woodpeckers and watch energetic dippers negotiating the rushing stream.

From the trailhead, the Baldy Creek Trail crosses a shaky two-log bridge across the North Fork John Day River, then heads through forest. The trail is lined with huckleberry bushes, which are food for grouse, bears, dogs, and humans. With a little encouragement, many dogs learn to eat huckleberries right off the bush. The advantage is that they will alert you to the presence of huckleberries, even off trail. The disadvantage is that they can find and eat them faster than you can.

In 1 mile the trail crosses Baldy Creek, providing humans with another informal two-log bridge—this is the last true "bridge" across the creek. From here on, rely on downed logs and/or waterproof boots.

For the next mile, the creek remains discreetly east of the trail but is accessible. At mile 2.1, the trail veers away from a burned area—the outer limit of the 1996 Sloan Ridge Fire. Here the trail wallows across the confluence of two streams. It next veers west, taking the high ground through a primitive forest of spruce and Douglas fir for the next 1.2 miles.

At 2.5 miles from the trailhead, the path rejoins the creek and plays tag with the stream for the next mile. The path steepens and the trail is rougher as it begins a serious climb from flat forest floor to the top of moraines and Baldy Lake. The approach of the switchbacking portion of the climb is signaled rather rudely when the trail ducks beneath a huge powerline. Switchbacks maintain an even grade and easy pace.

Once at the top of the climb, the trail flattens and contours to the southern end of the basin in another mile. Here, a spur trail leads to the right for

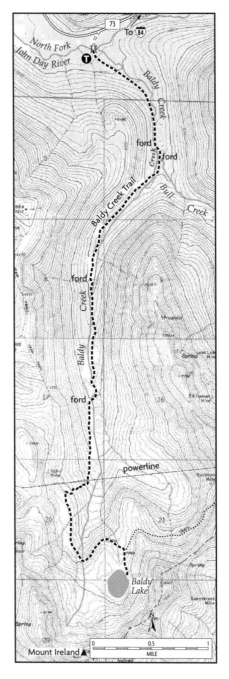

Pooped pup: Dundee rests on rocks above Baldy Lake.

another 0.25 mile south and 100 feet up to find Baldy Lake—surrounded by forest, but with a nice view of the imposing granite cliffs above that lead to the summit of Mount Ireland. Return as you came.

70. North Fork John Day Wilderness: Elkhorn Crest Loop

Round trip: 9 miles
Elevation range: 5870–7960 feet
Difficulty: Strenuous
Hiking time: 8 hours
Best canine hiking season: Summer
Regulations: Northwest Forest Pass required
Maps: USGS Crawfish Lake and Anthony Lakes 7.5' quadrangles
Information: Wallowa-Whitman National Forest, Whitman Ranger District, (541) 523-4476

Getting there: From Interstate 84, take exit 285 at North Powder. Drive west on County Road 101 marked for Anthony Lakes. In 3.5 miles, turn left (south) at a four-way intersection. Drive 0.6 mile from the intersection and turn right (west) onto the Elkhorn Scenic Byway. This road becomes Forest Road 73 when it crosses into the Wallowa-Whitman National Forest. Follow FR 73 for 24 miles from the I-84 exit past Anthony Lakes Ski

Resort (7500 feet) to FR 73/380 marked for Peavy Cabin, a historic ranger cabin. Turn left onto FR 73/380 and drive 3.4 miles to the trailhead at the end of the road 0.1 mile past Peavy Cabin. If you park closer to the cabin, you'll be a bit closer to the return trailhead.

This hike ranges from subalpine meadows to stark granitic ridge crests. Mountain goats live in this high country. Keep dogs under control. The hike provides a good lesson that a burned forest is not a dead forest. Deer, coyotes, kingfishers, owls, hawks, and woodpeckers are abundant, even though for the first 2 miles you hike through the bleached and skeletal remnants of a mixed forest that burned in the 1996 Sloan Ridge Fire.

From the trailhead, the trail almost immediately enters the North Fork John Day Wilderness to follow the North Fork John Day River. There are ample opportunities to visit the stream. Water is also abundant in small tributary streams early in the season. At 1 mile into the hike, the trail enters a wet meadow that is one of the main headwaters springs for the North Fork. The trail remains a respectful, but accessible, distance—between 20 yards and 0.25 mile—from the nascent river for the first 2 miles. Watch for woodpeckers cavorting in the snags and an abundance of flowers—including lupine, mules ears, paintbrush, and fireweed—that attract a proliferation of butterflies.

At 2 miles, the trail forks. Bear left here on Trail 1640. You'll be leaving your free-flowing, canine-cooling water supply behind for a time. This trail

Rocky Mountain goats like these can be found along the Elkhorn Crest Trail. Keep dogs close at hand to avoid harassing these rare goats and other wildlife.

scrambles away from the North Fork, gaining altitude rapidly. It navigates talus, then thin alpine soils where yellow buckwheat blooms in midsummer, arriving at the ridge crest (7500 feet) 1.7 miles from the junction. At the ridgetop, turn left (north) onto the Elkhorn Crest Trail (Trail 1611). This well-worn path follows the top of the ridge, providing cool breezes and exquisite views of Baker Valley and the Wallowa Mountains to the east and the Greenhorn and Strawberry ranges to the west. The trail continues for 3 miles along the ridge. Watch for white—and relatively tame—mountain goats. Control dogs in the event that you encounter them.

After an excursion west around the granitic pinnacle of Mount Ruth, the trail drops to Nip and Tuck Pass. Here, it meets the Cunningham Cove Trail, which heads to the left—and down. Within 0.5 mile of the junction, the Cunningham Cove Trail lowers you into a granite-lined emerald basin replete with springs. Below you and spread out across much of the landscape to the east are the gray snags of fire-killed trees. The Cunningham Cove Trail drops at a fairly steady and rapid pace, returning you to the Peavy Cabin and trailhead area in 2.5 miles, playing tag with Cunningham Creek on the way down.

71. North Fork John Day Wilderness: North Fork Campground to Granite Creek

Round trip: 26 miles
Elevation range: 3980–5200 feet
Difficulty: Moderate
Hiking time: 2–3 days
Best canine hiking season: Summer
Regulations: Northwest Forest Pass required
Maps: USGS Trout Meadows and Olive Lake 7.5' quadrangles
Information: Umatilla National Forest, North Fork John Day
    Ranger District, (541) 427-3231

Getting there: From Interstate 84, take exit 285 at North Powder. Drive west on County Road 101 marked for Anthony Lakes. In 3.5 miles, turn

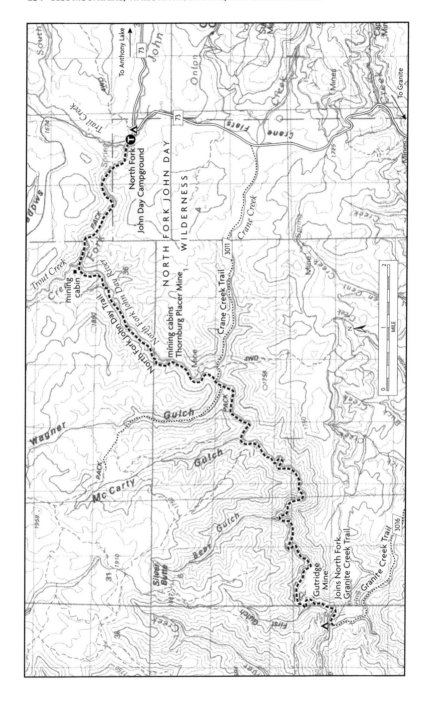

Meesha and the author cross a bridge near the confluence of the North Fork John Day River and Granite Creek.

left (south) at a four-way intersection. Drive 0.6 mile from the intersection and turn right (west) onto the Elkhorn Scenic Byway. This road becomes Forest Road 73 when it crosses into the Wallowa-Whitman National Forest. Follow FR 73 for 28.5 miles from the I-84 exit past Anthony Lakes Ski Resort (7500 feet) to the North Fork John Day Campground. The trailhead is at the campground entrance.

This trail has a civilized beginning that lures you into one of Oregon's wildest places. Expect bears and maybe even wolves here. The path follows the North Fork John Day River religiously. Water for canine cooling is almost always within easy reach.

From the campground entry, the trail heads across a grassy, pine-studded meadow. The landscape is fairly open for the first mile, and lodgepole pines dominate the trees. Look for lupines and spring camas here. An old mining cabin looms in a mile, and the trail becomes increasingly cloistered in the John Day's deepening canyon. The hike leads pleasantly through groves of ponderosa pine and Douglas fir.

At 2.5 miles, the trail finds another old mining cabin and crosses Trout Creek—a vigorous stream in early summer. Beyond the creek, the path slips around a bend and then crosses a broad floodplain where fragrant pines provide a great place to watch for deer. This is an area favored by does with fawns, so keep dogs close at hand in June and early July.

At 4.5 miles, the trail climbs along the outside of a steeply banked river meander. On the opposite bank you can glimpse piles of gravel. This is the abandoned Thornburg Placer Mine—worked in the late 1800s and early 1900s and yet another reminder that even when left alone, wilderness recovers slowly from human abuse. The trail clings to the hillside, then makes a switchbacking descent to the river at 5.5 miles into the hike.

Back at river level the valley opens, leading to meadows and open ponderosa stands. There are many suitable camping spots here. This is also a doe-fawn area, so be watchful, especially if you choose to camp.

At 6 miles, the trail meets the Crane Creek Trail and continues into the deepening canyon. Douglas firs and occasional spruce are more abundant now. The river is bigger and more serious. At 8 miles, the canyon bottom broadens briefly, opening into a grassy meadow that again invites thoughts of camping. Dogs accustomed to trotting along a forested trail might want a brief romp in this open grassy paradise.

But the trail quickly plunges into a starker canyon, where the forest that fringes the canyon top occasionally provides a skeletal reminder of past fires. At 9.5 miles, the trail crosses the North Fork on a narrow bridge. From this bridge to the junction with Granite Creek about 2.5 miles ahead, the path spends about half its time perched on slopes well above the river. At 13 miles, the path joins the Granite Creek Trail at a small open meadow where there are inviting campsites. Turn around here to return as you came.

72. Bonny Lakes and Aneroid Lake

Round trip: 13 miles
Elevation range: 6500–8400 feet
Difficulty: Moderate
Hiking time: 10 hours
Best canine hiking season: Summer
Regulations: Northwest Forest Pass required; register for wilderness entry
Maps: USGS Aneroid Mountain, Lick Creek, and Gumboot Butte 7.5' quadrangles
Information: Wallowa National Forest, Eagle Cap Ranger District, (541) 426-5546

Getting there: From the town of Joseph, 85 miles east of LaGrande on Oregon Route 82, travel east 8.3 miles on County Road 350 (Imnaha Highway) toward Imnaha. After the first summit, turn right on Salt

Creek Road (Forest Road 39), marked for Salt Creek Summit. Follow this narrow, paved road past Salt Creek Summit, a total of 12.8 miles, and turn right on narrow, bumpy, gravel FR 100. Follow this carefully—it's

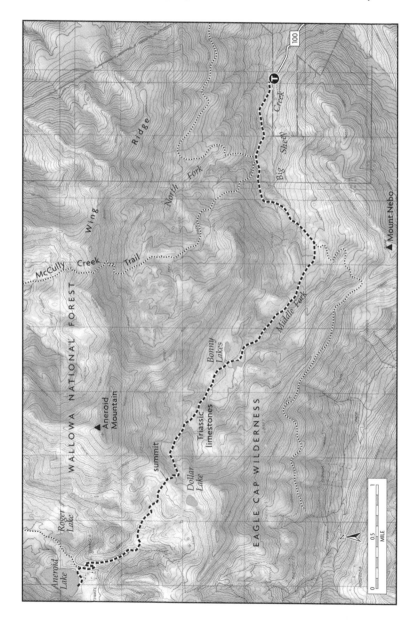

not fun without high clearance—for 3 miles to road's end and a parking area where the trail begins.

This trail can be hiked as a one-way trip if you can either leave a second vehicle at the Aneroid trailhead south of Wallowa Lake or arrange to be picked up there. The round-trip hike is slightly longer if you trek all the way to Aneroid Lake—but the scenery is worth it. The trip from the eastern trailhead provides fewer hikers and horses, along with abundant solitude, lovely scenery, and water.

The trailhead is in an open place torched by a major forest fire, the Canal Burn, in 1989 and now recovering as a thick stand of lodgepole pines; from here, the trail rambles across Big Sheep Creek and then clings to the north side of the valley. About a mile into the hike, watch for several other (small) trails entering from the north, and bear left at intersections to stay on the main trail. (The others go steeply uphill pretty fast—but the main trail climbs with less enthusiasm.)

Beginning about a mile into the trek, you'll find multiple crossings of Big Sheep Creek and its tributaries, as well as open riparian meadows. At 1.7 miles, bear right on the trail to Bonny Lakes as a path that leads to the Imnaha River (far, far away) continues straight. The trail to Bonny Lakes dives into spruce-fir forest and follows the Middle Fork of Big Sheep Creek closely; it is relatively flat until a short, steep climb at about 2.9 miles. You'll reach Bonny Lakes—two small but pretty lakes—at 4 miles at an elevation of 7800 feet. This makes a good destination—the gray marble and limestone here provide a scenic setting. It's also a favorite campsite for backpackers.

The trail beckons you onward and upward, to Dollar Lake, another mile of hiking across an open subalpine landscape and another 600 feet in elevation. This is the summit of the trail at almost 8400 feet. There are stunning views of Aneroid Mountain, Wing Ridge, Pete's Point, and the High Wallowa peaks from here.

Shooting stars (Dodecathon)—*members of the primrose family—are common late spring flowers in the Blue Mountains.*

To reach Aneroid Lake, continue west for 1.5 miles. You'll also drop from 8400 to 7500 feet. Here, the rocks are unabashedly granitic (granitelike), in contrast to the marble and metamorphosed sandstone you encountered at Bonny Lakes. There are cabins and a rustic lodge at Aneroid Lake so expect people in this pristine alpine setting.

You may continue to Wallowa Lake, still a steep, rough, dusty, horse-apple-strewn 6 miles ahead, or retrace your steps to the trailhead you started at 6.5 miles behind you.

73. Eagle Cap Wilderness: McCully Creek Trail

Round trip: 11.2 miles
Elevation range: 5550–7900 feet
Difficulty: Moderate to strenuous
Hiking time: 4–8 hours
Best canine hiking season: Summer, early fall
Regulations: Northwest Forest Pass required; register for wilderness entry
Maps: USGS Aneroid Mountain, Kinney Lake, and Lick Creek 7.5' quadrangles
Information: Wallowa National Forest, Eagle Cap Ranger District, (541) 426-5546

Getting there: From the town of Joseph, 85 miles east of LaGrande on Oregon Route 82, drive east on Country Road 350 (Imnaha Highway) toward Imnaha 5.4 miles. Turn right on Tucker Down Road (County Road 633). Drive south for approximately 2 miles—cross a cattle guard and bear left on gravel. Continue on this gravel road approximately 3 miles. You'll travel about 1 mile past the Ferguson Ridge Ski Area turnoff. Turn right on Forest Road 3920-012, marked for McCully Creek. The trailhead and parking area are approximately 0.5 mile from this intersection.

This hike takes you into truly wild country on the east side of the Wallowa Mountains, where bears and cougars and possibly wolves are sighted with some accuracy and frequency. Take precautions, and be

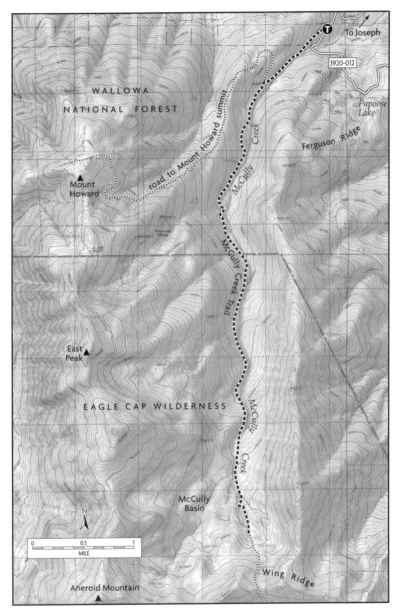

aware. However, take comfort in the fact that no one has ever had a bad physical encounter with wildlife on this trail, except for more ordinary skunks, porcupines, and harmless bull snakes. This trail is popular with

Kyla in spring snow along the McCully Creek Trail.

hunters, so it is best to avoid it during deer- and elk-hunting seasons, starting in mid-October.

From the trailhead, a narrow trail leads you 100 yards or so to a much broader trail—a now-abandoned gravel road that led to the top of Mount Howard and was used to build the Mount Howard Tramway. It is still used on rare occasions.

About 1 mile along this thoroughfare, the footpath leads left, following the slopes above McCully Creek into the forest. You'll have a good view of the 1989 Canal Burn that ravaged the adjacent forest here—including the lodgepole-rich woods at the trailhead. Soon, the main trail heads into dense spruce and fir woodlands that provide ample shade. At about 2.3 miles into the hike, you'll enter the Eagle Cap Wilderness.

The trail is well worn through most of its trip to the headwaters of McCully Creek and Aneroid Meadow. Expect a gradual, shaded rise punctuated by springs and seeps that are active until mid-July in most years. At 3.1 miles into the hike, the path dips slightly downward and you'll cross McCully Creek, then travel on the east slopes, with increasingly good views of Aneroid Mountain to the southwest, Wing Ridge to the south, and East Peak to the west, as the forest opens into meadows.

At about 4 miles, the forest morphs into scattered subalpine fir as you climb past 6000 feet elevation. There is a rocky stretch of steep going here that then flattens into meadows and scattered groves of trees. These meadows at the head of McCully Creek offer opportunities for wandering, and they are a favorite hideout for elk and deer. Especially if you are hiking in May and June, expect that baby elk (calves) and deer (fawns) may be near, and please be ready to control dogs. Once you've enjoyed the splendor here, return as you came.

74. Eagle Cap Wilderness: Hurricane Creek

Round trip: 6.4–24 miles
Elevation range: 5020–7700 feet
Difficulty: Moderate
Hiking time: 4 hours–2 days
Best canine hiking season: Summer
Regulations: Northwest Forest Pass required
Maps: USGS Chief Joseph Mountain and Eagle Cap 7.5' quadrangles
Information: Wallowa National Forest, Eagle Cap Ranger District, (541) 426-5546

Getting there: From the town of Joseph, 85 miles east of LaGrande on Oregon Route 82, turn west onto West Wallowa Avenue. In 3 miles, at the white Hurricane Creek Grange building, make a hard left onto a gravel road, the westward extension of Hurricane Creek Road. Continue 2.9 miles to the parking area at the end of the road.

This trail leads into the Lakes Basin of the Eagle Cap Wilderness. It is far less popular than nearby trails up the Lostine River or the path from Wallowa Lake but expect to meet other hikers along the trail. There is some use by horse packers. You might glimpse mountain goats on the slopes high above you.

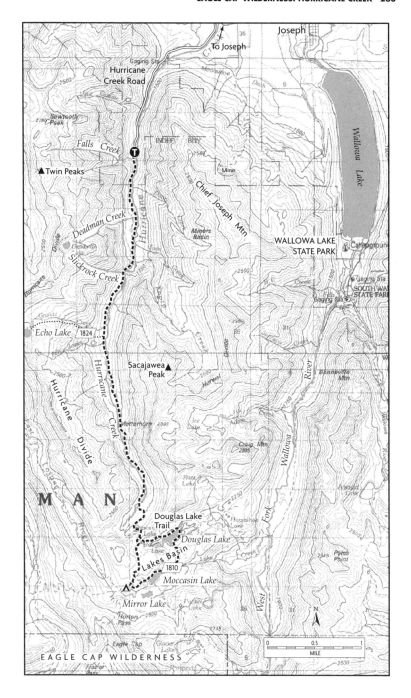

Joseph

To Joseph

Gaging Sta

Hurricane
Creek Road

Moccasin

Dash

Wallowa Lake

Sawtooth
Peak

Falls Creek

INDEP BDY

Mine

Twin Peaks

Chief Joseph Mtn

Deadman Creek

Divide

Miners
Basin

WALLOWA LAKE
STATE PARK

Campground

Slickrock Creek

Gaging Sta

SOUTH WAL
STATE PAR

Gaging Sta

Echo Lake 1824

Hurricane

Sacajawea
Peak

Bonneville
Mtn

Hurricane Divide

Creek

Matterhorn

Ice
Lake

Wallowa River

Craig Mtn

Razz
Lake

M A N

Douglas Lake
Trail

Horseshoe
Lake

Douglas Lake

West Fork

Lakes Basin

1810

Moccasin Lake

Pete's
Point

Mirror Lake

Horton
Pass

West Fork

N

EAGLE CAP WILDERNESS

Eagle Cap

Glacier
Lake

0   0.5   1
MILE

Horseback riders and packers frequently share the Hurricane Creek and other trails with hikers in the Wallowa Mountains.

From the trailhead, the Hurricane Creek Trail moves through lodgepole pine, tamarack, and grand fir forest for 0.3 mile to a water crossing of Falls Creek—getting across can be a challenge in early summer. Just upstream is a 70-foot waterfall. Informal trails lead to the base of this inviting cascade. This destination alone makes Hurricane Creek a worthy route.

Beyond this detour, the trail crosses a treeless expanse that appears to be a clear-cut. It is a natural clear-cut, however—a forest mowed down by snow avalanches in the 1960s. Beyond this natural, brushed-over area, the trail slips into lodgepole pine and larch woodland, then emerges into subalpine meadows at Deadman Creek 1.5 miles from the trailhead. The meadows offer views of Twin Peaks to the west and Sacajawea Peak to the south. If you watch the ridges to the west closely, you might see white dots—mountain goats frequent the rocky upper slopes.

Beyond Deadman Creek, the trail reenters a lodgepole-dominated forest for another 1.7 miles, switchbacking along outcrops, tiptoeing at the edge of an abrupt drop into Hurricane Creek, and emerging into the open as it nears Slickrock Creek. This stream comes by its name honestly.

The bedrock is coarse marble—a soft stone that has been polished and smoothed by running water. Approaching the Slickrock crossing (5780 feet), the trail teeters above cliffs and then crosses the slippery outcrops at the creek's junction with Hurricane Creek. It's a nice watering spot and, at 3.2 miles, a popular destination for day hikes.

At Slickrock Creek the trail steepens slightly, continuing through a forest increasingly composed of grand fir and Englemann spruce along with lodgepoles. Tamaracks are less abundant at this higher altitude. As you proceed up the trail, look for increasing numbers of spindle-topped subalpine fir.

At 5.1 miles from the trailhead, the path meets a junction with Trail 1824 to Echo Lake. This trail is steep and very rough, climbing about 2500 feet in 3.1 miles to the rocky alpine environment of Echo Lake (8372 feet). If you wish to put more grunt and challenge into your trip, this trail provides it. There is no water along the way, so if you choose to try this side trip, carry plenty for your dog.

Just past the junction with Trail 1824, the Hurricane Creek Trail jogs left and crosses Hurricane Creek. There is no bridge and few stepping-stones, so expect to wade through cold, knee-deep water. Use caution, as this crossing can be hazardous in early summer. There are numerous good camping sites near this junction and crossing, and many hikers make this crossing, combined with the crawl to Echo Lake, an early-summer backpacking destination.

After plunging across Hurricane Creek, the trail steepens and strays away from the stream, though it crosses two hefty tributaries in the next mile. It encounters several abandoned and decaying cabins at about 8.3 miles from the trailhead, where the path tempers its uphill pace and encounters pretty meadows of paintbrush and lupine as it climbs from 6800 to 7000 feet. Look for Clark's nutcrackers here and a stunning view up the adjacent rugged, glacially polished marble slopes of Sacajawea Peak. At the end of this series of meadows, the path steepens again for its final climb to the Lakes Basin.

At 9.4 miles the trail crests at 7700 feet. It then drops for 0.3 mile to meet a well-worn trail (Douglas Lake Trail) to the left (east). This trail, which heads for Douglas Lake and the Wallowa River, is also the beginning of a 4.3-mile Lakes Basin loop hike that makes a superb day hike during your stay here. To hike the loop, turn east onto this trail for 1.6 miles past Douglas Lake to a junction with Trail 1810. Turn right (west) at this sharply angled junction and follow Trail 1810 to Moccasin Lake at 2.6 miles and back (west) to Mirror Lake.

To reach campsites near Mirror Lake, continue straight here, toward Eagle Cap and the Lakes Basin 1.2 miles ahead. The Lakes Basin is an overused area with many campsites roped off for restoration. Choose campsites well away from lakeshores, and enjoy the stunningly beautiful landscape. Return as you came.

75. Eagle Cap Wilderness: Maxwell Lake

Round trip: 7 miles
Elevation range: 5430–7730 feet
Difficulty: Strenuous
Hiking time: 5 hours
Best canine hiking season: Summer
Regulations: Northwest Forest Pass required unless you are using a campsite; register for wilderness entry
Map: USGS North Minam Meadows 7.5' quadrangle
Information: Wallowa-Whitman National Forest, Eagle Cap Ranger District, (541) 426-5546

Getting there: From the town of Lostine, 55 miles east of LaGrande on Oregon Route 82, turn south onto Lostine River Road. Follow pavement for the first 6 miles, then gravel for the next 10.5 miles. As you approach Shady Campground, park in the signed "Trailhead Parking Area" on the left side of the road and walk to the trailhead unless you plan to camp in the Shady Campground.

This hike lures you upward with an easy, well-graded trail that ambles gently through shade and sun-splashed open patches for the first 2 miles before, as one fellow hiker noted, "It goes off its medication" and becomes a steep and much more rugged pull. It seems as though the first few miles were built by dedicated and patient crews, and the last mile was done with an "aw-shucks, let's just get to the top" budget plan. That said, the trail is worth the effort in the last mile, which provides

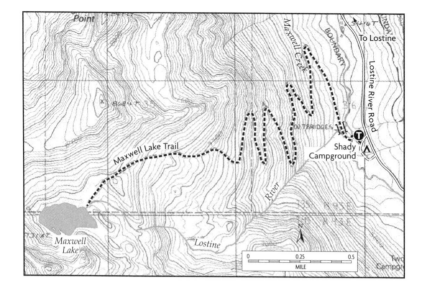

stunning views of the glacially carved Lostine valley, plus wildflowers galore. Horses are (understandably) prohibited on the trail, leaving it to hikers and dogs.

The trail begins in the aptly named Shady Campground, crosses the Lostine River on a sturdy footbridge, and leads through a patch of wetland before crossing Maxwell Creek. There's no bridge here, and in

Craggy granitic peaks rise above Maxwell Lake.

June the water roars. (By August, it's much tamer.) The evenly graded, genteel switchbacking ascent begins just beyond the creek. Springs and seeps provide places for cooling paws, but little reliable drinkable doggie water, until you reach the lakes.

At 2.6 miles from the trailhead, the trail rounds a bend and begins its manic ascent. While not a bad pace, it's notably steeper. This last 1000 feet and 1.5 miles provide plenty of excuses to stop and enjoy stunning views and wildflower-drenched meadows. In its home stretch, the trail tours roche moutonée—glacially sculpted granitic boulders—and ice-smoothed outcrops. The short descent to Maxwell Lake is welcome at 3.4 miles. You can explore the small Maxwell Lake basin, including a second smaller lake to the east, polished bedrock outcrops, and a huge dike (ancient vent system) of brownish Columbia River basalt near the smaller lake. Return as you came.

76. Eagle Cap Wilderness: East Fork Lostine River

Round trip: 6.4 miles to Lost Lake; 15.2 miles to Sunshine Lake/ Lakes Basin

Elevation range: 5584–7100 feet (Lost Lake); 5584–7595 feet (Mirror Lake); 5584–7700 feet (Sunshine Lake)

Difficulty: Moderate

Hiking time: 3 hours to Lost Lake; 7 hours to Sunshine Lake

Best canine hiking season: Late summer

Regulations: Northwest Forest Pass required; register for wilderness entry

Maps: USGS Eagle Cap and North Minam Meadows 7.5' quadrangles

Information: Wallowa-Whitman National Forest, Eagle Cap Ranger District, (541) 426-5546

Getting there: From the town of Lostine, 55 miles east of LaGrande on Oregon Route 82, turn south onto Lostine River Road (Forest Road 8210). Follow pavement for the first 6 miles, then gravel for the next 11 miles. The vast parking area is at the road's end, 17 miles from Lostine. The trail's

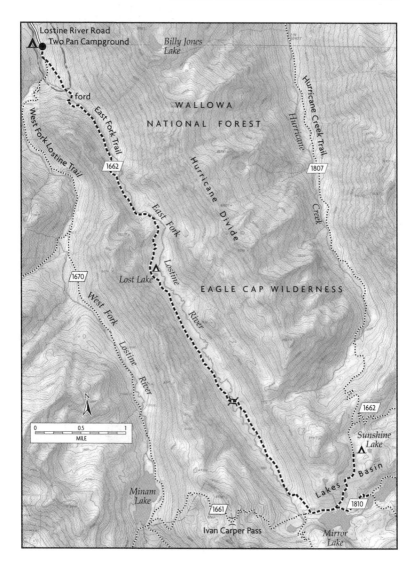

start is well marked near kiosks at the south side of the parking area. There is also a small eight-unit campground (called Two Pan) at the trailhead.

This trail is among the most popular in the Wallowa Mountains. It leads to the extraordinary glacially sculpted landscapes of the Lakes Basin. But beware: On weekends and even on weekdays, this is a crowded place.

Mirror Lake reflects Eagle Cap in its pristine water.

Hence, this guide encourages you to camp in locations other than Mirror Lake to help preserve both water quality and solitude there. You can hike trails along the lake, visit other parts of the Lakes Basin, and also camp in areas that provide greater privacy and comfort. The Forest Service wilderness rangers strictly enforce a ban on camping less than 200 feet from the lakes. Nice, quiet campsites that afford access to the Lakes Basin are present near Lost Lake, along the valley of the East Fork Lostine River, and beyond Mirror Lake near Sunshine Lake. They are great places for Fido to enjoy alpine splendor.

The Lostine River Trail begins as a single broad thoroughfare, providing a gentle grade for the first 0.5 mile. At a major trail junction, marked by a concrete trail sign, bear left and continue toward the Lakes Basin. Soon the path begins serious climbing to clear a talus slope. At 0.6 mile from the trailhead, the route crosses the broad Lostine River. Here, a log bridge washed out in 2009. Its replacement is in question (it's a wilderness area, after all . . .), so be prepared for a challenging wade in July and wet feet in August. It's a reasonable crossing but can be hazardous when water is high.

Beyond the river, the trail encounters another steep, switchbacking climb at 1.5 miles from the trailhead, then encounters a very pretty falls as the Lostine tumbles over granite outcroppings. At 2.8 miles, the trail emerges from the forest and begins a 2-mile-long trek on the western edge of the Lostine's broad, perfect, U-shaped glacial valley. Eagle Cap is alluringly visible for most of the remaining trek to the Lakes Basin proper. Lost Lake, a placid pond, is one of the first features you'll recognize, some 3 miles from the hike's start. This is a favorite camping area and a stopping point for hikers who are taking their time.

At 4.6 miles into the hike, the trail crosses the Lostine on an elegant bridge. An informal trail leads along the river, while the main trail to Lakes Basin heads into the trees, where it remains for the next 1.5 miles until you pop out onto granite outcrops and top out with a breathtaking view of Mirror Lake and Eagle Cap. For hikes with dogs, the side trail—and the meadows in general—offer wonderful places to explore and private, Fido-friendly places to pitch a tent. You can drop your packs here, pitch a tent, and then tour the Lakes Basin unencumbered.

Once you've reached the Lakes Basin at 7 miles from the trailhead, there's a junction with three other trails (#1661, 1810, and 1910). Continue east on the Lakes Basin–Mirror Lake trail #1810. The trail tours the tent-laden granite banks of Mirror Lake for 0.3 mile, then it turns south and clambers slightly uphill to the junction with a trail to Moccasin and Douglas lakes. Bear left and continue toward Sunshine Lake, which sits an easy 0.5 mile from Mirror Lake. Campsites await you here and on nearby meadows that overlook the lake—but you'll be comfortably distant from the Mirror Lake crowds. (Note: Moccasin and Douglas lakes areas also offer more secluded campsites. And the trail to these lakes also loops back to Sunshine Lake.)

You can return as you came, or travel a different route, over the Ivan Carper Pass (an initial 800-foot climb) for 3.4 miles on Trail 1661 to Minam Lake and the 6.1 miles on the West Fork Lostine River Trail (#1670) to the Two Pan trailhead. Or, if you have two vehicles, you could leave one at Hurricane Creek's trailhead, continue north from Sunshine Lake to meet the Hurricane Creek Trail, and follow it 10 miles down to the Hurricane Creek trailhead.

Five More Great Dog Hikes in the Blue Mountains, Wallowa Mountains, and Eastern Oregon

1. Summit Point to Crater Lake, Eagle Cap Wilderness, 14 miles round trip; 7 miles west of Halfway on Oregon Route 86, take Forest Road 77 to FR 7715 at McBride Campground then follow Trail 1885 north. Wallowa Mountain Visitor Center, (541) 426-4978.

2. Eagle Creek, Eagle Cap Wilderness, 12 miles round trip from Boulder Park to Eagle Lake; from Forest Road 77, approximately 30 miles west of the town of Halfway, follow FR 7755 approximately 5 miles to the trailhead, then follow Trail 1922 to Trail 1931 to Eagle Lake. Wallowa Mountain Visitor Center, (541) 426-4978.

3. Clear Creek to Fish Lake, 16 miles round trip; from Halfway on Oregon Route 86, take Forest Road 66 north 8 miles to FR 6610, and in 1.5 miles turn right on Spur Road 030 to the trailhead. Wallowa Mountain Visitor Center, (541) 426-4978.

4. Dutch Flat Creek to Dutch Flat Lake, Elkhorn Mountains, 14 miles round trip; from Interstate 84, 25 miles south of La Grande, take exit 285 at North Powder, then take Elkhorn Scenic Byway (Forest Road 73) approximately 20 miles west to FR 7307 to the trailhead. Wallowa-Whitman National Forest, Whitman Ranger District, (541) 523-4476.

5. Strawberry Lake, Strawberry Mountains Wilderness, 1.3 miles one-way, with access to several other longer trails; check locally for trail conditions. From John Day, at U.S. Highways 26 and 395, drive east about 10 miles on US 26; turn south on County Road 60 and follow it 12 miles south to a campground and the trailhead. Malheur National Forest, Prairie City Ranger District, (541) 820-3800.

APPENDIX A: CONTACT INFORMATION

Banks–Vernonia State Trail
(503) 324-0606
www.oregonstateparks.org/park_145
.php

Barlow Ranger District, Dufur Ranger
Station
780 NE Court Street
Dufur, OR 97021
(541) 467-2291
www.fs.fed.us/r6/mthood/projects
/index.shtml#barlow

Bend District Office, Oregon Parks
and Recreation
Administration, Recreation Services,
and Planning & Development
Hours: Monday–Friday, 8:00 AM–
5:00 PM
799 SW Columbia Street
Bend, OR 97702
(541) 389-7275
www.bendparksandrec.org

Bend–Fort Rock Ranger District,
Deschutes National Forest
1230 NE Third Street, Suite A-262
Bend, OR 97701
(541) 383-4000
www.fs.fed.us/r6/centraloregon

Cape Perpetua Visitor Center
2400 U.S. Highway 101 South
P.O. Box 274
Yachats, OR 97498
(541) 547-3289
TDD (541) 547-3251
www.fs.fed.us/r6/siuslaw/recreation
/tripplanning/capeperpetua/events
/index.shtml

Columbia River Gorge National
Scenic Area
902 Wasco Street, Suite 200
Hood River, OR 97031
(541) 308-1700, TTY (541) 386-8758
www.fs.usda.gov/crgnsa

Crooked River National Grasslands
813 SW U.S. Highway 97
Madras, OR 97741-9210
(541) 475-9272
www.fs.fed.us/r6/centraloregon

Deschutes National Forest
Headquarters
1645 U.S. Highway 20 East
Bend, OR 97701
(541) 383-5300
www.fs.fed.us/r6/centraloregon

Detroit Ranger District, Willamette
National Forest
Oregon Route 22
Detroit, OR 97342
Mail: HC-73, Box 320
Mill City, OR 97360
(503) 854-3366
www.fs.usda.gov/willamette

Diamond Lake Ranger District,
Umpqua National Forest
2020 Toketee Ranger Station Road
Idleyld Park, OR 97447
(541) 498-2531
www.fs.fed.us/r6/umpqua
www.fs.fed.us/r6/umpqua/contact/

Dufur Ranger Station, Mount Hood
National Forest
780 NE Court Street
Dufur, OR 97021
(541) 467-2291
TTY (541) 467-5170
www.fs.usda.gov/mthood

Eagle Cap Ranger District, Wallowa
Mountains Office
201 East Second Street
P.O. Box 905
Joseph, OR 97846
(541) 426-5546
www.fs.usda.gov/wallowa-whitman

Estacada Ranger Station, Mount Hood
National Forest
595 NW Industrial Way
Estacada, OR 97023
(503) 630-6861
www.fs.usda.gov/mthood

Gold Beach Ranger District, Rogue
River–Siskiyou National Forest
29279 Ellensburg Avenue
Gold Beach, OR 97444
(541) 247-3600
www.fs.fed.us/r6/rogue-siskiyou
and
Crissey Field Welcome Center
14433 U.S. Highway 101 South
P.O. Box 4580
Brookings, OR 97415
www.oregon.gov/OPRD/PARKS
/crissey_field.shtml

Hebo Ranger District, Siuslaw
National Forest
31525 Oregon Route 22
P.O. Box 324
Hebo, OR 97122
(503) 392-3161
www.fs.fed.us/r6/siuslaw

High Cascades Ranger District, Rogue
River–Siskiyou National Forest
47201 Oregon Route 62
Prospect, OR 97536
(541) 560-3400
www.fs.fed.us/r6/rogue-siskiyou
/index.shtml
and
730 Laural Street
P.O. Box 227
Butte Falls, OR 97522
(541) 865-2700

Hood River Ranger District, Mount
Hood National Forest
6780 Oregon Route 35
Mount Hood–Parkdale, OR 97041
(541) 352-6002
www.fs.usda.gov/mthood

Humbug Mountain State Park
39745 U.S. Highway 101 South
Port Orford, OR 97465
(541) 332-6774
www.oregonstateparks.org/park_56
.php

Lane County Parks and Recreation
Department
90064 Coburg Road
Eugene, OR 97408
(541) 682-2000
www.lanecounty.org/departments
/PW/Parks/Pages/default.aspx
online park reservations: ecomm
.lanecounty.org/parks/

Lookout Mountain Ranger District,
Ochoco National Forest
3160 NE Third Street
P.O. Box 490
Prineville, OR 97754-0490
(541) 416-6500
www.fs.fed.us/r6/centraloregon
/recreation/trails/trail-district-lookout
.shtml

McKenzie River Ranger District,
Willamette National Forest
57600 McKenzie Highway
McKenzie Bridge, OR 97413
(541) 822-3381
www.fs.usda.gov/willamette

Medford District, Bureau of Land
Management
3040 Biddle Road
Medford, OR 97630
(541) 770-2200
www.blm.gov/or/districts/medford
/index.php

Mount Hood Information Center,
Mount Hood National Forest
65000 East U.S. Highway 26
Welches, OR 97067
(503) 622-7674
http://www.mthood.info/

Mount Hood National Forest
Headquarters
16400 Champion Way
Sandy, OR 97055
(503) 668-1700

Mount Pisgah Arboretum
34901 Frank Parrish Road
Eugene, OR 97405
(541) 747-3817
www.mountpisgaharboretum.org/

North Fork John Day Ranger District,
Umatilla National Forest
P.O. Box 158
Ukiah, OR 97880
(541) 427-3231
www.fs.fed.us/r6/uma/nfjd/index
.shtml

North Umpqua Ranger District,
Umpqua National Forest
18782 North Umpqua Highway
Glide, OR 97443
(541) 496-3532
www.fs.fed.us/r6/umpqua

Ochoco National Forest Headquarters
3160 NE Third Street
P.O. Box 490
Prineville, OR 97754-0490
(541) 416-6500
www.fs.fed.us/r6/centraloregon
/conditions/recreport-win.shtml

Oregon Department of Forestry,
Tillamook State Forest, Forest Grove
District Office
801 Gales Creek Road
Forest Grove, OR 97116
(503) 357-2191
www.oregon.gov/ODF/FIELD/FG
/aboutus.shtml

Oregon Dunes National Recreation
Area
855 Highway Avenue
Reedsport, OR 97467
(541) 271-3611
www.fs.fed.us/r6/siuslaw/recreation
/tripplanning/oregondunes/

Oregon State Office, Bureau of Land
Management
333 SW First Avenue
Portland, OR 97204
(503) 808-6002
www.blm.gov/or/index.php

Oregon State Parks and Recreation
Department
1115 Commercial Street NE
Salem, OR 97301
(800) 551-6949, (503) 986-0707
www.oregon.gov/OPRD/

Pine Ranger District, Wallowa–
Whitman National Forest
General Delivery
Halfway, OR 97834
(541) 742-7511
www.fs.usda.gov/wallowa-whitman

Portland Bureau of Parks and
Recreation
1120 SW Fifth Avenue, Suite 1302
Portland, OR 97201
(503) 823-7529
www.portlandonline.com/parks/

Prairie City Ranger District, Malheur
National Forest
P.O. Box 337; Highway 26
Prairie City, OR 97869
(541) 820-3800

Prineville District, Bureau of Land
Managment
3050 NE Third Street
Prineville, OR 97754
(541) 416-6700
www.blm.gov/or/districts/prineville
/index.php

Rogue River–Siskiyou National Forest
Headquarters
Federal Building, 333 West Eighth
Street
Box 520
Medford, OR 97501-0209
(541) 858-2200, TTY (541) 858-2203
www.fs.fed.us/r6/rogue-siskiyou
/about/

Salem District, Bureau of Land
Management
1717 Fabry Road SE
Salem, OR 97306
(503) 375-5646
www.blm.gov/or/districts/salem
/index.php

Sauvie Island Wildlife Area
18330 NW Sauvie Island Road
Portland, OR 97231
(503) 621-3488
www.dfw.state.or.us/resources/visitors
/sauvie_island_wildlife_area.asp

Silver Falls State Park
(503) 873-8681
www.oregonstateparks.org/park_211
.php

Siskiyou Mountains Ranger District
6941 Upper Applegate Road
Jacksonville, OR 97530-9314
(541) 899-3800
www.fs.fed.us/r6/rogue-siskiyou/
and
645 Washington Street
Ashland, OR 97520-1402
(541) 552-2900

Sisters Ranger District, Deschutes
National Forest
U.S. Highway 20 and Pine Street
P.O. Box 249
Sisters, OR 97759
(541) 549-7700
www.fs.fed.us/r6/centraloregon
/wildlife/sites/34-sisters.shtml

Siuslaw National Forest Headquarters
4077 Research Way
P.O. Box 1148
Corvallis, OR 97339
(541) 750-7000
TDD (541) 750-7006
www.fs.fed.us/r6/siuslaw

Tillamook County Parks Department
8000 Cedar Street
Rockaway Beach, OR 97136
Mail: P.O. Box 633
Garibaldi, OR 97118
(503) 322-3477, reservations/
registration (503) 322-3522
www.co.tillamook.or.us/gov/parks
/default.htm

Tryon Creek State Park
(503) 636-9886
www.oregonstateparks.org/park_144
.php

Umatilla National Forest Headquarters
2517 SW Hailey Avenue
Pendleton, OR 97801
(541) 278-3716
www.fs.fed.us/r6/uma/about/

Umpqua National Forest Headquarters
2900 NW Stewart Parkway
Roseburg, OR 97470
(541) 672-6601
www.stateparks.com/umpqua
_headquarters.html

Waldport Ranger District, Waldport
Office
1130 Forestry Lane
P.O. Box 400
Waldport, OR 97394
(541) 563-3211
www.fs.fed.us/r6/siuslaw/

Wallowa Mountains Visitors Center,
Wallowa-Whitman National Forest
Enterprise, OR 97828
(541) 426-4978
www.fs.usda.gov/wallowa-whitman

Wallowa-Whitman National Forest
Headquarters
1550 Dewey Avenue
P.O. Box 907
Baker City, OR 97814
(541) 523-6391
www.fs.usda.gov/wallowa-whitman

Whitman Ranger District, Wallowa-
Whitman National Forest
3285 11th Street
P.O. Box 947
Baker City, Oregon 97814
(541) 523-4476
www.fs.usda.gov/wallowa-whitman

Wild Rivers Ranger District, Rogue
River–Siskiyou National Forest
2164 NE Spalding Avenue
Grants Pass, OR 97526
www.fs.fed.us/r6/rogue-siskiyou
/index.shtml
and
26568 Redwood Highway
Cave Junction, OR 97523
(541) 592-4000

Willamette National Forest
Headquarters
211 East Seventh Avenue
P.O. Box 10607
Eugene, OR 97440-2607
(541) 225-6300
TDD (541) 465-6323
www.fs.usda.gov/willamette

Zigzag Ranger Station, Mount Hood
National Forest
70220 East U.S. Highway 26
Zigzag, OR 97049
(503) 622-3191
www.publiclands.org/explore/site
.php?id=3782

APPENDIX B: RECOMMENDED READING

Acker, Randy. *Field Guide: Dog First Aid Emergency Care for the Hunting, Working, and Outdoor Dog*. Belgrade, MT: Wilderness Adventures Press, 1994.

Cameron, W. Bruce. *A Dog's Purpose*. New York: Forge Books, 2010.

Carlson, Lisa, and James M. Giffin. *Dog Owner's Home Veterinary Handbook*, 3rd ed. Hoboken, NJ: John Wiley and Sons, 1999.

Coren, Stanley. *The Intelligence of Dogs: A Guide to the Thoughts, Emotions, and Inner Lives of Our Canine Companions*, reprint ed. New York: Bantam, 1995.

———. *The Pawprints of History: Dogs and the Course of Human Events*. New York: The Free Press, 2002.

Duno, Steve. *Last Dog on the Hill*. New York: St. Martins Press, 2010.

Fogle, Bruce, and Amanda Williams. *First Aid for Dogs: What to Do When Emergencies Happen*. New York: Penguin, 1997.

Horowitz, Alexandra. *Inside of a Dog: What Dogs See, Smell, and Know*. New York: Scribner and Sons, 2009.

Katz, John. *Katz on Dogs: A Commonsense Guide to Training and Living with Dogs*. New York: Random House, 2005.

Knapp, Caroline. *Pack of Two: The Intricate Bond Between People and Dogs*. New York: Bantam Dell, 1998.

McConnell, Patricia. *The Other End of the Leash*. New York: Ballantine Books, 2003.

Pryor, Karen. *Don't Shoot the Dog: The New Art of Teaching and Training*. New York: Bantam Dell, 1999.

Rugaas, Turid. *On Talking Terms with Dogs: Calming Signals*. Wenatchee, WA: Dogwise Publishing, 1997.

Stein, Garth. *The Art of Racing in the Rain*. New York: Harper, 2010.

Townshend, Emma. *Darwin's Dogs: How Darwin's Pets Helped Form a World-Changing Theory of Evolution*. London: Francis Lincoln Ltd., 2009.

INDEX

Snow is no excuse to stay inside!

About the Author

Ellen Morris Bishop is a photographer, writer, and geologist. She is the author of several books on geology and the outdoors, including *Hiking Oregon's Geology*, second edition (The Mountaineers Books, 2004). Since she was five, dogs have accompanied her on virtually all her hikes, field work, and outdoor adventures. Her dog Meesha is a certified Therapy Dog and has provided canine companionship to Alzheimer's patients, nursing home patients, and worked in the Read to the Dogs programs in public libraries. Both Meesha and Dundee have earned Basic Obedience and Agility certificates. Ellen's previous work with dogs includes working with stock dogs and training a Newfoundland to be a certified Water Rescue Dog. Ellen works as a photographer and writer, and also teaches geology at the college level. Her photographic specialties are geologic landscapes and portraiture. Her website is www.ellenmorrisbishop.com. She lives in Central Oregon with her husband, David, two dogs, Meesha and Dundee, and their border collie sidekick, Megan.

The perfect dog hike includes water for wading, shade for napping, rabbits for sniffing, and, of course, a nice easy chair for a rest along the trail.

THE MOUNTAINEERS, founded in 1906, is a nonprofit outdoor activity and conservation organization, whose mission is "to explore, study, preserve, and enjoy the natural beauty of the outdoors . . . ." The Mountaineers sponsors many classes and year-round outdoor activities in the Pacific Northwest, and supports environmental causes through educational activities, sponsoring legislation and presenting educational programs. The Mountaineers Books supports the organization's mission by publishing travel and natural history guides, instructional texts, and works on conservation and history.

Visit www.mountaineersbooks.org to view our complete list of more than 800 outdoor titles:

The Mountaineers Books
1001 SW Klickitat Way, Suite 201
Seattle, WA 98134
800-553-4453
mbooks@mountaineersbooks.org

The Mountaineers Books is proud to be a corporate sponsor of the Leave No Trace Center for Outdoor Ethics, whose mission is to promote and inspire responsible outdoor recreation through education, research, and partnerships.

The Leave No Trace program is focused specifically on human-powered (nonmotorized) recreation.

Leave No Trace strives to educate visitors about the nature of their recreational impacts, as well as offer techniques to prevent and minimize such impacts. Leave No Trace is best understood as an educational and ethical program, not as a set of rules and regulations.

For more information, visit www.lnt.org or call (800) 332-4100.

OTHER TITLES YOU MIGHT ENJOY FROM THE MOUNTAINEERS BOOKS

Best Hikes with Dogs Inland Northwest
Craig Romano & Alan Bauer
From the Selkirks and the Blue Mountains,
to the Canadian Okanagan Highlands—
75 trails for dogs to roam the terrain

**Best Hikes with Dogs
Western Washington,
2nd Edition**
Dan Nelson
85 hikes around the state for all
skill levels of dog and owners

Best Hikes with Kids Oregon, 2nd Edition
Bonnie Henderson and Zach Urness
Easy day hikes for the whole family covering
the coast, Portland metro area,
Mount Hood, and the Eastern Oregon.

100 Classic Hikes in Oregon, 2nd Edition
Douglas Lorain
A full-color guide to Oregon's
finest trails, written with a conservation
ethic, and featuring the best hikes in the state

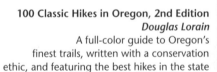

**The Mountaineers Books has more than
800 outdoor recreation titles in print.**
For more details, visit
www.mountaineersbooks.org.